THE ATTITUDE FACTOR

THE ATTITUDE FACTOR

EXTEND YOUR LIFE BY CHANGING
THE WAY YOU THINK

Thomas R. Blakeslee

Thorsons
An Imprint of HarperCollins*Publishers*

Thorsons
An Imprint of HarperCollins*Publishers*
77–85 Fulham Palace Road,
Hammersmith, London W6 8JB

Published by Thorsons 1997

1 3 5 7 9 10 8 6 4 2

© Thomas R. Blakeslee 1997

Thomas R. Blakeslee asserts the moral right to
be identified as the author of this work

A catalogue record for this book
is available from the British Library

ISBN 0 7225 3546 5

Printed and bound in Great Britain by
Creative Print and Design (Wales), Ebbw Vale

This book is dedicated to my dear mother, who first aroused my interest in why attitudes change with age. I have tried my very best to make this the book that I wish she had read 40 years ago.

CONTENTS

PREFACE

I want to thank Dr Ronald Grossarth-Maticek for his kind hospitality, his important insights and his decades of scientific research on the connection between attitudes and longevity. His work proves that the mental rejuvenation produced by applying the 'attitude jogging' principles of this book can do much more than just increase the joy in your life – they can significantly improve your physical health and longevity as well.

Over the past three decades more than 10,000 people have answered Dr Grossarth-Maticek's attitude questionnaires. By correlating these test scores with health status many years later, he has shown that attitude factors can have an incredibly strong effect on both health and longevity. Even more important, his controlled experiments have shown that attitude factors can be changed – even late in life – to extend life expectancy while simultaneously improving the pleasure in life.

To keep the book easy to read, I have covered the scientific evidence only briefly. Readers with a scientific bent are encouraged to read the important additional details of these exciting experiments and those of many other researchers in the Notes and References chapter of this book. More details, and copies of important medical journal articles, can be found on my web site (www.attitudefactor.com). If you are a web user you can use this site to administer, score and analyse automatically the tests in the Appendices. In 5 – 10 years I plan to analyse this test data to prove scientifically that people who read this book carefully and stay with their attitude jogging exercises will live significantly longer than people who don't (*see page 208 for more details*).

Attitude jogging is a lifelong process that becomes effortless once you have established the right mental habits. Since change becomes more difficult with age, I have directed this book at people in their thirties, forties or fifties, whose mental habits are still easily changed.

My sincere thanks to Mel Walsh, Sandra Cleary, Rhonda Balzan, Marianne Harms, Jamie Catto and Richard White for their helpful comments on the manuscript. Also, a special thanks to Lynne Franks, whose love and support have brought my feelings of pleasure and well-being to a new level.

KEEPING YOUR YOUTHFUL JOY

My grandfather, at the age of 85, once cracked open the sheet of ice on a motel pool to take his morning swim. I consider myself lucky to have been exposed to his role model because, as I watch my less fortunate friends grow old, I see that my grandfather gave me a priceless gift. The attitudes he taught me by example have allowed me to continue savouring life with a youthful enthusiasm that few people my age still enjoy.

Nobody teaches us how to age in school. We all learn by good or bad examples from our parents and other role models. But why should such crucial learning be left to chance? By developing a basic understanding of how attitudes develop and why they naturally tend to decline, you can learn to take control of many aspects of your own ageing process.

Attitudes are crucially important to happiness because they define the way we react to the world. They can make the difference between pleasure and pain, happiness and misery, even good health and bad. Attitudes are like well-worn paths in the mind that gradually evolve as a result of thousands of little choices we make every day of our lives. They define our experience to such a degree that different people often have opposite reactions to the same thing. A film, book, painting or person can induce pleasure or pain – depending entirely upon your attitude. As people age, changing attitudes often make them hate the very same people or things they once loved. Attitudes make the difference. Look at the list of reactions below and consider the fact that your attitudes alone can take you all the way from the negative to the positive extreme.

Negative Reactions	→	Positive Reactions
Pain	→	Pleasure
Hate	→	Love
Boredom	→	Fascination
Fear	→	Excitement
Annoyance	→	Enjoyment
Misery	→	Happiness

Ideally, as we gain experience with life our attitudes should evolve in a direction that enhances our happiness. As we learn to appreciate more and more things, our capacity for joy should continue to *grow* with age. Unfortunately, the ironic reality is that most people's attitudes do quite the opposite: After a period of growth in early life, a gradual decline usually begins in the early thirties. Though the cumulative effect of this decline is often painfully obvious to children and grandchildren, it is almost never noticed by the victims themselves.

Attitude decline is the gradual tendency of attitudes to slip from positive towards negative. Attitude jogging is a kind of mental exercise which can reverse this downward spiral and increase the sources of joy in your life while reducing pain, fear, annoyance and boredom.

THE INVISIBLE DISEASE

The symptoms of attitude decline gradually accelerate with age until they are like a disease that robs you of joy and actually shortens your life. Yet, ironically, victims of this disease are never aware of its symptoms. The reason we don't notice attitude decline is that **we use our attitudes to make judgements about our attitudes**. If we hate cats, our attitude about cats tells us that we *should* hate cats. The natural result is like circular logic: Our attitudes always *seem* to be exactly what they should be. No matter how much they detract from our enjoyment of life we will always vigorously defend our own attitudes because we use an attitude to judge itself.

This circularity is at the very root of the problem and the reason attitudes can decline so much, without our knowledge. People with serious phobias can become so fearful that they remain trapped in their own home for decades, yet they will defend their attitude as a necessary precaution against the dangers outside. Examining your own attitudes is extremely deceptive because you can't help rationalizing. We are all good at it because we have had a lifetime of practice. Rationalization is more than just a defence mechanism – it is the basic way we make sense out of our own behaviour.

Everyone has unique values and tastes, so I will be very careful not to judge your attitudes with mine. We all enjoy different things, but since everybody wants to be happy and healthy, let us agree right now on an objective goal for attitude jogging: *To develop attitudes that will maximize health and happiness.*

ATTITUDES, HEALTH AND LONGEVITY

Many people think that feeling good is just a shallow luxury, but recent scientific research has shown that it is actually a vital necessity for good health and long life. Feelings of pleasure and well-being are actually signals of satisfaction from the same ancient part of your brain that controls important bodily systems such as your immune system and cardiovascular system. When your instinctive needs aren't met, these systems are seriously compromised and your defences against germs, viruses and cancer cells are weakened.[1]

You have probably noticed that colds and other illnesses often come a few days after an emotional upset. What most people don't realize is the amazing degree to which major diseases, heart disease, infections, cancer and even accidents are affected by your basic emotions. Even more important are the habitual attitudes that affect your overall ability to experience joy. The graph on page 4 summarizes the amazing results of a massive experiment by Dr Ronald Grossarth-Maticek.[2] In 1973 his assistants gave a *pleasure and well-being* test to some 3,055 elderly residents of Heidelberg, Germany. This 15-question test (reproduced in

Appendix I) measures how intensely and how often you experience feelings of pleasure and well-being.

Twenty-one years after the test was given, the health status of the people who had taken the test was checked and it was found that ***people who had scored highest on the test were 30 times more likely to be alive and well than those who had low scores***.[3] This amazing correlation between feelings of pleasure and well-being and later good health tells us that being happy is truly more than just a luxury. It's a matter of life and death!

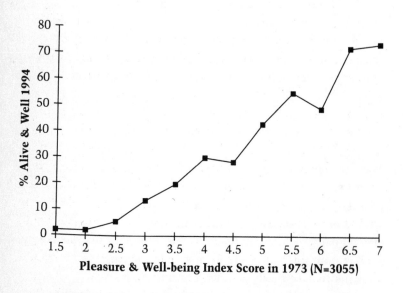

Pleasure & Well-being Index Score in 1973 (N=3055)

Your habitual ability to experience feelings of pleasure and well-being can predict future good health with amazing accuracy. The graph above shows the results of a 1973 experiment where over 3,000 elderly people took the pleasure and well-being test (see Appendix I). As the graph shows, the percentage still alive and well 21 years later varied from only 2.5 per cent of the people with scores of 2 or less to 75 per cent of the people with scores of 6.5 or better. Attitude jogging is directed at improving this important ability.

Your ability to feel pleasure and well-being is strongly influenced by the mental habits and attitudes which you have learned in childhood and continue to develop throughout your life. Often as people

age their capacity for pleasure declines, reducing the pleasure in their lives. The ultimate result is often a weakened immune system, poor health and premature death.

Attitude jogging is a way to prevent this decline and gradually improve your capacity to live life with a maximum of healthy feelings of pleasure and well-being. By increasing the sources of joy in your life, you improve your attitude factor and with it your chances of staying in good health and living to a ripe old age.

THE 'USED TO' TEST

One of the first symptoms of declining attitudes is a narrowing of the range of things you enjoy and an expansion of the things that bore, frighten or annoy you. Children joyfully play with almost anything, while cranky old people are annoyed by virtually everything. Attitude jogging is a way to keep that youthful exuberance alive.

I have devised a little test which is worth some time and effort on your part. I call it the 'used to' test because it helps you to evaluate objectively your own attitude changes since your days as a student (in primary, secondary or higher education). Please use your will-power to overcome the very natural tendency to skip over this test, because it will challenge your rationalizations. As you take it, try to be coldly objective and resist the strong natural desire to rationalize and be defensive. Assessing the problem is the important first step towards solving it.

Get a pencil and paper right now and make yourself a list, in a vertical column on the left, of all the *things you enjoyed doing* in your final year of schooling.

As an aid in remembering what you used to enjoy, here are some items from my list, which you are welcome to copy:

- dancing
- swimming
- singing
- acting silly
- standing out in the rain
- putting your bare feet in mud

- getting wet or dirty
- camping
- exploring
- skinny dipping
- building a sand castle at the seaside
- riding a merry-go-round
- French kissing
- roller coasters
- climbing trees
- long walks
- taking a bus
- driving nowhere in particular
- picnics
- plucking the petals from a daisy
- watching insects
- skipping rope
- playing
- sledging
- skating
- writing poems
- *really* listening to music
- playing a musical instrument
- doing art projects
- getting carried away
- parties
- hobbies
- concerts
- impulsively changing plans
- not noticing that the water or air is cold
- smoking pot
- playing sports
- skipping
- staying up all night
- playing pretend games
- falling in love

LIST OF SOURCES OF JOY	✔ STILL	REASON I NO LONGER ENJOY IT

It may take you a few days to really complete your list since you will have to jog your memory by trying to remember all of the good times you used to have. You can expand the list later but, when you've finished a first pass, move on to step two and put a tick next to each item on the list that you still enjoy regularly.

Now for the third and most important step: Write down the reason you no longer enjoy each item you didn't tick.

This is the toughest step of all because you must resist the normal rationalizations that will instantly come to mind. Try playing devil's advocate and giving brutally honest answers.

Remember that 'too old' is a totally unacceptable answer – be specific. If you can't think of any good reason, simply write in a question mark.

If you find the result depressing, welcome to the club. To be fair, you can make another list of new things that you now enjoy doing regularly. If this list is longer than the list of 'used to's', congratulations – you have probably already been using some of the principles of attitude jogging without knowing it.

WATCH THOSE RATIONALIZATIONS!

Please keep your list and add further items as you think of them. We will refer to it frequently in future chapters. One goal in exploring the attitude development process is to understand why 'I used to' becomes such a common phrase as people age. The good news is that once you understand how attitudes evolve, you will be able to use your will-power at crucial times to take control and actually reverse this downward spiral.

One big advantage of the 'used to' test is that it identifies things that *you* used to enjoy. Everybody has different tastes, so it would be wrong of me to tell you that you should enjoy something that *I* happen to enjoy. However, it is safe to say that you would clearly be happier if all of your 'used to's' were still sources of joy. Of course it is perfectly natural for your tastes to change as you grow. Unfortunately, if you are not adding at least as many new sources of joy as you are losing, you are on a dangerous path that can ultimately lead to a narrow, cranky old age.

Rationalization is a useful defence that helps us to make sense out of life. In interpreting the results of this test it is extremely important that you use all of your critical-thinking powers to see through the ingenious explanations that will naturally come to mind to explain away your 'used to's'. For example, people often blame babies or job pressure long after the child has grown or the job has changed. Sports injuries that healed long ago are another one. Be sure to keep your reasons *in the present*.

Another possible rationalization for a long list of 'used to's' is that you have improved your focus so that you are now getting more enjoyment from fewer things. To a point this could be a valid argument, but make sure you aren't fooling yourself. You probably enjoyed things pretty passionately in your youth. Are you really more passionate about your interests now? Generally passion creates energy, so the more things you are enthusiastic about the more energy you will have to do them all. Lack of time is a valid excuse only if you don't spend hours each day on passive pursuits such as watching television or sleeping long hours. (Caution: Rationalization will defend this use of your time, as it does all attitudes.)

REALLY BAD ATTITUDES

While losing the ability to enjoy an activity is sad, there is an even worse possibility: being annoyed at seeing others do things that you used to enjoy. Declining attitudes can truly turn pleasure into pain. Most neighbourhoods have a cranky old couple (or individual) who get annoyed by the sound of children playing and spend their days looking for things to complain about. This is a perfect demonstration of where the downward spiral can ultimately lead. Yet, if you ask crotchety people if their attitudes need improving they will almost certainly be annoyed and angrily insist that they are 'doing just fine, thank you'.

Another extreme example of how attitude decline can ruin your life is the amazingly common mental illness called phobia. People with phobias are severely disabled by unnatural fears that prevent them from flying, driving, being in crowds, and even from leaving their own home. Just as we rationalize our own negative attitudes, people with phobias usually convince themselves that their phobias are nothing more than wise precautions.[4] The process by which phobias develop is similar to the one that produces the normal attitude declines exposed by the 'used to' test. The good news is that excellent new treatments have been developed for phobias, which are equally effective against 'used to's' (more on this in Chapter 8).

One of the reasons negative attitudes can develop so easily without our knowledge is that our natural tendency to rationalize conceals them. Since attitudes develop very slowly as a result of many seemingly insignificant experiences, your rationalization stories can also gradually evolve to maintain the illusion that everything is fine. Even major changes are very difficult to detect when they happen gradually over several decades.

A NEW VIEW OF YOURSELF

To improve your attitude factor, you must learn a new self-critical way to look at yourself that will see through your own rationalizations. This can be a difficult challenge, but the payoff is worth it. Besides being a lot less expensive than paying a therapist, self-analysis can be considerably more effective because other people's insights always carry less weight than our own. When you do have a private insight you can act on it with immediate enthusiasm. The key to success is in learning a healthy scepticism about your own comfortable rationalizations.

If you have a special friend or lover who is interested in attitude improvement, you can both benefit greatly by making a pact to help each other. A good start is for you both to take the 'used to' test and then help each other to examine your answers critically. It is always easier to see through others' rationalizations, though sometimes harder to get them to accept your insights. By making a pact to engage in respectful *mutual* criticism, you can reduce your natural defensiveness. Changing attitudes is a long process which can be fun if you have a special friend to do it with you.

If you found as many 'used to's' as I did, you may be asking yourself 'How could I have let this happen?' In the next chapter I'll show how we are all victims of a cruel trick of nature: Because humanity's unique ability to think in words has only been a recent evolutionary addition, we are often totally unaware of the true basis of our attitudes. In the next chapter we will show how a correct understanding of how your mind really works can help you to reverse dramatically the tendency towards attitude decline.

Exercise One

1. Take the pleasure and well-being test in Appendix I. Be sure to be completely honest in your answers and avoid rationalizations.
2. Calculate your score by adding up the numbers you have circled and dividing by 15.[5]
3. Look up your score in the figure on page 4 to determine your current outlook for being alive and well when you are 79.
4. Diligent attitude jogging can improve your score on the test. How much would your health outlook improve if your score increased by 1? By 1.5? Hint: According to figure 1, improving your score from 4 to 5 makes the difference between a 30 per cent chance of being alive and well at 79 and a 44 per cent chance. If you can get your score up to 5.5, your chances go up to 57 per cent. (Web surfer's note: www.attitudefactor.com will lead you through this entire exercise automatically.)

Exercise Two

1. Make a list of things you 'used to' enjoy in your youth.
2. Pick one of the items that you used to enjoy but now feel negative about.
3. Write down the first reason for your current dislike that comes to mind.
4. Pretend you are a youngster and that your parents have just given you that reason. Poke holes in the rationalization as a typical know-it-all kid would.
5. Try the same thing with any negative attitudes you have. In this case do your hole-poking by role-playing as someone with a positive attitude about the same thing.

Exercise Three

1. Have your friends or children ever accused you of being cranky or judgemental?
2. If they have, try to remember the last time they said it and relive the discussion with the roles reversed. Like an actor playing a role, try to act as your own critic.
3. Try the same trick in a real situation in the future. The idea is to practise the ability to see through your own rationalizations.

Exercise Four

1. Make a co-commitment pact with a close friend or lover to help each other work on attitudes.
2. Help each other with the role-playing in the above two exercises. Make it a real discussion, with one of you acting as devil's advocate poking holes in your partner's rationalizations.
3. Make it a game to point out any usage of phrases like 'used to' and 'too old' in conversation. Challenge yourself or your partner for a more specific explanation.

CHAPTER SUMMARY

1. Attitudes make the difference between happiness and misery, yet we allow them to develop by chance.
2. Our own attitudes always seem OK because we use an attitude to judge itself. No matter how much misery our attitudes cause, we will always defend them.
3. Rationalization is the basic way we make sense of life, yet it hides our bad attitudes by justifying them.
4. Attitudes naturally tend to decline, beginning at the age of about 30, unless effort is made to prevent their decline.
5. Feelings of pleasure and well-being are strongly predictive of future good health. Take the test in Appendix I.

6. Making a list of things you 'used to' enjoy is a good way to measure attitude decline.
7. Often the reasons we give for 'used to's' are rationalizations or events of the past that are no longer valid.
8. Cranky people never agree that they are cranky, though it's obvious to all non-cranky people around them.
9. Making a pact to work on attitudes with a close friend can be fun and very rewarding.

WHY ATTITUDES DECLINE

My cat is a real character. She won't eat fish but loves dry cat food. She hates dogs and getting wet or dirty, and loves to sit purring on people's laps or sleeping stretched out in the sun. In her younger days she used to love playing with balls or yarn and going for walks with me in the woods. Without any help from language, she has developed definite attitudes about virtually everything in her world.

Like all animals, my cat learned her attitudes by behavioural conditioning. Pleasant experiences reinforced her preferences, while unpleasant ones reinforced her dislikes. With no power of language, she expresses her attitudes entirely through her behaviour.

Animals have fully-developed non-verbal attitudes which include strong likes and dislikes, fears and prejudices. As evolutionary descendants of animals, our attitudes work the same way but we also have a new language-based system which discusses its own logical version of our attitudes.

For us humans, life is not so simple. Evolution has given us the unique and powerful ability to think in words and discuss our attitudes. This gives us tremendous power but also causes much confusion because our attitudes, behaviour and emotional reactions to things continue to be determined by conditioning – just like my cat. Though we try to use our ability to think logically to express our attitudes in words, our deeds often don't match our words.

One reason things get so confusing is that the logical, verbal part of the human mind is capable of overriding conditioned behaviour and seizing control. We have a name for this: we call it **self-control** or **will-power**. *The only time we act totally consistently with the attitudes we discuss and arrive at logically is when we are exercising self-control.* Since we only use self-control occasionally, it is not surprising that we are often confused about our own attitudes.[1]

We all develop a verbal self that speaks for us and explains and justifies our behaviour to ourselves and others. Using words and logic, we create a model in our mind of a self that knows about and controls much more than it really does. We strongly believe that we can use introspection to look at our own thoughts, *but the thoughts that we see are only the thoughts of our verbal self.* After a lifetime of believing the rationalizations of our verbal self, it is very difficult to learn to take these insights with a grain of salt. Learning a healthy scepticism for this verbal version of your attitudes is the first and most difficult step towards real self-improvement.

The confusing reality is that evolution has given us two fundamentally different modes of thought which are separated by an unbridgeable language barrier: Our verbal self thinks in words, while natural behaviour is based on wordless sensory images.

HOW DID WE GET INTO THIS MESS?

As a former computer designer I can well understand how the human brain got to be such a messy arrangement. Because of the way evolution works, each change had to be added on top of the existing structures without ever disturbing their function. No 'shutdown for reorganization' was ever possible because every single generation in our genetic lineage had to survive or we would now be extinct. As mammals evolved from reptiles and as we evolved from mammals, improvements in brain capabilities had to be accomplished by tacking new structures on top of the old without disturbing their function or organization.

After hundreds of millions of years without a single chance to reorganize, the result is what an engineer would call a kludge – a very messy and far from optimum collection of tacked-on additions. The latest addition to the human brain, called the cerebral cortex, sits on top of two complete structures that we inherited from our reptile and mammal ancestors. Although these separate evolutionary levels have continued to co-evolve, the lower levels of our brain still look and work a lot like the brains of reptiles and lower mammals. More importantly, they continue to control much of our behaviour.

Most of the behaviour and the feelings we call attitudes originate in these older parts of our brain. The newest part of our brain adds the language and logic capabilities, and here is where the problems start. Since the behaviours in the lower levels are not in words, they are untranslatable and invisible to introspection. This language problem means that the verbal part of your brain is forced to do its best to deduce plausible rationalizations to make sense out of the behaviour it observes.

Swallowing is something we all know how to do, yet take a moment right now to explain verbally how you do it. Unless you are a throat specialist, you will probably find that you have surprisingly little verbal understanding of your swallowing behaviour. You will probably have to resort to actually swallowing and watching yourself to deduce and describe what you are doing! The behavioural and feeling parts of all of your attitudes are similarly only accessible to your verbal self by observation and deduction.

GUESSING ABOUT EMOTIONS

Your verbal self is continually observing your own behaviour and making statements based on observation and guessing rather than direct knowledge. For example, if a friend asks you to join him for dinner and you've already eaten, you may agree but warn him that you're not really hungry. As the meal progresses you may surprise yourself by eating a lot and even ordering a pudding. This might cause you to say, 'I must have been really hungry.' After observing your own behaviour, your verbal self is forced to correct its faulty assessment of your own current attitude about eating.[2] Though your verbal self can feel the effects of adrenaline, endorphins and other chemical messengers in your bloodstream produced by lower parts of your brain or body, it is often forced to guess at the interpretation of these sensations.

This was clearly demonstrated in a classic experiment[3] where human subjects were injected with adrenaline (the natural substance that increases heart rate in emergencies and emotional arousal) and asked to describe how they felt. Each subject was put in a room with another person who had secretly been told to act either euphoric (happy) or angry. When the experimenters asked the subjects how the drug made them feel, almost all of them mirrored the feelings of the other person. If the person in the room with them acted angrily, they reacted with anger. If the person sharing the room acted euphoric, they felt euphoric. Clearly this shows that we habitually guess about our feelings, using whatever clues are to hand.[4]

The things we fear are not logical decisions but rather the result of observing our own reactions. If we run in panic from something, or break out into a sweat when we see it, our verbal self takes note of what it saw to bring its verbal version of our attitude into sync with reality. The conditioned behavioural response comes first and then the verbal rationalization tries to make sense of it.

We continually adjust our verbal model of our own attitudes to agree with our observed behaviour. When I say, 'I *must be* in love' it is usually based on observations about my own behaviour. I may notice that my pulse races when I am with the object of my love and that I am continually going out of my way to be with her. It is our own *observed* behaviour that helps us deduce that we are in love.

Sometimes, we are even mistaken in our verbal assessment of our own feelings. People may say that they hate somebody when they really love them. The mistake is usually obvious to friends. The reason friends' observations are often more accurate is that they are observing the behaviour more impartially. When we observe our own behaviour we often interpret it in a self-serving way. When you try to examine your own attitudes you must be extremely careful not to be fooled into accepting these rationalizations as actual knowledge.

SELF-CONTROL AND WILL-POWER

One reason we get so confused about our separate attitude systems is that either one is capable of taking control of our actions. When we use self-control or will-power, our verbal self takes control away from and overrides the behavioural system. Remember that the verbal self talks logically about attitudes, while most *behaviour* is controlled by other parts of the brain which know no language and learn like an animal, by conditioning.

Since the verbal self is usually not in control, it isn't surprising that people often behave in ways that are not consistent with their stated beliefs or attitudes. Only when self-control takes over do we consistently act according to our stated beliefs. If we logically convince a businessman that he shouldn't be prejudiced against women, he may still show prejudice in the way he treats his workers – except when he exercises self-control. To change his behavioural response will require more than just words.

No wonder we have such trouble with attitudes when our basic understanding is so flawed. We actually use rationalization almost continually to try to deduce a model of how our own mind works. Like a press secretary, our verbal self gives confident explanations which are really just plausible guesses. After a while we begin to believe that our fabricated explanations are real. The fact is that *conditioned behaviour uses no words, so there is nothing there that our verbal self can understand*. The rationalization that we use to try to make sense of our actions is based only on wishful thinking and observation of our own behaviour. All the complexities of a behaviour such as walking are accessible to your verbal self only by watching yourself walk. Our feeling that we have direct knowledge of our behavioural attitudes is simply an illusion resulting from the fact that we have had a lifetime of practice watching our own behaviour. We feel the same way about anything we practise a lot. Just as a chess master begins to 'feel' the effect of moves in advance, we get a false sense that we have direct knowledge of our own behavioural attitudes.[5]

WHY SELF-HELP OFTEN FAILS

When you read a self-help book, the words affect only your verbal self. Books can teach you to *talk* differently about your behaviour but the behavioural problem itself remains except when you override it with self-control. Since the animal part of the brain understands no language, it can learn only by experience – like an animal.

This brings us to one of the major insights of this book: **To really change your own attitudes your verbal self must learn to be like the animal trainer of your own behaviour**. By using your self-control briefly at critical moments, you can set up the needed learning experiences to retrain your own behavioural attitudes.[6]

Though primates and humans both throw stones at their prey, **only humans practise their throwing ability.** Even small children in primitive tribes have this ability because they have a language-based verbal self that can take them beyond reactive animal instincts. When we practise throwing, we use self-control to set up the learning situation, though the throwing itself is done by the lower parts of the brain. Conditioned behavioural learning from successes and failures gradually improves the throwing skill. Though your verbal self understands the concept of practice, it has only the poorest understanding of how to actually throw a rock. It is simply the trainer.

When you practise anything non-verbal, you are using your self-control as a trainer for a behavioural skill which your verbal self only poorly understands. Your skill may improve, but your verbal self probably won't have any access to the new knowledge. Most of a sports coach's job consists of simply putting his team in practice situations that allow their conditioned behaviour to learn from experience.

A dog trainer can't *tell* a dog how to jump through hoops but she can set up learning experiences to modify the dog's behaviour. A good trainer rewards the dog for achieving small sub-goals that eventually lead to the final result she wants. She doesn't expect the dog to immediately start jumping through hoops. What she does instead is hold up a hoop in front of the dog and reward it every time it steps through. By then raising the hoop a little higher each time, the trainer can soon have the dog jumping quite high through the hoop.

Animal trainers teach by setting up learning experiences. Since books deal in words, they change only the logical, verbal version of your attitudes. To really change your behaviour, you must use self-control to set up learning experiences for your behaviour.

This behavioural conditioning process used on animals is exactly the same one your verbal self must use to modify your own behaviour. For instance, if you wanted to gain confidence in public speaking, you would start by practising on one friend, then work your way up by speaking successfully to a tiny group and then ever-larger audiences. Your verbal self's job is to set up manageable challenges and be firm and supportive to maximize your chances of success.

The part of your mind that can read and understand this book is a new addition tacked on very recently by evolution. To make effective change it must learn to face the fact that most of your behaviour is determined by older parts of your mind that don't understand words, time or logic. Your logical self must learn to be a trainer, not a controller. Animal trainers have developed very effective techniques which you must learn well if you are to succeed.

As you develop your skills as a trainer, you will become more and more effective at making deep changes to your own behaviour and attitudes which will eliminate the need for self-control. Self-training creates attitude changes at the deep emotional level while it helps you develop co-operative teamwork between your verbal self and other parts of your mind and body.

ANIMAL TRAINING TIPS

(apply to deep human behaviour too)

- Be consistent in immediately rewarding good behaviour and punishing bad. Don't allow exceptions that may confuse the training. Remember that animals don't understand complex logical distinctions or thinking in the future or past.
- Repeat conditioning with ever-increasing difficulty till you create a well-worn path. Subdivide major goals into achievable sub-goals that lead to the desired final result. Let the animal step through the hoop first and then raise it a little each time till it becomes a high jump.
- Don't over-control. Be decisive in your commands but let the animal be in full control as much as possible so that confidence and autonomy will develop and maximum learning will occur.
- Develop a good rapport with your animal based on mutual respect and support. Have fun together.

ANIMAL ATTITUDES DECLINE TOO

If you watch the older animals in the zoo you will get a good idea of what naturally happens to untrained behavioural attitudes. Nature tends to take the path of least resistance, so each animal finds a comfortable niche where it can exist with a minimum of effort. Sleeping all day is common for mature zoo animals and house pets. Only wild animals exposed to daily challenges remain vital into old age without training. Our behavioural side, being derived from lower animals, has inherited this same tendency. Without training help from our verbal self, our behaviour gets lazy and spoilt, just like a spoilt house pet. Well-trained dogs, horses and other animals retain vitality into old age. Attitude jogging is purposeful training, undertaken by your verbal self, directed at keeping your youthful joy alive and improving your attitude factor for a longer, happier life.

Unfortunately, most people's verbal self is like an animal trainer who hasn't been taught how to train animals. When the animals get lazy, the best she can do is try to keep her job by making up excuses for them. Rationalization is simply an honest attempt to make the best of a bad situation when you don't know how to revitalize your menagerie or even that you have the power to do so. This book will help you to open up your verbal self to its own power and show you how you can train your attitudes back into vitality. Breaking the lifelong habit of covering for them with rationalizations will be the most difficult part of this job.

As a victim of misinformation you need feel no guilt. You were raised with a false understanding of the mind which ignores the true source of most behaviour and blames your verbal self for everything you do. What else could you do but try to make up excuses? Unfortunately, correcting this misunderstanding is just a start, because lifelong habits are not easily broken. Changing bad habits is hard work, but the reward of a longer, happier life is well worth it.

LONG-TERM GOALS AND SELF-CONTROL

Behaviour is conditioned by rewards and punishments, so its time horizon is quite limited. If you punish your dog a week after he has ruined the living room rug, the lesson will be wasted. Only humans have the gift of language which makes logic and long-term planning possible. Our own conditioned behaviour is as short-sighted as a dog's, but self-control gives us the power to make short-term sacrifices to achieve long-term goals.

Most of the time we are controlled by the simpler non-verbal kind of thinking we share with other animals. This conditioned behaviour is always present-orientated. Eating sweets provides pleasure in the short term, thereby reinforcing the behaviour. However, in a longer time-frame continuing to eat sweets can make us ill. In an even longer time-frame it will make us fat. This is why most people use self-control to stop themselves after a few sweets, even though their conditioned behaviour would drive them to continue eating. Binge eaters are unable to use self-control to override their short-term conditioned behaviour and therefore suffer the consequences.

Gambling and shopping are similar situations where most people use self-control to prevent long-term consequences beyond the time-frame of conditioned behaviour. Since the bills don't arrive for a month or so, the corrective punishment comes too late to be effective for behavioural conditioning. In fact, self-control is our only defence against long-term consequences. It intervenes at crucial moments in our lives to protect us from consequences that are beyond the short time-perspective of conditioned behaviour.

WHY ATTITUDES DECLINE

We all know the consequences of eating too many sweets or buying too much on a shopping spree, so most of us learn when to use self-control to protect ourselves. Few people have a similar awareness of when they make the seemingly harmless decisions that ultimately lead to attitude decline. It is much like eating sweets without knowing that they can cause obesity. Since our behaviour is conditioned by short-term rewards, our only hope for preventing attitude decline is by using self-control to intervene at these crucial moments to prevent a long-term disaster.

Since attitude decline often takes decades, and even then our rationalization conceals it, few people are even aware of the problem. Attitudes decline as the cumulative result of thousands of innocent-looking decisions to seek comfort and safety in the short term. Much of this book will focus on developing an understanding that will help you to recognize these important moments where self-control must intervene to protect your long-term interests.

When we exercise self-control our verbal self takes over and directly controls our actions. This self-conscious behaviour is sometimes crucial for keeping us out of trouble, but tends to be stiff, excessively logical and unfeeling. Self-control is therefore best used minimally and decisively – as a brief exception to normal behaviour rather than a sustained mode of living. The lower parts of our brain are the primary source of joy and meaning in life. When they are in control we are 'in the moment' and fully experiencing life.

It is therefore extremely important to learn to use self-control only during the really critical moments of your life when it will make a major difference. These critical moments are usually only one or two seconds long, yet they can determine your whole future.

Learning to recognize these magical moments takes practice. In the next chapter we will explore some important new scientific insights into the amazingly complex process by which attitudes develop.

Exercise One

1. Try to think of a friend who talks one attitude but whose behaviour conflicts with that attitude (e.g. a male chauvinist pig or bigot who claims to be liberal).
2. Discuss the inconsistency with them and observe their reaction.
3. Acting the role of a sceptic, examine your own attitudes for such inconsistencies.

Exercise Two

1. Try to describe in words how you sneeze, one step at a time.
2. Did you find yourself trying to visualize or observe yourself to figure it out?

Exercise Three

1. Watch a pet or other animal for signs of non-verbal attitudes and emotional reactions to people, food and other animals and external objects. Observe the 'subtitles' that are possible with no language ability at all.
2. Practise visualizing your own non-self-controlled behaviour as originating in an evolutionary remnant of lower animals in the lower part of your brain.
3. Notice when you shift to self-control how easy it becomes to verbalize what you are doing and why.

Exercise Four

Practise using self-control to override your natural behaviour and feeling the different conscious sensations. For example, while eating, stop the fork in mid-air as you are about to take a bite. Just freeze in that position and notice how easily you can verbalize what you are doing. When you return to your normal eating pattern notice how you can easily think about other things and are almost unconscious of the act of eating.

CHAPTER SUMMARY

1. Our verbal explanations for many things are based on observing our own behaviour and then making up plausible rationalizations.
2. The human brain evolved from lower animals without a single opportunity for major reorganization.
3. Language, logic and long-term-planning evolved long after basic behavioural attitudes and emotional responses were well established in lower parts of the brain.
4. Cats, dogs and monkeys have complex attitudes and emotional responses without language.
5. Our verbal self's version of our attitudes doesn't necessarily agree with our behavioural attitudes, which are in control most of the time.
6. The only time our verbal self is in control is when we use *self-control* or *will-power*.
7. Changing your mind about an attitude from reading or discussion will not change your behaviour except during self-control.
8. Introspection shows us only our verbal self's version of our attitudes. Our faulty understanding of the mind makes us expect our behaviour to agree.
9. Books speak only to your verbal self; to change your behaviour you must use self-control to set up conditioning experiences as an animal trainer would.
10. Only your verbal self can consider long-term side-effects of your behaviour, so self-control is the only way to prevent the attitude decline that often results from pursuing short-term goals (e.g. feeling good through overeating, shopping, etc).

CHAOS AND ATTITUDE DEVELOPMENT

On the day you were born you already had an attitude towards nipples. You loved nipples and would instinctively suck and knead anything that vaguely resembled a breast. During the first few months of life the newest part of your brain, which is now the basis of your language, logic and verbal self, was only partly developed and still not functional. However, behavioural learning in the lower parts of your brain began almost immediately as you developed a preference for the smell of your own mother's breast (or the rubber teat of your bottle). This preference was reinforced each time you got a nourishing meal.

Throughout life, behavioural attitudes continue to develop by this same process of reinforcement. Every time a specific behaviour pattern succeeds, that pattern is reinforced, making it more likely to be used in the future. Bad experiences cause negative reinforcement, making them less likely to be tried in the future. Basic behaviour patterns, including your attitudes, are thus developed much as you would train an animal – by the conditioning of reward and punishment.

Each positive experience actually causes chemical and electrical changes in your brain which make it more likely that the pattern will be repeated in the future. This is actually a form of learning, with a final result much like the well-worn paths animals create through the meadows and woods. Every time the path is used makes it easier to follow that path in the future. As the path becomes well worn, it becomes more and more difficult to change.

WHY ATTITUDES REINFORCE THEMSELVES

Attitudes determine the way we feel about and react to specific things. Our likes and dislikes are created by experiences: We tend to like things we associate with good experiences and hate things we associate with bad experiences. Herein lies another key reason attitudes can become such a problem: When you have a negative attitude about something, that attitude almost guarantees that your future experiences with it will be unpleasant. Since these unpleasant experiences condition you to hate it even more, there is no escape. Once you start disliking something, the dislike tends to reinforce itself. On the other hand, things you like produce pleasant experiences, further reinforcing your attraction to them. This leads us to one of the major reasons attitudes so easily run amuck: *Attitudes are inherently self-reinforcing*.

Because of this self-reinforcing tendency, your first encounter with anything new is a very important event. On your first ever encounter, liking or disliking is often a matter of chance; the weather, your mood, other people's attitudes, encountering a particularly good or bad example the first time are all chance factors that could get you started on the like or the dislike path. Since reinforcement usually simply strengthens likes or dislikes, the difference between a lifelong hate and a lifelong love is often nothing more than chance.[1]

Pets provide an amazing example of how existing attitudes reinforce themselves by changing our reaction to things. I have many friends who love dogs and cats so much that when their pets defecate or vomit on the floor this is not even perceived as a bad experience. These friends seem to love the animals even more. Yet a person who fears cats will consider it a horrible experience if a cat simply sits on his or her lap and purrs. In both cases the existing attitude is reinforced by what should be an attitude-changing experience.

The same self-reinforcing tendency that perpetuates an attitude can also magnify attitude changes – particularly in the negative direction. A single bad experience can frighten you so that you get a negative feeling each time you encounter anything related to the cause of the bad experience. Often the negative reaction spills over and affects your reactions to other related things.

Likewise a very positive experience with something you thought you hated can cause a reversal of attitude which is then reinforced. Unfortunately this is not as common in everyday life because of the principle known colloquially as 'shit happens': Things naturally tend to break but they seldom fix themselves. Since negative mishaps and accidents are far more common than dramatic reversals in the positive direction, attitudes naturally tend to decline unless we make a conscious effort to improve them.

With attitude jogging your self-control will learn to intentionally set up positive experiences to offset the effects of the inevitable negative mishaps and accidents that are a part of life. The 'shit happens' aspect of real life guarantees that your attitudes will decline if you don't put forth some conscious effort to offset this effect. While you're at it, a little extra effort can actually put you in an upward spiral where attitudes improve with age.

FALLING OFF A HORSE

As you go through life, accidents happen to you or your friends which make you cautious or fearful. These negative experiences accumulate and cause your attitudes to generally decline unless you expend some effort to reverse the process. If you fall off a horse it takes effort and self-control to overcome your fear and get back in the saddle. Anyone who currently rides horses will confirm that this is what you must do. *People who 'used to' ride horses may disagree.*

Using your will-power to get back on a horse after a spill is a perfect example of a 'critical moment'. Your logical self must intervene just long enough to get your foot in the stirrup. After that the lower parts of your brain take over the actual riding and you have a positive riding experience that offsets the negative conditioning of the fall. Your self-control is the animal trainer holding up the hoop, and your conditioned behaviour responds by jumping through it.

If you miss the critical moment and decide not to remount the horse, it will take much more will-power to overcome your fear later. This is why it is so important *to learn to recognize your critical moments and get in the habit of seizing them without hesitation.* The first opportunity is always the easiest.

CHAOS AND COMPLEXITY THEORY

For most of this century scientists have been deluding themselves into thinking that they were on the verge of solving almost every imaginable problem. In the 1970s a new awareness began to emerge that science had been unconsciously limiting itself to a tiny subset of the world's problems. In the past two decades a new approach to science has been developing which attempts to attack a whole world of much more complex real-world problems where nothing is reversible. The new sciences of complexity and chaos theory[2] have provided important insights about important irreversible processes: world-wide weather patterns, the world economy, new technology trends, and even human personality development.[3] In each of these problems, each moment is affected in very complex ways by all previous history, so seemingly insignificant changes at *critical moments* can drastically alter final outcomes.

One of the most important insights of this new thinking is that in any complex development over time there are long periods of relative stability punctuated occasionally by critical moments where a slight change in conditions can have a major impact on all future development. In chaos theory they call these critical moments *bifurcations.* At these critical decision points, seemingly insignificant random external influences can make dramatic differences to the final outcome.

For example, the action of waves lapping a sandy shoreline will naturally develop into large, uneven scallop shapes, even on a long, even beach. The location of these massive arcs of sand is initially defined by tiny initial variations in the sand. A sand castle left at the right time and place on the beach can eventually develop into one of these massive shapes. The large meanders in a river are similarly initially started by tiny rocks or bumps.

The mathematicians call this extreme sensitivity to small changes the *butterfly effect* after a famous example relating to weather: A butterfly in Beijing can be the indirect cause of a storm two weeks later in New York. Here is how it would happen: If the breeze from the butterfly's wings breaks the stillness of the air in Beijing, that breeze could eventually build into a tiny cyclone. This cyclone of air may eventually grow till it causes a storm. As that storm interacts with world-wide weather patterns, an eventual result could be a storm in New York two weeks later. Actually the New York storm would also depend on many other critical moments, but without the butterfly in Beijing, the complex chain of events that led to the storm would never have happened.

ATTITUDES AND COMPLEXITY

Your attitudes today also have many complex causes based in your historical past. They are the result of many critical moments that could have gone one way or the other depending on chance variations in your life circumstances. Each decision point is like the branching of a tree. As you climb the tree you make decisions at each branching. Where you are right now is dependent on every single decision point that led you there.

Whether you like to ride horses today depends upon a whole complex sequence of critical moments: Did your Uncle have a horse? Did you say yes when he offered to let you ride it? Was it a gentle horse? Did your mother cancel your first riding lesson because of a luncheon engagement? Did you get back on the horse when he threw you the last time you went riding? Each of these critical moments lasted only a second or two, yet each, and hundreds more, had a major effect on your present attitude towards horses.

HOW ATTITUDES DEVELOP

As a child, your first encounter with a cat may be a positive or a negative experience depending upon whether the cat purrs or scratches you. This critical moment is like the first branch on a tree which leads to your current attitude about cats. If the cat scratched you, your attitude branches towards the cat-hater side of the tree. However, this does not doom you to forever hating cats because subsequent critical moments where you have good experiences with cats can eventually take you over to the cat-lover side of the tree. However, since each critical moment builds upon the effect of previous ones, early experiences have a leverage advantage. Since memories naturally fade, recent experiences also have an advantage.

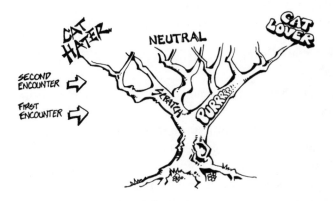

Your behavioural attitude towards cats develops by conditioning. Each time you experience a cat makes you like them more or less, depending upon whether the experience is positive or negative. Each experience biases your reaction to future experiences so that, if you've been scratched a few times, you will tend to be conditioned negatively even if the cat is friendly.

Each of your attitudes has its own developmental history, with critical decision points determining your final attitude. These critical moments in your life correspond to the bifurcation points of mathematical chaos and complexity theory. At these critical moments a tiny change in conditions can make a enormous difference to your future. These are the turning points where life changes can be triggered by seemingly insignificant events. One of the principles of attitude jogging is learning to use self-control at these sensitive moments to take control of and direct your own attitude development.

Attitudes determine how we react to general categories of things, like cats and animals, but we also develop related but more specific short-term attitudes. For example, we may have an attitude about a particular cat, a particular film or a particular dinner party that may differ from our general attitude about that category. The mechanism is the same but the time-scale is shorter. Each specific attitude contributes to a longer-term general attitude about that category. Your attitude towards this particular dinner party is strongly affected by your general attitude about parties. If this party turns out to be exceptionally enjoyable, your general attitude about parties and other social gatherings will move up a notch.

WHY YOU CAN'T GO BACK

Wouldn't it be nice if you could go back and undo the damage done at some of the critical moments in your life? Unfortunately this is as impossible as stopping a storm in New York by taking a butterfly net to Beijing. The problem is that *each critical moment affects all of the future decision points.* Many psychotherapists waste their patients' time and money by focusing excessively on past events. Some even try to take the patient back to relive critical times with different reactions. While this may be a useful visualization exercise, the idea of changing the effects of past events by returning to the past is wishful thinking. The problem is that the crucial moments that change your life do so primarily by their effect on *later* critical moments. To erase the effect of a childhood trauma, you would have to erase much more than the memory of that trauma. You would also have to change the memories of all of the thousands of critical moments which followed that were affected by that initial trauma.

To look at it differently, if you think of the development of an attitude as climbing a tree, then each critical moment is a branching point where you took one path or the other. If you now find yourself on the 'afraid of cats' side of your 'attitude towards cats' tree, you will never be able to make yourself love cats by reliving your first encounter with a cat. The problem is that you will still have all of the memories of the other negative encounters that were made negative by that first bad experience. Fortunately, the tree is still growing. All you can really do now is to continue on up the tree and accumulate some positive cat experiences as you proceed. With time, you can work your way over towards the other side of the tree.

It would certainly be nice if we could really time-travel and change the past, but the hard reality is that we can only control the present. If you have had 20 years of bad experiences with cats it will take some time to undo them. The good news is that when you understand the attitude development process you can plan intentional experiences to take you where you want to go. These can be extremely powerful against the haphazard, random experiences that led your attitudes to their present state.

In Chapter 8 we will cover some of the amazingly effective techniques which cognitive-behavioural therapists have developed for correcting phobias. Since phobias are essentially pathologically bad attitudes, we will adapt these techniques and use them against the less dramatic but more widespread problem of attitude decline. But first, we'll look (in the next chapter) at some other cultures to witness the amazing power of attitudes to define our very reality.

Exercise One

1. Think of a long-held belief that you once had which you now feel is false. In other words, think of something you have changed your mind about.
2. Now think back and remember how that belief seemed to be reinforced by your experiences before it changed.
3. Now think about how your *new* belief seems to be reinforced by experience.

Exercise Two

1. Make a list of critical moments that happened in the past week (e.g. breaking/sticking with your diet, making/catching yourself

about to make a wrong turn, saying/not saying something in a hurtful way).

2. Did your self-control intervene at the critical moment to your satisfaction?

Exercise Three

1. Make a list of bad experiences in the past year which have made you more cautious or made you dislike something you liked before.
2. Make a list of positive experiences in the past year which have made you like something that you didn't like before.
3. Are you on an upward or downward spiral when it comes to positive attitudes?

CHAPTER SUMMARY

1. Attitudes begin as instinct and then gradually evolve based on experiences in life. They are like well-worn paths.
2. Attitudes are inherently self-reinforcing because they tend to support themselves in the direction they started out.
3. Critical moments in your life push your attitudes in one direction or the other. Self-reinforcement perpetuates these choices into long-lasting preferences and dislikes.
4. Bad experiences that make you afraid of things are more common than mind-opening experiences that make you like things you previously disliked. As a result, attitudes tend to narrow and decline with age, unless you work on them.
5. Chaos and complexity theory shows how critical moments alternating with long stable periods are common in all complex irreversible processes.
6. We can control attitude development by learning to recognize the critical moments and using self-control to push us briefly in directions that will benefit our long-term attitude growth.

CHAPTER
4

PAIN, PLEASURE AND PLACEBOS

The Sherpa of Nepal traditionally act as porters for Western mountain climbers who climb mount Everest. They uncomplainingly carry 77-pound packs up the mountain wearing simple cold-weather gear even in freezing temperatures. Their culture takes pride in their ability to endure pain and hardship without flinching. The climbers, on the other hand, experience great hardships covering the same routes – even after years of training and conditioning and with hi-tech thermal wear, oxygen, and much lighter packs.

In 1982 two American psychologists[1] performed a series of controlled experiments on six Nepalese and five Western trekkers. They found that the Nepalese were just as sensitive to stimuli as the Westerners and just as able to make discriminations between high- and low-intensity stimuli. The only difference was found to be in the interpretation of painful stimuli: What the Westerners would call unbearable pain, the Sherpas would accept stoically. Their learned attitude towards pain was simply different to that of the Western trekkers.

The experience of pain feels so basic that we tend to think of it as permanently wired into our nervous system by evolution. One of the reasons for this misconception is that we tend to learn attitudes from our culture. Since we all tend to imitate the cultural norm, we see a deceptive uniformity of response which makes that response seem 'normal'. When we study other cultures, however, we see an incredible variation in even basic responses to pain and pleasure, which proves that such attitudes are largely learned by example. Our parents and others around us teach us our attitudes by their example.

In Bavaria today it is considered inappropriate to ask for anaesthesia when you have a tooth filled, yet 200 miles to the north most Berliners consider it a necessity. In many African tribes virtually everyone painfully mutilates their body without complaint. Subcultures within our own society enjoy piercing their bodies and even bondage and torture.

It is common for people with serious injuries who are absorbed in important survival actions not to feel the pain until they are safe and able to focus on the pain. In wartime, soldiers often suffer severe wounds including the loss of limbs and open abdominal wounds without complaining about the pain. Some soldiers with major injuries actually react with euphoria at the thought of being able to leave the battlefield and go home.

In Lamaze natural childbirth classes, mothers are taught to experience the pain of childbirth positively. The group setting of these classes helps establish a new cultural norm within that group. One of the techniques used is to practise plunging your hand into ice water and tolerating it for longer and longer periods, feeling the sensation as intense but natural. After such training, many mothers can then deliver their babies happily without any pain-relief medication.

Though we are all affected by the culture we find ourselves in, individual attitudes can vary widely from the norm. Dentists will confirm that even within one culture people's tolerance for pain varies greatly. A nonconformist attitude can take people far from the cultural norm. An example of extreme variation in attitude towards pain would be the masochist, who actually enjoys pain. The process by which this kind of attitude develops is of great interest because it illustrates how pain can be turned into pleasure and also how we can free ourselves from cultural norms about ageing. More about this later.

Even animals learn their basic attitudes by imitating the examples of their parents. A Canadian study[2] showed this in an experiment sure to be unpopular with dog lovers. They raised dogs from birth in a protected and isolated environment where they had no contact whatsoever with older animals. Deprived of learning by experience or example during early development, these dogs seemed to be insensitive to pain. Presented with a lighted match, the dogs would fearlessly approach it, nuzzle it and even repeatedly snuff it out by sniffing it. They also repeatedly licked extremely hot central heating pipes without showing any evidence of pain. Even after two years of unrestricted existence some of the dogs continued to exhibit this casual attitude towards pain.

ATTITUDE: THE DIFFERENCE BETWEEN PAIN AND PLEASURE

Imagine a loud outdoor rock concert where thousands of young people are ecstatic with pleasure listening to the music. A mile away, an elderly couple calls the police to complain about the intolerable noise level. Both are hearing the same sounds, yet their reactions to it are totally opposite because of different attitudes. What seems intolerably loud noise to the old couple is actually thousands of times softer than the sound level bringing intense pleasure at the concert, yet their attitude turns pleasure into pain.

Any sound above a certain threshold is perceived as pain, but certain sounds are more annoying than others. A barking dog is naturally more upsetting than chirping crickets. If the dog has ruined your sleep all week, it sounds even more annoying. The insignificant noise of a dripping water faucet can be agonizing if your mental attitude makes it so.

Our reaction to smell is also a learned response. The first person to eat Gorgonzola and Limburger cheese must have been hungry indeed. After years of eating them I have begun to find their smell interesting where it was formerly repulsive. Burning leaves always had a nostalgic smell during my childhood, but now many consider it air pollution.

The smell of the seashore at low tide is often essentially rotting seaweed and dead fish, but it smells quite romantic and nostalgic to some people. We have become very fussy about the smell of human excrement, but in European cities before the turn of the century everybody emptied their chamber pots into the street, making a smell that would certainly make us sick today.

Food preferences also vary tremendously with culture. Eating live grubs, termites, steer eyeballs or sea cucumbers may seem disgusting to us, but all are enjoyable delicacies to the majority in some cultures. Even a nice juicy steak can look absolutely disgusting to a strict vegetarian who sees it for what it is – a piece of a dead animal.

The things we love and the things we hate all seem to us to be inherently lovely or hateful, yet they are all really nothing more than learned attitudes – which are remarkably changeable. The things that we now find hateful, uncomfortable or even boring can all be seen as challenges which attitude jogging can overcome. In Chapter 6 you will see how.

ENJOYING A SAUNA

The aboriginal people of Tierra del Fuego close to the Antarctic circle lived essentially naked in the freezing cold when the Europeans first encountered them. In the deserts of north Africa, tribesmen live with *average* summer temperatures of over 110°F (43°C).

Everybody has a range of temperatures in which they feel comfortable, but this comfort range can vary tremendously with conditioning. Your comfort range changes significantly with the seasons as exposure to extremes of cold and heat condition you and alter your concept of what is a 'normal' temperature. People who live in cold climates often rejoice at unseasonably 'warm' winter weather and remove their coats to enjoy temperatures which they would call uncomfortably cold in late summer. This drastic change in attitude after six months' gradual conditioning illustrates just how amazingly changeable your comfort range is.

In Finland over half of the homes have saunas where people intentionally expand their comfort range by alternately experiencing the extreme heat of the sauna and then rolling in the snow or jumping into icy water. The result is a healthy, vigorous attitude towards temperature extremes which allows the Finns to enjoy both hot and cold. Since the human anxiety response works by the same mechanism as our response to cold, there is good evidence that toughening ourselves to temperature changes also effectively reduces depression and anxiety.[3]

The sauna is an excellent demonstration of how attitudes can turn pain into pleasure. In a sauna people go to considerable trouble and expense to sit in a hot, humid atmosphere for the sheer enjoyment of it. On a hot, humid day people usually complain bitterly that they hate the heat – the difference is simply one of attitude. Our choice of words to describe temperature extremes reflects our attitude. 'Balmy' or 'sultry' weather is really the same as 'sweltering' or 'miserably hot' weather except for the attitude factor. 'Freezing cold' weather can just as well be perceived as 'invigorating' or 'brisk'. The difference in the experience is essentially the difference between pain and pleasure.

Later in this book I will show you how to work on your own attitude towards discomfort, heat and cold, and make significant changes in your own reactions. Your body's physical reaction to cold is identical to its reaction to fear, challenge, embarrassment and stress. When your face flushes and your heart pounds, it's the same reaction you have when you jump in cold water, so toughening exercises can be very effective against fearfulness. Once you understand the principles of attitude development, you will be able to widen your own comfort range and learn to enjoy yourself while others around you are miserable and complaining.

THE PLACEBO EFFECT

The placebo effect is an amazing demonstration of the power of mental attitudes to improve health and eliminate pain. Placebos are sugar pills that do their work entirely by the power of suggestion. The placebo effect is so strong that experiments have shown placebos to be as effective as eight milligrams of morphine for relief of pain.[4] For about one third of the population, a placebo will give 50 per cent pain relief.

Since the relief is entirely a result of changing expectations, placebos are much more effective if they are strongly recommended by a doctor. A recent British study found that brand names helped increase the effectiveness of placebos given as headache remedies. Unbranded placebos significantly helped 40 per cent of the subjects, while 50 per cent were helped if the placebos had a brand name. In the same study, 56 per cent were helped by generic aspirin, while 60 per cent benefited from identical brand-named aspirin.

Placebo injections are more effective than capsules, and placebo capsules more effective than pills. Even the colour of the pill has been found to make a difference. Small yellow pills work best for depression, while large blue pills make the best sedatives. One of the reasons drug testing is so expensive is that *any* illness, including cancer, can be helped by *any* treatment if it is confidently given because of the amazing power of the placebo effect.

To find out if treatments *really* work, it is necessary to do double-blind testing. In this type of test some of the subjects, called controls, are secretly given placebos. If the new treatment doesn't work significantly better than the placebos, the treatment is not considered effective. It has been found that results end up being biased significantly if either the examiners or the patients know who is getting the placebos. Apparently, subtle non-verbal cues and unconscious errors in data collection will otherwise unfairly favour the real treatment. With double-blind testing this bias is eliminated by requiring that both the examiners and the patients are totally unaware of who gets the placebos.

The placebo effect is so pervasive that double-blind testing must be used to evaluate even such things as surgery and psychotherapy. Many treatments which seem to be very effective with uncontrolled testing turn out to be totally ineffective when evaluated properly under double-blind testing.

Surgery also has a strong placebo effect. To evaluate a new surgery properly it is necessary to do controlled experiments where *dummy surgery* is actually performed on some randomly-selected volunteers: An incision is made but the internal corrective work is secretly not done on some of the subjects.[5] Unless the real surgery produces significantly better results than the dummy surgery, the treatment must be considered ineffective. One formerly popular surgery for asthma was performed by one doctor on 3,914 patients with 65 per cent reporting moderate to marked improvement. Later double-blind testing showed that a dummy incision and stitches in the same location was equally effective.[6]

The amazing benefits of placebo treatments are a direct result of the attitude changes which result from changed expectations. Placebo cures are extremely effective for alleviating pain and for curing and preventing virtually any mental or physical disease. They dramatically demonstrate the power of attitude changes to improve your health and happiness.[7] With attitude jogging we try to bypass the sugar pills and go to work directly on the attitudes themselves.

Many alternative medical treatments are undoubtedly effective simply because they bring hope to a hopeless situation. People who are told that they have a terminal disease go into a state of hopelessness that essentially shuts their immune system down. When someone confidently offers them a cure, the hopelessness is alleviated and his or her immune system often rallies. As long as such treatments are inexpensive and don't turn people from proven medical treatments, they are probably useful.

Some kinds of meditation can apparently enhance your immune response. In fact, a recent experiment demonstrated that focusing your mind on 'thoughts of appreciation' measurably increases your immune response as measured by the IgA antibodies in your saliva.[8] An even stronger increase was measured when special 'designer music' was played at the same time. The average increase for all 10 people tested was 141 per cent with the music and 50 per cent without it. The type of music used made a big difference, with by far the best results obtained with the special 'designer music' on a best-selling American CD called *Heart Zones*.[9] Some people can get as much as a 250 per cent increase in immune activity in just 15 minutes. I have tried it myself and I got an amazing increase after just 15 minutes of focusing on thoughts of appreciation of my mother.

The proper technique is to focus your positive feelings on the area of your heart and sustain them for 15 minutes while you listen to the music. It is probably not coincidental that prayers of appreciation are amazingly similar to this technique. Though the experimenters didn't try religious music, I wouldn't be surprised to find that it works as well as the designer music.[10] People with faith in God have been found to live longer and to have a better prognosis when they have heart disease or cancer. The reason may well be a combination of the real power of prayer on the immune system and the fact that their religious faith makes them feel less hopeless.

THE MIND-BODY CONNECTION

The amazingly strong connection between mental states and good health has only recently been re-discovered. For decades, specialization in the medical profession led orthodox medical practitioners into a false sense of separation of the mind from the body. Medical researchers working in their separate specialities had identified and given separate names to chemical messengers in the nervous system, the endocrine system and the immune system. This perpetuated the misunderstanding of these three systems as separate entities. Recent discoveries have shown that the conceptual separation of these systems is nothing but a historical artefact.

We now realize that they are richly interconnected by chemical messengers. Some 60 – 70 different molecules called peptides have been identified which travel through the bloodstream and keep the brain, the glands and the immune system in constant communication. This invisible communications network is now being mapped using new techniques which can find and identify the receptors for each type of peptide molecule.

Endorphins, for example, were originally thought to be produced only in the brain, but turn out to be produced also by glands and immune cells. White blood cells have been found to have receptors for virtually all of the peptides and can also produce peptides themselves. Each immune cell is thus in continuous two-way communications with the brain and the glands that produce it. The regulation of the quantity and the activity of the immune cells is thus determined by delicate feedback loops, which are strongly affected by emotional factors.

Peptides are still called by many names: neurotransmitters, hormones, endorphins, growth factors, etc. depending upon the specialist who first discovered them. The same peptides are used by all three systems, which are not separate at all but act together as an integrated network. Your entire intestine, for example, is lined with peptide receptors – which is why you can feel your emotions 'in your gut'. The mind and body aren't really separate at all – just the disciplines which study them.[11]

Beta endorphin is a peptide produced by the ancient parts of the brain as a reward for following instinctive drives. It is called an opioid because it gives us feelings of pleasure just like opium. It also has been found to increase natural killer cell activity, which is an important immune defence against cancer and disease.[12] Emotions such as pleasure and well-being can thus directly increase production of immune cells and send messages to activate them. Likewise, feelings of helplessness have been shown to reduce immune activity.

Have you ever noticed that you usually get colds a few days after a setback or bad experience in your life? A recent experiment reported in the *New England Journal of Medicine*[13] confirmed that this is no mere illusion. The researcher gave psychological stress questionnaires designed to measure helplessness and negative emotions to 394 healthy subjects. He then gave them nose drops containing several types of cold virus. The chances of getting cold symptoms turned out be amazingly predictable from the test scores over an almost two-to-one range. Major diseases, cancer and even accidents have been similarly linked to emotional reactions.

Evolution works by culling the weak and preserving the strong. Mating battles in some species allow only the strongest to reproduce. Predators cull the weak in others. Perhaps the weakening of the human immune system by feelings of helplessness is nature's way of culling to improve the breed. One massive study in Finland examined the health records of 96,000 widowed people and found that ***their probability of dying was actually doubled*** in the week after losing their mate.[14]

Feelings of pleasure and well-being have the opposite effect. They tell your immune system that you are thriving; it responds by working at peak efficiency so that you can survive and reproduce. The feeling of exultation that follows successfully dealing with a challenge actually energizes your immune system. Stress which can be dealt with thus actually helps you to maintain good health.

We are fortunate to be able to use this new understanding of mind-body interactions to our own advantage. By directing our attitude jogging efforts at developing attitudes which are scientifically proven to be healthy, we can maximize not only the quality of our lives but its quantity as well.

Exercise One

1. Think back to the last time you were ill. Was your life running smoothly during the few days before you fell ill?
2. Next time you are ill, think back a few days and try to recall a negative event which may have weakened your immune response.

Exercise Two

1. Make a reservation at an ethnic restaurant which serves food that you have avoided because you consider it 'creepy' (such as raw fish in a Japanese restaurant, sea slugs in a Chinese restaurant).
2. Order something that pushes your comfort zone just enough so that you can succeed in eating it.
3. Watch the other diners enjoying their food and try to copy their enthusiasm.

Exercise Three

1. Take a long hot shower and then turn off the hot water to make it go suddenly cold. Count the seconds and see how long your self-control can prevail and keep the cold water on.
2. The next time you take a shower, try increasing the time you take the cold water by one second.
3. After you have built your tolerance up to four times as long as on the first day, shorten the cold part of the shower back to what it was on the first day. Notice how easy it is now.
4. Note: if it's Summer now, do the exercise by plunging your hand in a bowl of ice water. This is a long-term difficult exer-

cise which can pay off handsomely by strengthening your self-control and building up your resistance to catching cold. If you have a heart condition, however, consult your doctor before attempting this exercise.

Exercise Four

1. A researcher found that small children laugh an average of 450 times a day, while adults average only 50.
2. Count your laughs for a whole day to see how you are doing.

CHAPTER SUMMARY

1. Our response to pain is learned from our culture, though it seems to be inherent in our neural wiring.
2. Many likes and dislikes that seem fixed to us are also really learned from our culture. Live termites taste good to some people.
3. Temperature comfort ranges vary greatly between cultures and with conditioning as the seasons change.
4. We can change our attitude towards things we are bored or annoyed by and turn them into sources of pleasure.
5. The placebo effect is as effective as 8 milligrams of morphine for pain relief for one third of the population.
6. The placebo effect is so strong that testing of all new drugs and surgery must use expensive double-blind procedures.
7. Since placebos affect only the attitudes of the patient, all of their power to cure disease and relieve pain is really just the power of attitudes.

THE PRINCIPLES OF EXERCISE

Remember the adverts in the old magazines that showed a scrawny runt at the seaside getting sand kicked in his face by a muscular bully while his girlfriend looked on, clearly impressed by the brute? When I was 10 I sent away for their literature and found it very convincing. The brochure was full of 'before-and-after' pictures showing runts even scrawnier than I who had become very impressive musclemen. The fact is, *anyone* can develop big muscles if they just have the self-control to follow a basic exercise programme. As the pictures showed, your starting point is not very important. In fact, many of the Mr Universe winners have started out as runts who got sick of getting sand kicked in their face.

Self-control is a kind of mental strength that develops in exactly the same way as physical strength. Just like muscular strength, self-control gets stronger when you exercise it and it atrophies when you don't use it. If you overstress it, you can strain it and make it weaker. To build it up, you have to stress it a little more each day – just enough to avoid overstress.

The mind and the body are made of similar stuff, yet for some reason most people think of them as two separate and unrelated domains. Body-building is so well understood that most people accept the fact that virtually anyone can build themselves into a muscleman simply by following an exercise programme. A less well-known fact is that will-power, self-control and mental attitudes all respond to the same kind of training programme you would use to build up your biceps.

If you have very weak biceps now, no problem. You simply start out lifting a smaller weight. The final result may take longer but will still be the same. To build your biceps, you start with a weight which is difficult to lift but not too difficult. You lift that weight enough times to stress the muscle slightly and then you take a day or two for recovery. Each session you increase the weight slightly so that the stress stays at the same significant but tolerable level. Your muscle adapts to the gradually increasing demands by growing stronger during each recovery period. *The ultimate strength you can develop has practically nothing to do with where you started out.*

EXERCISING YOUR SELF-CONTROL

Your mind has the same ability to adapt to demands made upon it as the body. The same 'use it or lose it' principle applies. You build mental strength by successfully taking on difficult but achievable challenges. Overtraining is as bad as undertraining, so you must choose your challenges well and also be sure to let up on the pressure periodically and just relax and enjoy yourself. In attitude jogging you must learn the limitations of your self-control at its current state of development. If you choose too difficult a goal, your failure will leave you weaker than before. Choose your battles well. You must learn to recognize your golden opportunities and seize them without hesitation. These opportunities are the critical moments where minimum effort will produce maximum results. The recovery will come naturally, during the long periods between critical moments.

The satisfaction of overcoming obstacles is a reward you may find addictive. Self-confidence, self-esteem, self-satisfaction and mental strength are all feelings you will have when your self-control successfully negotiates a critical moment. Assertiveness and self-regulation follow naturally from the mental strength you will develop. Whenever you accomplish a goal, you please yourself by accomplishing something that *you* wanted to do. Just as weight-lifters enjoy the feeling of pumping up their biceps, your self-esteem will feel a rosy glow every time you demonstrate your own power. In fact, self-control is the real accomplishment of champion athletes because that is what allows them to stay with their rigorous training routines. Sports records have been shattered in all fields in recent years because trainers have learned to put heavy emphasis on the development of mental strength and positive attitudes.

Though we still have many more concepts to cover, we are finally at a point where we can try some attitude jogging. In the exercise that follows it's extremely important that you assume the role of a no-nonsense animal trainer. Remember that when you try to change habitual behaviour you will feel a resistance that comes from the lower parts of your brain. You must resist your habitual response to that feeling, which is to try to cover up for it with rationalization. Saying that you tried your best but obstacles prevented you from succeeding is not acceptable. To succeed you must adopt the 'no excuses' attitude of a good trainer.

REGAINING A 'USED TO'

The list of 'used to's' you compiled for the test in Chapter 1 gives us an excellent starting point for our first experience with attitude jogging. We will work on regaining one of your 'used to's' as a source of enjoyment. Please pick a fairly easy one from your list. Think of each of the items on your list as a weight to be lifted. We will start with a weight that is not too difficult and gradually build up to the really hard ones. As you build up your mental strength and cleverness at recognizing critical moments, the harder items will become easy. Just as a weight-lifter gradually builds up the size of the weights he or she lifts, we will gradually build up to harder and harder attitude goals.

This is a good time to buy yourself a nice notebook and label it 'Attitude Journal'. If you already have a journal or diary, you can create a special section in it. Now re-copy, in pencil, your list of 'used to's' in a column on the left-hand side of the first page. Sort them in order of difficulty, with the easiest one on top and the hardest on the bottom. Leave plenty of space on the right and between items, because in later chapters we will be covering other types of attitude work. Use a pencil so that you can easily rearrange them as you gain more experience. Starting to make this list is a critical moment for you because it commits you to the process of continual improvement of your attitude factor. Your future happiness, good health and longevity depend on it!

As a simple example of a first attitude exercise, let's assume that you 'used to' enjoy giving dinner parties, but haven't done so for years. Decide on the date for your dinner party and write it to the left of that item on your sorted 'used to' list. Another critical moment. Now telephone your first guest and invite him. Notice that placing the call is a critical moment which ends when you enter the first digit. The actual conversation takes no will-power except for a brief instant when you begin the first sentence about the party. Another critical moment.

Notice that the critical moments when you used self-control were all no more than a few seconds long. They were the moments when your self-control set things into motion and committed you to a new direction. The rest of the time you can simply let your normal behaviour take its course.

BEWARE OF SETBACKS

Usually, you can expect a few snags in this kind of exercise which will require a couple more zaps of self-control. When one of the guests calls to say that he must go on a business trip you will have an excellent excuse to cancel the party and blame the failure on somebody else. Another critical moment. Two seconds of self-control and you begin a sentence suggesting rescheduling the dinner.

These inevitable unplanned critical moments are the real key to success or failure. Your verbal self must develop a knee-jerk reaction to recognize these moments which could sabotage your efforts and, without hesitation, jump in with the needed self-control to keep things on track. Remember that your conditioned behaviour is like a badly trained animal trying to resist your training. You will feel its resistance as an emotional response. Be firm and don't let it suck you into making excuses for it. Your natural habit of rationalization is a formidable enemy. As your self-control gets stronger this will get easier and easier.

Once the dinner party is under way, you have set up your behavioural side with a pleasant evening which should positively reinforce your natural party-giving behaviour. However, there are still dangers. If your behavioural side has a bad attitude about parties, you may have to use self-control again to make a change of direction to liven up the party by putting on some dance music or some other ploy. Another critical moment. Another effective strategy is 'acting as if' you really love parties. If you really get into the role as a good actor would, your behaviour is tricked into following suit. Always try to stay in the moment, because that keeps your verbal self quiet. Really focusing on what your guests are saying *now* helps to keep you in the present. Worrying about the future, or self-conscious behaviour (e.g. Will they like the food? Are we having fun?) defeats the purpose of the exercise.

After the exercise is over, you should close the loop by logging the results in the extreme right of the entry in your Attitude Journal. Another critical moment.

As a final step, set up a free-form comments section about one-quarter of the way into your Attitude Journal. Use this to write down insights, feelings and comments about your attitude exercises, and anything else that comes to mind. Mark each entry with a date. These notes to yourself will help you to think clearly about the changes you are making and where you want to go next.

Behavioural conditioning usually has to be repeated to be effective. If your guests didn't already offer to return the favour, you should write in the date and goal for another party exercise as soon as you finish logging the results. Another critical moment. Depending upon how you feel you can either set yourself a more difficult goal like a larger party or a theme party, or just relax and enjoy a repeat of your triumph.

THE WORST THAT CAN HAPPEN

If you hated the party, don't despair. A wise person once said that if you never make mistakes you must not be trying hard enough.

Anytime you undertake an attitude jogging exercise you should anticipate the possibility of failure and even plan your escape route before you start. In fact, let's refine your Attitude Journal by putting the following heading at the top of the page:

DATE	GOAL	WORST OUTCOME	ESCAPE PLAN	RESULT

By thinking in advance about the worst possible outcome and an escape plan, you can greatly reduce your anxiety about undertaking any attitude exercise. Often our 'used to's' contain some element of fear which is caused by behavioural conditioning. Your verbal self won't be caught off guard and is much better prepared to handle those feelings if it has already thought out the true dangers in advance. For example, the 'worst outcome' for a dinner party is that everyone will be bored and go home early – hardly something to panic about. The escape plan also prepares your verbal self to deal with any behaviour-based feelings of dread. In the case of a dinner party your escape plan can be to warn guests in advance that it will be an early night because you have an early morning appointment. If things turn out to be fun, everyone will forget the warning – if not, you can just remind them. The full entry in your Attitude Journal for the dinner party exercise would then look something like this:

DATE	GOAL	WORST OUTCOME	ESCAPE PLAN	RESULT
2/2	Dinner Party	Everyone bored and goes home	Excuse for ending early	Smashing success

Of course your first attitude jogging exercise doesn't have to be a dinner party, but you should follow this basic framework. If you don't succeed, don't panic. You may have tried to lift too heavy a weight. Figure out an easier goal which will build your confidence towards success at the larger one and schedule it right now. If your dinner party for six was a disaster, try another with only one or two good friends and then work up from there. Try making it less formal, or doing it in a restaurant at first. The key is to build confidence one small step at a time. Any goal can be split up into a sequence of more modest steps. 'Divide and conquer' is the basic principle to follow. If at first you don't succeed – subdivide! As you build confidence about specific tasks and learn to enjoy things again, you will find your general level of self-confidence rising also. This will make even unrelated 'used to's' easier to conquer.

YOUR MOST IMPORTANT ATTITUDE

As you begin to work on your attitudes, it is extremely important that you start out on the right foot. As you work on specific problems you are also altering your most important attitude of all – your attitude towards challenges and change. Vital people are excited by challenge and change, and that is the attitude you should work towards. As you experience success, allow yourself the joy of gloating and basking in the glory of your own accomplishments. That warm glow of accomplishment is what really builds self-esteem. Life should be fun, so go ahead and enjoy it.

Learn to love the feeling of facing challenges with excitement. By selecting just the right level of challenge you can almost guarantee success, yet still feel that warm glow when you succeed. If you do it right, you'll find it addictive. As you build mental strength you will find yourself proudly flaunting it and actually seeking challenges for the pure joy of overcoming them. Just as mountain climbers look for higher and higher mountains to climb, attitude joggers are always on the lookout for weaknesses in their own ability to enjoy life to the maximum.

The worst possible attitude towards challenge and change is to look at it with dread. Many people have a long-standing bad habit of using their verbal self's ability to look into the future in a negative way. Instead of using it to make constructive plans, they focus on the negative and worry about what may go wrong. A good animal trainer must project a calm confidence which the animals can sense. A trainer who vacillates and shows uncertainty will surely lose this rapport.

Worrying and working yourself into a state of anxiety can be avoided by using your logical ability to examine the real risks coolly. The columns we added to the Attitude Journal entry about the 'worst outcome' and the 'escape route' are designed to help you to do this. In the heat of battle, conditioned behaviour can give you feelings of panic or dread which your verbal self will naturally try to rationalize. If you have previously *briefly* prepared yourself by calmly using your logic to examine the real risks, you will be better prepared to deal with these feelings. People with bad mental habits often get carried away with depression or fear because they haven't clearly thought out the reality of what they are dreading.

IRRATIONAL DREAD

Embarrassment, for example, is unpleasant but short-lived and definitely not life-threatening. If you do an exercise where the main risk is embarrassment, like trying to dance, sing or create art, try doing it with total strangers. Your exit strategy can then be to simply leave and never see them again. This is the worst that can happen – hardly something to work yourself into a state about.

For years I was terrified of dancing because I thought I would make a fool of myself. Then I began to watch the bad dancers on the floor and realized that they were having a good time anyway and that *nobody was even paying attention to them*. Feelings of self-consciousness are based on a gross overestimation of other people's interest in how *you* look. The fact is that people are far too self-absorbed even to bother to look at you most of the time.

People with phobias often have the bad habit of worrying that they will pass out or panic and act crazy. The fact is that they never do. When people jump off of tall buildings it's never because they had a fear of heights, yet many people misinterpret the normal surge of adrenaline they get when they look over the edge of a precipice as an urge to jump. The verbal part of our brain does its best to make up explanations for gut feelings, but often it gets started on the wrong track and the result is a phobia.

Many 'used to's' are a direct result of parental training. Most of us have been taught to monitor our actions continually and use self-control to make sure we *keep clean, dry and warm and always clean up our plate*. These over-learned rules can significantly reduce your capacity for joy. Attitude jogging exercises where you intentionally override this negative conditioning can weaken its power on you so that you can be free of its tyranny and enjoy life. It's nice to know how to 'act like a grown up', but doing it all the time kills the joy of many innocent pleasures. If you're wearing old clothes, getting them dirty has no serious consequences, yet most people can't help but dread and avoid getting dirty. This dread is just as irrational as the phobic's dread of passing out. It has been conditioned into most people's basic behaviour by parental training.

A fun exercise is to put on some old clothes and then have fun destroying them. Doing this with a friend or lover is particularly delightful. Roll in the mud, squirt each other with a hose, and even tear each other's clothes. Really let go and play like a child. With a little practice you will be able to violate these taboos spontaneously and have great fun doing it. Even if you occasionally ruin some decent clothes, the price of the fun you'll have is cheap compared to a concert ticket – and you'll have a lot of fun. Since the ability to enjoy things is what attitude jogging is all about, let yourself enjoy it. Always approach your exercises with a sense of delightful anticipation.

'Acting as if' is an effective technique for overcoming negative feelings. Just as a method actor puts herself into a role by becoming the person she is portraying, you must *become a person who enjoys* the thing you're working on. Visualize the feelings of this person and feel them yourself. If you're rolling in the mud, visualize and become a child. If you're attending a loud rock concert, watch the people who are ecstatic and become one of them. If your ears feel uncomfortable, push through the discomfort and enjoy it anyway. You'll be amazed at how much your body can adapt if you push it in the right direction. 'Use it or lose it' applies to more than just muscles. It applies to your very ability to enjoy life.

Exercise One

1. Pick carefully from your list of 'used to's' one that is just hard enough that you will be almost sure of success but will still need to use a little will-power. Write it down in your Attitude Journal.
2. Use your imagination to rehearse the desired outcome.
3. Now imagine the worst thing that can happen if your exercise fails. Write it down.
4. Think about what you could do for each possible thing that could go wrong. Rehearse in your mind and write your escape plans down.
5. When the exercise is finished, write down the results and what you have learned.
6. Pick your next exercise. Make it harder if you can.

Exercise Two

If you are the least bit overweight, make a resolution always to leave something on your plate when you finish eating. Think of it as an offering to the god of slimness who will starve to death without your regular offerings.

Exercise Three

1. Think of the one thing about the one personal limitation or fear that you would most like to change.
2. Think of how you could take a first small step towards over-coming that fear or limitation.
3. Rough out a step-by-step plan that might lead you to your eventual goal in small, manageable steps.

Exercise Four

Plan a holiday or evening out that will push your comfort zones a bit. Use some of the tricks we have discussed to push through the discomforts you encounter.

CHAPTER SUMMARY

1. Champion body-builders who started as runts prove that your starting point is no limit to the ultimate effects of exercise.
2. Self-control can be built up by exercise – one small step at a time, as with physical exercise.
3. Self-confidence, self-esteem, assertiveness and self-regulation are all improved by successfully taking on challenges.
4. Choose your challenges well, because just as overtraining strains muscles, overly difficult challenges cause setbacks.
5. Set up an Attitude Journal and use it to regain some of your 'used to's.'
6. Think out the worst that can happen and an escape route before any exercise, to reduce chances of panic.
7. Your most important attitude is your attitude towards challenge. Learn to welcome and enjoy it, and enjoy your successes.
8. Learn to overcome your irrational fears and free yourself from an overlearned compulsion to be neat and clean.
9. 'Acting as if' is a very effective way to modify conditioned behaviour by acting out the desired behaviour till it begins to feel natural.

EXPANDING YOUR COMFORT ZONES

My first exciting discovery of the power of attitude jogging came when I moved to the beach in California. I began to swim in the ocean every day as a relaxing midday break in my work. As the winter approached and the water gradually grew colder I found that, if I calmly walked into the water without hesitation, I would feel only a few seconds of discomfort before the water would feel pleasantly invigorating. I continued to enjoy my daily swim throughout the winter.

The surprising thing was that *as the water got colder the effort required stayed the same.* Apparently my body and my mental attitude were adapting to the cold as quickly as the ocean was cooling down. Each day the water was slightly colder but my comfort range was wider so the will-power required remained the same.

I was pleasantly surprised to find an added bonus. My widened comfort range in the water also made me more comfortable on land. Instead of freezing on the cold days, I now enjoyed the briskness of the cold air. My resistance to colds and flu also seemed to improve as I no longer caught the colds my friends frequently had.[1] Rather than suffering through the cold water, I found it crisp and invigorating. My entire body had a glow. While others waited for summer to again enjoy the beach, I continued to enjoy it all winter.

That experience opened my mind to the possibility of similarly widening my comfort range in other areas of my life. By judicious use of self-control at critical times I have since learned to enjoy many things that I previously found unpleasant or boring.

The most exciting discovery was that the critical times where I needed self-control were amazingly brief. As I walked into the cold ocean I simply relaxed, focused on the surf further out, and ignored the cold for about 10 seconds. By the time the second wave broke over me, the need for self-control had passed – I was actually enjoying the brisk water.

Ocean water changes temperature very slowly as winter approaches, and this is the key to widening your comfort range painlessly: Each confrontation should challenge you a little, but not too much. By taking small, manageable steps you minimize the strain on your will-power. It would take incredible will-power to suddenly start swimming in the ocean in the middle of winter, but the tiny increments of cold I faced as the temperature changed gradually day by day were relatively easy to handle.

Readers who live in places with really cold winters may find my references to cold air in the Los Angeles winter amusing. This only illustrates my point further. Since they have no option but to confront the cold air daily as they leave the house, people in cold climates are forced to expand their comfort range in the winter. I remember visiting Chicago one February, during a 'heat wave' where the temperature reached 40°F (4.5°C). Everyone was running around in their shirtsleeves remarking about how warm it was. After months of expanding their comfort zone downward, 40° was solidly inside of theirs. The 'cold weather' people suffer with in Los Angeles starts at about 60°F (15.5°C). *Your comfort zone is continually shrinking. Its width is determined by the stretching effect of challenges successfully met.*[2]

WHY ATTITUDES SHRIVEL

If you've ever worn a cast on a broken bone you have seen how amazingly quickly the body can atrophy when it is completely protected from stress. A broken arm can shrivel in a couple of weeks to a frail shadow of its former self. Attitudes have a similar tendency when they are totally protected from challenge. When you seek nothing more than comfort and luxury in life, it's like putting a cast on your attitudes.

Comfort and safety seem like reasonable goals, yet many of the worst effects of ageing are a direct result of their pursuit. The problem is that following these short-term goals often produces unintended long-term consequences. *Every time you avoid discomfort your comfort range shrinks a little*. The ironic result is that in the long run *avoiding discomfort ultimately makes you less comfortable.*

Cheerful, flexible people have a wide comfort range, developed by years of accommodating and adjusting to challenges. At the other extreme are cranky people who are miserable most of the time because they have let their tolerance range narrow through years of refusing to adapt. The more we can stretch our mental flexibility by adapting to the things we dislike, the more we will be happy with whatever life hands us.

Comfort is a relative term. It is as dependent on your own comfort range as it is on the external environment. Each person's comfort range is the result of decades of conditioning. Over the years these tiny changes in attitude, not noticeable in themselves, gradually result in a significant narrowing of your comfort range. The final ironic result is that in the long run *avoiding discomfort ultimately makes you less comfortable*.

If you always take the path of least resistance your attitudes shrivel just like the muscles inside a cast. Though you can create special exercises to widen your comfort zone intentionally in areas that you feel are weak, confronting the challenges of normal life should be your first priority. Vital people actually enjoy confronting these challenges because they understand their importance to long-term happiness.

THE CONTORTIONIST

Contortionists can virtually tie their bodies in knots. They can put their head between their legs by bending their back either forwards and backwards. This bizarre ability is not very useful unless you want to join the circus, but it illustrates our amazing ability to extend flexibility by exercise. If you want to become a contortionist, all you have to do is push your flexibility limits a little bit each day. Each day you will find that the same effort pushes your flexibility to new limits. Before you know it, you will be able to comfortably assume positions that would have caused extreme pain before you first started.

Contortionists develop their amazing flexibility one small step at a time by pushing their comfort zones repeatedly with time for recovery in between. Attitudes can be made flexible in the same way.

Your mind has the same amazing power to adapt as your body. The problem with attitudes is that no one ever told us that it takes effort to keep them from shrivelling. Each of your attitudes has a comfort range which has been defined by a lifetime of stretching, but each has a continual tendency to shrivel too, just like your bones and muscles. Your reactions to temperatures, noise levels, smells, tastes, physical discomfort and even intellectual challenge all have their own comfort zone, which is continually trying to shrink.

The degree to which comfort zones can adjust is awesome. Indian fakirs and street performers amaze us by sleeping comfortably on a bed of nails, while people accustomed to luxury complain if the hotel sheets aren't silky smooth. The same sheets that are considered intolerably rough by a rich person would be considered the height of luxury by someone accustomed to sleeping on the pavement.

The amazing range of adaptability of human attitudes is every bit as impressive as the physical flexibility demonstrated by the contortionist. The important difference is that flexible attitudes are the very basis of happiness and good health. Attitude jogging makes it possible to *enjoy yourself in situations where others are miserable*. This ability to enjoy more and hate less can be developed without any painful exercises. All you have to do is learn a new way to respond to the normal discomforts of life.

RISING TO CRITICAL MOMENTS

Whenever your comfort zone is challenged, you naturally feel a negative emotion. If you give in to that negative feeling you condition yourself to react even more negatively to the same situation in the future. With attitude jogging we learn to recognize the challenge as a critical moment and use our self-control to push through the discomfort. This turns the negative experience into a positive one based on the satisfaction of success. Instead of reinforcing a dislike, you expand your comfort range and at the same time give a boost to your feelings of self-control and self-confidence.

Pushing through a feeling of discomfort is a skill which improves with practice. In the next chapter we will cover some very effective techniques for developing this ability.

A REAL EXAMPLE

Enough talk about theory! Let's look at some real-life examples of attitude jogging: Imagine yourself on a romantic holiday with your lover where the water in the hotel pool is slightly cold. This is a critical moment. You can complain to the management and stay out of the pool, or use about two seconds of self-control to dive into the water. If you dive in, the water will soon feel comfortable and you'll have an enjoyable swim. You will also have widened your comfort range a bit so that tomorrow you may not even find the water cold. In fact, later in the week you may even find that you prefer having the water a little brisk. Two seconds of self-control at a critical moment can thus make the difference between a disappointing holiday and a happy one. Even more important, the cumulative effect of thousands of little critical moments like this over a lifetime can make the difference between a happy, vital old age and a miserable, crotchety one. Every time you use your will-power to push your comfort zone past its present limits, you widen your comfort limits one more notch.

Your most important attitude of all is your attitude towards challenge and change. One of the basic goals of attitude jogging is to condition you to welcome these challenges and enjoy the thrill of conquering them. This thrill is far stronger than the mild discomfort of a few seconds of self-control. The idea is to make a game of learning to recognize life's little discomforts as critical-moment opportunities and delight in the satisfaction of turning them to your advantage.

WHAT ABOUT VALID COMPLAINTS?

Some readers may resist the idea of 'going with the flow' rather than complaining about cold hotel pools and other such discomforts. Let me just point out that grouchy, unhappy people always think they are doing a service to the world by standing up to the incompetence they see everywhere. The amazing power of rationalization to make our attitudes always seem correct makes this feeling very convincing. Be careful!

The fact is that most complaining is not very successful. Restaurants and hotels with bad service will continue to have bad service in spite of your complaints. The problem again is rationalization: Rude waiters think that *they* are OK and the irascible patrons have an attitude problem. Perhaps the best plan is to make the best of it and then vote with your feet by never returning. In the long run the only way bad service gets corrected is through the good old free market system.

One way to look at it is that you always put your energy into the thing that *can* be changed – your own attitude. You can't change the world, but you can change your reaction to it. The results are amazingly similar. As you put the energy you used to waste on complaining into improving your own attitude factor, you will find that it gets easier and easier to enjoy things instead of hating them. It's a little like finding that the incompetence in the world has suddenly gone away.

An important skill to develop is the ability to *recognize the difference between the things you can change and things you can't.* Once you learn this distinction you can take all that energy you were wasting on useless complaints and focus it on something important that really *can* be changed. Give people a little slack and save yourself grief by understanding that their rationalizations fully support whatever they are doing, even though it annoys you. Assertiveness is a good quality. You deserve the best and you should stand up for yourself at certain times. It's unhealthy to suffer in silence just because you don't want to make trouble. However, by learning to be flexible you can often eliminate the unpleasantness at its source. With a positive attitude you can *truly enjoy* situations that less flexible people would hate.

One useful trick for enjoying things that you find substandard is to learn to enjoy 'funkiness'. Funky originally meant strong-smelling, but jazz musicians began using it to mean low-down, dirty, simple and from the heart. Many hotels, restaurants and even art can be enjoyed if you look at them as 'funky'. You'll find the experience much more pleasant than hating them for being 'substandard'. A waiter's bad mood can be a source of secret amusement or annoyance – the choice is yours.

ROMANIAN TOILET PAPER

I once stayed at a hotel in Romania where the toilet paper was so stiff that I used it as stationery to write letters to all of my friends. Once I realized that the whole population of Romania happily uses that loo paper and considers it normal, the challenge was simply to think like a Romanian and get used to it. After a few days it did start to feel normal.

This trick of imagining yourself in the place of the people who enjoy things you find annoying is very effective. Often you will see other people around you enjoying the object of your annoyance. If you see people joyfully swimming in the cold pool, you can use them as your role models. In some situations, however, you will have to use your imagination as I did in Romania. Humour is another very useful tool. If you find yourself getting sucked into a

feeling of discomfort, try stopping yourself and intentionally looking for the funny side of the situation.

BOREDOM

Being bored is a challenge that can be dealt with easily with a little
practice. If you find yourself stuck in a boring waiting room waiting
for a doctor or an aeroplane, try watching the other people and making up stories about what they are doing. Take a cue from small children, who can entertain themselves anywhere by simply using their
imagination. If you always grab a magazine or other distraction, you
soon lose the ability to entertain yourself in your own imagination.
Think of the prisoners who kept their sanity through years of solitary confinement by using their imaginations. Simply remembering
events of the past can provide you with a rich repertoire of films in
your mind. Try remembering past attitude jogging triumphs.

Often people are bored because they have tuned out of what is
happening. Deciding that you're not interested or can't understand
is a common source of boredom that is curable. If you're in a lecture
on insects, you may find yourself drifting off because the subject is
outside of your comfort zone of knowledge. Perhaps you didn't like
biology in secondary school. Open up your mind. Pretend you love
biology. Really listen carefully to just one of the lecturer's points
with the expectation of being amazed. Try another one, and another.
You may find that you have a new interest in insects. When you
really try to get into things that seem boring to you, your reward
may ultimately be much more than just a temporary relief from
boredom. It may even turn out to be a critical moment leading to a
new hobby or career. Learning to like something that previously
bored you or filled you with loathing is an amazingly satisfying
experience for a true attitude jogger.

Another possible reason for boredom is that the speaker himself is a really boring person. After you have tried your best to
really appreciate what he is saying, you can at least salvage the
moment by focusing your attention on what makes him so boring.
Try to observe the small details of what he is doing, how he looks,
his gestures and inflections. Delight in your own observations and

resolve never to make those mistakes yourself. Pretend you are making a study of what makes people dull. Note every tiny mannerism that contributes to his boringness. Look at his gestures and body language. Feel sorry for the poor man and think about his parents and school experiences that made him that way. After you have exhausted all of these possibilities, you can always resort to that old standby for self-entertainment, daydreaming.

CHARTRES CATHEDRAL

Sometimes we are bored as a result of our own stupidity. I vividly remember my trip to Chartres cathedral in France. Because it was the zillionth cathedral I had seen, I saw nothing exceptional about it. I had heard that the stained-glass windows were wonderful but they actually seemed rather faded compared to others I had seen. I happened to find myself standing behind a group listening to an Englishman who was telling the history of the windows and describing them in detail. A wonderful thing happened as he made the windows come alive with rich stories and wonderful insights about their design and meaning. Gradually, I began to see their beauty. It turned out that the guide was a famous expert on these particular windows who had written books and spent decades enchanting visitors. My own lack of sensitivity and knowledge had turned this priceless masterpiece into just another church.

Just about anything is fascinating if you pay attention and open up your mind. Insects are fascinating, art is fascinating, music is fascinating, mechanisms are fascinating, even parasites are fascinating. We all carry with us an invisible list of things we have decided are not interesting. These things are outside of our comfort zone of knowledge. With a little self-control, we can regain them and experience them anew.

Once you learn to make a game out of overcoming challenges to your comfort zone, you actually become immune to most kinds of discomfort. Each positive experience takes you up the attitude tree in the positive direction and builds your feeling of control over your life. This giddy feeling of control energizes your immune system like no other attitude. It is the opposite of the victim mentality or the feeling of hopelessness, both of which lead to bad health and unhappiness.

PLAYING ADVENTURE GAMES

One of my fondest travel memories is the time I ran out of petrol on the motorway just outside Paris and had to hitchhike to a petrol station. My one term of French was just enough to get me into trouble, but the experience turned out to be exhilarating because I kept my cool and treated it as an imaginary adventure. The fact is that most such experiences are only adventures in our own imagination. If I had seen it as a terrifying experience, as many people would, what would the real dangers be? Getting kidnapped and sold into white slavery?

The real danger in such situations is panic. Once panic sets in it's easy to forget the reality of the situation. The 'worst outcome' column in your Attitude Journal entries is a useful thing to remember in situations like this. The worst outcome in this case would probably be nothing but a long walk. One good trick for enjoying such adventures is to think about the fun you'll have retelling your exciting experience. The more interesting twists of fate, the better. Life is full of mundane and forgettable experiences, but the memory of a real adventure endures forever and adds richness to your life. If your holiday goes perfectly and you just sit next to a nice warm pool, what do you have to talk about or remember?

Getting lost is a terrifying experience to some people, but what is the worst that can happen? Being in a strange place where all of the hotels seem to be booked can seem frightening in your imagination, but the fact is the worst outcome is probably sleeping in your car. I heartily recommend that you try intentionally sleeping in your car in a strange place as an attitude jogging exercise. Once you have actually done it you will realize that it's not really so bad. In fact, if you recline the seat it's a lot more comfortable than sleeping in an aeroplane – the seat is wider and things are a lot quieter with no announcements or people climbing over you to go to the toilet.

If you get lost in a strange city, relax and enjoy it. You will see parts of the city you never would have seen otherwise. Just be patient, stay calm, and think of it as another adventure that will make a good story. Try to solve the problem calmly, as you would a puzzle. If you find yourself in a bad neighbourhood, remember that all of the residents of that neighbourhood are there every day and are still alive. Your brief visit is really not all that risky if you keep your cool. When you live in a super-safe neighbourhood, your comfort zone for danger can shrivel to a really irrational point.

WHY OLD PEOPLE HATE ROCK CONCERTS

The quiet of suburbia can make your comfort range for noise contract to the point where simply visiting a big city becomes a real problem. People who live in the city sleep through sirens, noisy motorcycles, loud music and other distractions without a problem, and so can you. You simply have to push through the discomfort and be patient. Your natural adaptability will soon widen your comfort range until you can sleep through anything.

Going to concerts may bring about a similar effect. People who regularly attend loud concerts or dance clubs have a widened tolerance for the high volume. If you use self-control to push yourself through the pain for a few minutes and feel the enthusiasm of the other fans, your comfort will begin to improve within minutes. If, on the other hand, you retreat by leaving because you can't stand the volume, you will have even more trouble at your next concert because your comfort range will have contracted. Many people lose their ability to enjoy concerts or dance clubs at some point in their lives because once they begin running from loud music, their comfort zone contracts more with each episode. The first time you retreat from any challenge is extremely important, as we will see in the next chapter.

Exercise One

1. Go right now to the video shop and rent the excellent film *Two for the Road*. This film, starring Audrey Hepburn and Albert Finney, demonstrates attitude decline more effectively than any book ever

could. It starts with a bored, spoilt couple travelling in luxury through the south of France. It periodically cuts back to their previous travels in the same area when they were poor students and full of the fun and joy of life. The contrast between joyfully living as back-packers and fussing about luxury hotel conditions vividly demonstrates what the Attitude Jogging is all about. Enjoy it!

2. When you're done with the film, throw some old clothes and a toothbrush in a small bag and try a little adventure weekend of your own. Don't make reservations. Be spontaneous and flexible. Have fun no matter what happens. Have fun getting lost. Have fun sleeping in a creaky, lumpy bed. And if the pool is cold, just dive in. Instead of a fancy restaurant, buy some nice French bread, cheese, paté, a bottle of wine and a beautiful piece of fruit. Find a beautiful spot on the ground and have a picnic. No picnic table required. All you need is a corkscrew and a knife. No plates, no spoons, no glasses, and the shopping bag is your rubbish bin. Keep it simple and there's no preparation and no clean up. Take a nap in the sun when you're done, climb a tree, or splash in the water like Hepburn and Finney. If it rains, take a walk in the rain. The important thing is to have fun *no matter what happens*. With practice you'll find that it gets easier and easier.

Exercise Two

Plan a travel adventure this week that will push your comfort zone just enough that you are fairly certain to succeed. Camping out, taking a bus or driving into the city, a major hike in the country or town.

Exercise Three

Plan something that will expand your intellectual comfort zone. A lecture, a ballet, an opera, a play – or a night course in anthropology, computers, sculpture or whatever.

Exercise Four

If you didn't do Exercise 1 in Chapter 4 (the cold shower exercise), think about it again. If you really want to build up your self-control, your resistance to colds and your emotional stability to advanced levels, this exercise will do the job.

CHAPTER SUMMARY

1. Your temperature comfort zone will expand as the seasons change if you don't run from the challenge.
2. Comfort zones always tends to shrink unless you challenge their limits.
3. Attitudes shrivel when challenge is avoided, just like a broken arm shrivels in a cast.
4. If you always seek comfort, you will be *less* comfortable in the long run because your comfort zone will shrink.
5. Self-control is best used at critical moments, usually only one or two seconds in duration.
6. Learn to adjust without complaint and enjoy things that you can't change. Use the energy saved to change a few well-chosen things that you really *can* change.
7. Delight in your ability to adjust to and enjoy things that would make other people miserable.
8. Remember that nobody admits to being cranky. Since attitudes are used to judge themselves, they always seem reasonable to their owner.
9. Expand your comfort zone of knowledge by really listening to something you thought was boring. 'Act as if' you are fascinated and soon you will be.
10. Expand your adventure comfort zone by enjoying a real-life adventure as if you were in a film. Enjoy the thought of retelling it to friends.
11. If the music seems too loud, stay anyway. Your comfort zone will widen.

CHAPTER
7

THE ART OF MINIMAL SELF-CONTROL

Since words in a book can have no direct effect on your non-verbal behaviour and attitudes, self-control becomes your all-important link for change. By learning to use it skilfully you can keep your attitudes vibrant and positive without sacrificing the joy of living unselfconsciously.

Spontaneity is a positive quality we associate with joyful living. It is usually associated with behavioural impulses and is very much 'in the moment'. Self-control is usually quite the opposite – self-conscious behaviour driven by the verbal, logical part of the brain which is very aware of long-term consequences but not very joyful or spontaneous. Continuous self-control means you are living completely rationally – like a robot. Self-control is best used in short bursts, which are just long enough to turn down that second piece of cake and get you back on the right track. With practice you can develop a style of self-control which is crisp and decisive and almost seems spontaneous. With this skill you can prevent long-term attitude decline without spoiling the joy of living with passion and feeling. The idea is to improve the teamwork between your self-control and behavioural thinking, so that each can do what it does best. Also, as we will see in Chapter 9, scientific studies have shown that 'rationality and anti-emotionality' can greatly increase your risk of early death from major disease.

A karate master can break bricks and boards with his bare hand, while a less skilled person would only injure himself. The secret lies in using quick, decisive action. Self-control can similarly be made to seem effortless and non-intrusive. Skilled surgeons use a similar trick to remove a large adhesive bandage from your body almost painlessly. Yet unskilled people torture themselves just removing a plaster because they gradually pull it away millimetre by millimetre. The skilful way to remove a bandage is quickly and decisively, with no hesitation – rip! – and the bandage is off.

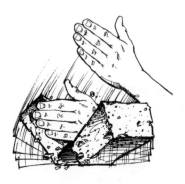

Self-control is best used quickly and decisively to maximize its effectiveness and minimize discomfort.

The anticipation of pain is often more unpleasant than the pain itself, so acting without hesitation is extremely important. I once had a wisdom tooth pulled by a dentist who fooled me by pretending to be examining the tooth while he coolly pried it out. When he told me that he had already pulled the tooth, I was amazed. When you learn to do the little acts of self-control you need for attitude jogging with this kind of finesse, they can be equally painless.

The principle of minimizing the time duration of discomfort is a sound one. In fact, I would gladly submit to the most excruciating pain possible if it lasted only one microsecond. Moving quickly to 'seize the moment' without stopping to deliberate eliminates the pain of anticipation, while acting decisively minimizes the duration of the discomfort.

GETTING INTO COLD WATER

Let's use the example from the previous chapter where impulsively diving into the chilly hotel pool saved both the holiday and the attitudes. Entering cold water is a good way to practise your technique. Just like all acts of self-control, it's easy if you do it right and miserable if you don't.

Dawdling over feeling the water first is a big mistake because it starts you thinking about and dreading the coldness. You can die a thousand deaths in your mind while you think about what you are about to do. Better just to get on with it and dive in impulsively and without hesitation. You can jump into a cold pool with only about one second of self-control – the time it takes for your feet to leave the ground.

Just before you jump, focus your mind intensively on swimming nice purposeful strokes. This will distract you from feeling the discomfort. When your mind has something to focus on, it won't dwell on the discomfort of the cold water. Reaching the end of the pool should be your only thought. Keep focused on doing laps until the water begins to feel normal. Then you can enjoy gloating about your accomplishment. One second of self-control can do a lot. In this case it started your jump and focused your attention on swimming laps. The rest was conditioned behaviour which, though sceptical at first, could not help but be impressed when the water eventually felt good.

If you wanted to teach your dog to swim, you could throw his ball in the pool and then push him in. Training your own behaviour is done in the same way. If you practise this technique on manageable challenges, you will be surprised at how good you can get at overriding conditioned behaviour quickly and painlessly – with a quick karate-chop of self-control. The effectiveness of your will-power and self-control will be strengthened amazingly.

RECOGNIZING CRITICAL MOMENTS

One of the basic principles of attitude jogging is to make your self-control count by learning to use it without hesitation when the golden opportunities where it will have maximum effect arise. With practice you can develop an instant knee-jerk reaction and an alertness to these situations. Certain phrases should act as triggers because they almost always signal that attitude decline is about to occur if you don't intervene. 'Used to' is one of the most common ones. If you hear yourself saying it, you should instantly use your self-control to take a change in direction.

'Too old' is another phrase to look out for. By itself it is never a valid reason for not doing something. Maybe you can't play tennis because your right leg is paralysed as a result of a degenerative disease. If so, you can't play tennis because your leg is paralysed, not because you are too old. Many people play tennis into their seventies.

Many critical moments occur when one of your comfort zones is being challenged. If the challenge is something you can handle, learn to push yourself without hesitation to take it on. Anything unfamiliar or slightly more challenging than what you usually do is a golden opportunity. We can create artificial attitude jogging exercises to expand our comfort zones, but by far the best exercises are the opportunities that come up in the course of normal life. When a friend invites you to do something a little outside of your comfort zone, *all you have to do is say yes*. One second of self-control.

When you are in a comfort-zone-expanding situation and you feel a negative reaction coming on, fight it. Use your self-control to make a change in direction which will rescue the experience and make it end positively. The fight is between your conditioned behaviour, which doesn't like to exceed comfort zones, and your verbal self's knowledge of the dangers of attitude decline, which is verbal and logical and therefore reachable by this book. The stronger of the two will prevail, but remember, strength of will can be built up by exercise. That's why attitude jogging gets easier the more you do it.

THE POWER OF FIRST TIMES

Some moments in your life are more than just critical. Some are exquisitely critical, where the mere flap of the proverbial butterfly wing can start a storm that changes your life. These extra-critical moments are often *first times*. Because of the basic self-reinforcing nature of attitudes, first opportunities are always easier than later ones. This is why it is so important to develop a habit of acting decisively in your attitude jogging.

Learn to say 'yes' instinctively whenever a friend invites you to do something new like play tennis, take a dance class, go to a party with a new crowd, go to a lecture, or anything outside of your normal pattern. One second of self-control the first time may be all it takes to open up your life to a whole new world of experience. If the first time is successful, it may require no willpower at all to say yes when you're invited again. **First-time opportunities are like magical pressure points in your life where a tiny push has amazing power.**

In our previous example of the chilly hotel pool, it was quite easy to jump impulsively into the cool pool on first arriving. A 'first-time' opportunity. Ten minutes after backing away from the first impulse to jump into the pool, the problem is much bigger. Now you have a debate going on in your mind whether to jump in or not. In your imagination you have already suffered the cold water more than you would have if you had just jumped in the first place. The first moment by the pool on the second day, you have another opportunity. It's still more difficult than the first day because your mental suffering has raised your anxiety level, and negative conditioning has occurred. With each succeeding day the self-control required to jump into the pool grows. The first opportunity is always the easiest, so learn to be decisive and seize it.

PARTIES AND CRITICAL MOMENTS

I recently went to a party where I left early because I began feeling isolated from the fun. My big mistake came early on when somebody asked me to dance. I was involved in a conversation so I didn't join in, though it would have been easy at that moment. A lot of people did start dancing and they started getting silly and forming a conga line. Again I didn't join in, though this time I was aware that I should have. Many more opportunities to join the fun arose as the party progressed, but the will-power necessary to join in got greater and greater with each one. The gulf between my mood and the festive mood of the dancers got wider and wider the more opportunities I missed. Finally I left the party because I could tell the gap was insurmountable.

The more I thought about that party the more I realized that it illustrated a basic principle about the use of self-control: 'The first time is the easiest,' whether you are talking about joining in the fun, striking up a conversation, jumping in a cold swimming pool, asking someone for a date, quitting smoking, cleaning up a mess, staying at a loud concert, really listening to a lecture, straightening out a misunderstanding, asking for a pay rise or virtually anything that requires self-control.

This book would never have been written if I hadn't pushed myself slightly to tolerate the cold ocean water as I went swimming a year ago. If I hadn't moved to the beach in late autumn, I wouldn't have been so desperate to swim in spite of the cold water. If I had backed off that first day and cancelled the swimming it's doubtful I would ever have tried it again until the next summer. The first time is always the easiest because of behavioural conditioning and the fact that self-control is weakened by failure and reinforced by success. That moment in the ocean was an ultra-critical moment for me because my impulse to swim in spite of the cold changed my life and started me down a path of discovery that resulted in this book.

MY MOTHER'S WALKS

Another personal experience that helped to inspire this book also relates to first times and temperature comfort zones. My mother is a very healthy 85-year-old who lives near Orlando, Florida. She used to be a lot healthier because she took walks regularly on Park Avenue, which is lined with interesting shops and is only two streets from her home. The last time I visited her she said it was 'too hot' to walk, even though it was only 80°F (26°C). The streets were full of people walking, many of them much older than she. She hadn't taken a walk for six months because of the heat, even though she 'used to'.

On the first warm day in April a critical moment had occurred which was also a first time. As she began her walk she noticed that the day was very hot, so she made a fateful decision – she went back inside. If she had continued her walk she would have stretched her comfort zone a bit, but by turning back she made it shrink. The next day it was hot again, so again she returned home. As summer gradually came on, the days got hotter and hotter and my mother continued to stay inside. Her comfort zone, which in previous years had grown wider as the weather got hotter, continued to shrink. Taking walks became a 'used to'.

The air-conditioner controls the temperature to within a few degrees in her home, so her comfort zone is now so narrow that walks are only possible a few days of the year – when the temperature outdoors falls within that narrow range. On that first warm day a little self-control could have pushed her to continue that walk in spite of the heat. It might have changed her life and extended her years of vitality.

The first time you run from a challenge rather than face it is an unfortunate missed opportunity because the failure gives you negative conditioning which makes standing up to that challenge harder next time, and harder still each time you fail. This basic fact of life is a direct result of the fact that attitudes are inherently self-reinforcing. Once you start down a path, it gets harder and harder to stray from that path. When critical moments present themselves, you must be ready to act spontaneously and immediately, because later opportunities will only be more difficult. As the old saying goes, 'There's no time like the present.'

BEING ANNOYED

The first time anything gives you a negative reaction is a golden opportunity to use two seconds of self-control to push through that negative feeling and turn your reaction around. Two seconds of self-control are usually all it takes to overcome the impulse to retreat from a challenge. Once you have pushed yourself in the right direction, behaviour quickly adapts to the discomfort and your comfort zone ends up being widened instead of shrunk. Just as a horse only needs a brief tug on the reins at a fork in the road, your own behaviour can often be redirected with the briefest nudge from self-control.

For example, the first time your new neighbour plays loud music late at night, if you use a moment of self-control to push through your impulse to complain or get upset it may be a crucial moment in your life. Just a little push from self-control to relax and refocus your thoughts onto something pleasant and you may just drift off to sleep. Having done this, your comfort zone for sleeping through noise will widen a bit so that next time it happens you'll find it even easier to deal with. Eventually, hearing the music becomes a non-event, just like hearing cars in the street are for any city dweller.

If, on the other hand, you try to change your neighbour's behaviour by complaining, you will have started down a path which could make your life, and your neighbour's, a living hell. Once you start down the confrontational path your sensitivity to noise will actually increase with each confrontation because you will be conditioning yourself to be vigilant and listen for the noise. This actually narrows your comfort zone.

Pushing through the discomfort on that first night could be the best investment of self-control you ever make. By widening your own tolerance you eliminate not only the problem with this noisy neighbour but also with all other annoyingly noisy situations in the future. Long after the neighbour has moved, the effects will remain in your attitude towards noise, your tolerance of others and your lack of crankiness.

If you have teenage children you are faced with similar critical moments regularly. Children can keep you young and flexible, or drive you deeper into obstinate inflexibility. Often first-time critical moments determine which way this interaction will go. Of course, children need to be taught consideration for others and reasonable limits, but often if you relax you will find that your comfort zone can stretch to accommodate their needs. They can help you to grow as much as you help them. Striking this balance is one of the real challenges of parenthood.

Learn to be alert for first-time situations where you feel a nega-tive reaction to something that you may not be able to change easily. Widening your own comfort zone is often the wisest choice. Mental flexibility protects you from discomfort in the long run, just as flexibility of the body does. Both tend to shrivel if they aren't stretched occasionally.

MATHS ANXIETY

Another kind of first-time challenge to be alert for is a challenge to your knowledge comfort zone. When you are exposed to some-thing new and you feel a negative reaction, try pushing through that negativity. The first time is definitely the easiest, as people with 'maths anxiety' can tell you. Maths anxiety usually begins at a critical moment in early childhood and then gets worse and worse because the initial difficulty with maths steadily grows as the student falls further and further behind his or her classmates. A perfect example of a self-reinforcing attitude.

When you are exposed to something new and it seems diffi-cult, use your self-control to push through that difficulty. It will never be easier than it is the first time. Computers, VCRs and other new gadgets may seem incomprehensible when you are first exposed to them, but if you don't push through the dif-ficulty it will get a lot worse in the future. Acceptable ques-tions on your first exposure will become dumb questions later, so ask them now. Look at new areas of knowledge as an atti-tude jogging challenge and enjoy the satisfaction when you pre-vail over them. Often the critical moment is just the one second it takes to ask the first question instead of tuning out and getting left behind.

As an adult you may have to deal with the bad effects of criti-cal moments in the past where you took the wrong path and closed your mind to new knowledge – or even a noisy neighbour. This means it will take extra work now, but as you develop your self-control and confidence you'll find it easier and easier to take on difficult challenges. The key is to divide the challenge into manageable steps and conquer them one at a time. If you already have established a pattern of complaining about your neighbour's noise, try cutting him a little slack on a night when the noise isn't so bad. As your comfort range widens you can give him more and more slack by pushing through each new level of challenge. You might even end up gaining a good friend.

If you've been left behind by the computer revolution, try starting with something easy and asking questions until you master it. As your comfort range stretches you will find that you can push yourself into more and more difficult challenges. Most important of all, be alert for first-time opportunities where questions are expected anyway. The first time is always the easiest.

Exercise One

1. Make a list of major, first-time critical moments in your life (e.g. first kiss, getting caught stealing or lying).
2. Think about the most crucial one and visualize how it would affect who you are today if it had gone differently.
3. Now think of all the other related critical moments that followed that moment in your life which would have to be changed if you wanted to undo the effects of that first critical moment.

Exercise Two

1. Pick something that you're normally afraid to do, like asking for a pay rise, going bungee jumping, jumping in cold water or talking to a beautiful stranger.
2. Rehearse it in your mind and anticipate the worst thing that could happen.
3. Do it decisively and without hesitation.

Exercise Three

1. Think of a bad habit that you would like to break.
2. Visualize yourself using a decisive karate-chop of self-control to stop yourself whenever you are about to do it.
3. Put yourself in the situation that usually triggers the bad habit, while staying in the present with your self-control primed to intervene decisively when needed.
4. Repeat the experience in ever more tempting situations until your behaviour is re-conditioned.

Exercise Four

Next time a friend invites you do something challenging, say yes and then push through any temptations to find excuses to cancel or drop out.

CHAPTER SUMMARY

1. Minimize your use of self-control and enjoy living in the moment and spontaneously.
2. Use self-control crisply and decisively and only to get yourself on the right track at critical moments.
3. Minimize the discomfort by being quick and decisive – like a karate chop or pulling a plaster off in one quick go!
4. Don't torture yourself by debating the use of self-control. Develop a knee-jerk reaction when you see a critical moment.
5. As you confront a discomfort, focus intently on the present action, not the pain (e.g. on the swimming, not on the cold).
6. Be alert for excuses and rationalizations which might let you off the hook. Don't take no for an answer.
7. First-time critical moments are your most powerful opportunities. They only happen once, so don't let them get away.
8. Push through first-time discomforts and try to adapt. Next time it will be easier.

NEW CURES FOR PHOBIAS

In the late 1950s I served three years in the US Navy as an electronic technician. One of my duties was to maintain the radar antennas at the very top of the ship's mast. I can still remember the wave of terror and my sweaty palms as I looked down from the top of that mast the very first time. My mind reeled as an image of my hands releasing their grip on the metal handholds flashed through my mind.

I had to climb the mast every week to do my maintenance check, often with the ship rolling in heavy seas. As the weeks rolled by, my palms got less and less sweaty. I began to actually enjoy going up the mast. As months passed, the tiny platform at the top of the mast became one of my favourite places to hang out. I even sunbathed there on nice days. My natural instinctive fear of heights had gradually been reconditioned into a pleasant and comfortable affection for the place.

That first day at the top of the mast was a critical moment for me that could as well have been the beginning of a serious case of acrophobia (fear of heights). Phobias are often the result of a kind of downward attitude spiral that begins with a retreat from fear and ultimately leads to inappropriate and disabling behaviour. Phobias are surprisingly common in our society. But new methods have been developed for treating them which are amazingly quick and effective. These methods are of great importance to attitude joggers because most of the so-called 'normal' symptoms of ageing are nothing but mild phobias.

HOW PHOBIAS DEVELOP

A 1991 study by Duke University[1] in North Carolina found that over 13 per cent of respondents between the ages of 45 and 64 had experienced symptoms of simple phobia within the previous six months. They also found that 2 per cent had suffered from social phobia, and over 7 per cent had suffered agoraphobia. Agoraphobia is literally 'fear of the marketplace'. In its milder form, it makes people panic when they are in large crowds. Many victims have ended up spending decades being terrified to venture out of their own homes.

Agoraphobia is not a disease that attacks you suddenly. It develops slowly, in a process similar to attitude decline. Once the downward spiral begins, the self-reinforcing nature of attitudes causes a vicious circle where panicky overreactions cause behavioural conditioning that makes the negative reactions grow worse each time.

Feelings of panic, which are a critical part of the vicious circle, are often caused by a simple misunderstanding of normal body reactions. You can demonstrate the cognitive difference between people who experience panic attacks and other people by simply injecting them with sodium lactate, a chemical that causes rapid, shallow breathing and heart palpitations. About 70 per cent of the people who have a history of panic attacks will experience one after such an injection. In normal people, the injections rarely produce panic.[2]

Most panic victims' verbal self has developed a bad habit of misinterpreting and overreacting to their body's normal response to emotional discomfort. Therapists use the word *cognition* to refer to the 'self-talk' of the verbal self. As we discussed in Chapter 2, the verbal self must often guess about the meaning of physical and chemical responses caused by the emotions. Panic victims have developed the bad cognitive habit of misinterpreting these reactions. In essence their problem is based on a *fear of the natural feelings produced by fear*. It is fear of fear.[3] One survey of people with phobias about specific animals found that 91 per cent feared their own panic.[4] Making a fool of yourself, going crazy, having a heart attack, losing control of bowels or bladder, scream-ing, fainting are other common fears. Most phobics rationalize their behaviour with some kind of internally consistent story that makes the fear seem logical to them.

Once this habit begins, a vicious circle is created between the cognitive and the behavioural response. A mild source of behavioural discomfort is made catastrophic by the verbal self's overreaction. The result is behavioural conditioning that makes the reaction grow worse with each exposure. Eventually, what was a mild psychic discomfort grows into a full-blown phobia.

We all feel negative behavioural reactions to certain things. Some of these reactions are programmed in by evolutionary sur-vival. Fear of heights, snakes, spiders, storms, drowning and suf-focation all have a natural survival value. The problem comes when bad cognitive habits cause these normal fears to be magni-fied, driving the victim's self-reinforcing attitudes to psychotic extremes. The first time you panic and run from a challenge can turn out to be a critical moment for you if it begins this vicious circle towards a phobia.

About 60 per cent of all object phobias begin with a specific bad experience with the object of fear.[5] The other 40 per cent have a more vague origin, often involving a friend's misfortune or watching someone else overreact. After a bad first experience, the real critical moment may come on the next exposure to the feared object. Failure to push through the fear can be the begin-ning of a gradual downward slide into a real phobia. People who develop a habit of confronting challenges to their comfort zone without hesitation are virtually immune from phobias.

HOW TO DEVELOP AGORAPHOBIA

Large, impersonal mega-supermarkets offer great selection but they give me the creeps. More than once I have felt an unpleasant flush of anxiety while shopping in one. I can easily imagine some-one who habitually runs from obstacles running out of the shop in panic. Giving in to this feeling would create a bad experience that would negatively condition their behavioural attitude towards the shop and also make a strong negative impression on their verbal self's attitude. It may be a critical moment. The next time they try to go in the shop it will be much more difficult to keep their cool. If they run out again, it may be very difficult ever to return.

Retreating now to a smaller shop, their shattered confidence may cause a bad reaction even in there. Again, a retreat from the challenge takes their attitude towards shopping in public down another notch. Soon the panic attacks begin in other public places until, in the end, the only place they feel safe may be at home. This scenario is not a rare occurrence. Millions of Americans are trapped in their homes right now as a result of this disorder, and many more are already in the vicious circle that leads to it. The US National Institute of Mental Health (NIMH) estimates that 23 million Americans, or 13 per cent of the population, now suffer from anxiety disorder.[6]

UNDOING THE DAMAGE

Recent breakthroughs in the treatment of phobias have allowed therapists to achieve rapid cures in about 80 per cent of the cases.[7] This new therapy, called *cognitive-behavioural* therapy, uses a two-pronged approach: The *cognitive* side involves teaching the patient's verbal self new ways to interpret the physical reactions and tricks for keeping thoughts in the present while confronting the feared situation. Bad cognitive habits are identified and corrected. At the same time, the patient's *behavioural* conditioning is turned around by exposing the patient to the object of his fears and showing him that no harm ensues. This repeated exposure to the feared situation without bad consequences reconditions the patient's behaviour and gradually eliminates the expectation of disaster. After repeated exposure, confidence builds and the patient unlearns the fear response. An important principle in this kind of therapy is to teach the patient to face the feared situation intentionally and *feel the fear without retreating from it.*

The most effective therapy is done 'in context', with the therapist actually accompanying the patient into the fearful environment and giving him or her support and encouragement. Homework assignments between therapist visits teach the patients how to confront the problem by themselves. Being in the real context that causes the problem is extremely important because our attitudes are dependent on context. We all have sub-personalities that may have different attitudes towards the same thing,[8] so it's important to work on the right one.

One important principle in this kind of therapy is to take small manageable steps in confronting the phobia. If an agoraphobia patient is afraid to leave the house, the therapist and patient first stand in the doorway for an extended period of time until the patient feels comfortable that nothing bad will happen. The next session they may work on standing out on the sidewalk. Each small step builds confidence for the next until they are actually able to work up to challenges that would have seemed terrifying at the start of the therapy.

GRACE: A REAL CASE HISTORY

Jerilyn Ross, a former phobia sufferer who is now a therapist and president of the Anxiety Disorders Association of America[9] has written an excellent book called *Triumph Over Fear* (Bantam 1994). In it she describes many case histories, including the amazing story of a 60-year-old woman named Grace who remained trapped in her house with agoraphobia for *over 30 years*.

Grace's fear of the outside was so great that she once even stayed inside in spite of a fire in her block of flats. She was discovered by an alert social worker when she called about getting at-home work to pay her long-overdue rent. When Jerilyn first called on her, Grace would agree only to let Jerilyn stand outside the door so she could look her over. Gradually, they progressed from standing in the doorway together to quickly putting one foot out the door, and finally both feet. By the end of the first session Grace was standing at the kerb touching Jerilyn's car for the count of 10. After a week of doing 'homework' with an assistant, the project for the second week was walking to the corner postbox.

Within a few weeks Grace was able to ride in Jerilyn's car to a record shop and buy a record. Next came a trip to a restaurant and a meal. Within five months they were able to cut Grace's therapy down to an occasional 'booster' session. By then she was holding down a job, doing her own shopping and even going to the pictures by herself. A year after the therapy had begun, Grace was enrolled in a night class where she got straight A's and eventually graduated with honours. As with many such cases, she still has an occasional panic attack, but she has learned to push through the feelings and function in spite of it.

Grace's amazing recovery shows what can be accomplished by dividing a massive attitude problem into tiny steps. Confidence can be rebuilt from an amazingly weak starting point.

WHY COGNITIVE-BEHAVIOURAL THERAPY?

The field of psychotherapy has a chequered past that is rife with dissension and infighting between the various schools of thought.[10] Freudian psychoanalysis recognized that the lower parts of the brain had effects that were outside the reach of our consciousness. It was a breakthrough in its time but with it came many quaint ideas that greatly oversimplified and oversymbolized the simple learning of the ancient parts of our brain. Its focus on verbally uncovering critical moments from childhood and expecting this to magically undo their effects prevented it from ever being really effective in curing phobias.[11]

The behaviourists essentially took over the field of psychology between 1920 and 1970. After showing that most introspection was unreliable fabrication, they took the position that consciousness had *no* effect on behaviour. They instead studied in great detail the process of animal learning called conditioning. By understanding animal behaviour and learning, they hoped to understand human behaviour. Behaviour modification training would then correct aberrant human behaviour. Their results were, however, disappointing.

What the behaviourists didn't understand was that some introspection *is* accurate. The conscious stream of verbal thoughts of the verbal self, which we call cognition, *does* control behaviour at crucial times, and introspection does accurately reflect this process. In the 1970s a new kind of therapy appeared called cognitive therapy. It proved to be quite successful in treating depression and panic attacks. By identifying bad patterns of verbal thought and teaching patients how to break these habits, they achieved speedy cures in only a few months.

Some illnesses such as phobias, compulsions and eating disorders don't respond well to cognitive therapy because behavioural conditioning makes the problems persist even after the faulty cognitive habits of the verbal self are corrected. To break the vicious circle between bad cognitive habits and bad conditioned behaviour, a dual-pronged approach is required. By simultaneously working on the cognitive habits and creating behaviour-modifying experiences, excellent results have been achieved with only a few months of treatment. Cure rates for phobias of 80 and even 90 per cent have been reported using this method.[12]

The psychoanalysts' dire predictions that phobias treated with cognitive-behavioural therapy would simply resurface as different symptoms has simply not proven to be true.[13]

SOME COGNITIVE TECHNIQUES

Attitude jogging is based on the same cognitive-behavioural techniques used to cure phobias. While this book works on correcting the cognitive misunderstandings and bad habits that cause attitudes to decline, your own real-world exercises give you in-context *behaviour* modification to undo the damage already done. Since 'used to's' are often nothing more than minor phobias disguised by rationalization, many of the techniques used in cognitive therapy may prove quite useful.

People's cognitive attitude towards fearful situations can vary all the way from the delight felt by sky divers and mountain climbers to the dread and panic felt by phobics. If yours tends towards the phobic side, here is some useful information. Normal anxiety produces shortness of breath, chest pain and sweating. Any mountain climber enjoys this sensation and seeks it out.

You may also feel slightly faint while your pulse is racing. The reason for this is that your body is providing more blood to your muscles. Some phobics panic because they think they are fainting when they feel this sensation, but their fear is misplaced because fainting occurs when your blood pressure is *low*. The fact is you are *less* likely to faint when your pulse is racing.

You can practise calmly feeling some of these symptoms by breathing rapidly into a paper bag. The build-up of carbon dioxide will give you shortness of breath just like anxiety. Realizing the true meaning of these physical reactions and learning to function normally in spite of them can permanently cure anxiety attacks. They are only frightening if you misinterpret them.

Even if you aren't phobic, your attitude towards the physical feelings of anxiety may cause you trouble. If you're lost and late for an appointment, you may tend to panic and become less effective. Some people tend to engage in catastrophic thinking about what *may* happen in the future. At the very least this decreases your effectiveness in the present and may make you stay lost. Cognitive therapists have developed some useful tricks for getting people with panic attacks to focus on the present. Here are a few of them:

- Putting a rubber-band on your wrist and snapping it when you feel yourself having catastrophic thoughts.
- Counting backwards by threes or fours, etc. This requires concentration by the verbal part of your brain – keeping it out of trouble.
- Monitoring your current level of anxiety by assigning it a number between one and ten. This keeps that part of your brain occupied and too busy for catastrophic thinking.
- Doing diaphragm breathing by keeping your chest still and letting your stomach area do the work. This prevents hyperventilation and gives you something in the present to focus on.
- Remember the 'worst outcome' you entered in your journal entry. Usually, it's not worth panicking about.

RUMINATION

One of the bad mental habits that is often a significant factor in phobias and depression is called rumination. Rumination is what cows do when they regurgitate food into their second stomach, called the rumen, to digest it a second time. For a cow this is useful, but for attitudes it's a disaster. Mental rumination is 'Thinking too much'. It can make you worry unnecessarily and it can magnify bad experiences and even alter your memory of them. The automatic thoughts of your verbal self serve a useful purpose in moderation but, like salt on food, they are good only if used sparingly.

When you stay in the present, fear, uncertainty, worry and regret have no meaning. The present has *complete certainty* because what is happening right now is *exactly* what is happening right now. Feelings of fear and uncertainty are always a result of future thinking because only the future is uncertain. Regret exists only when you think about the past, and depression is a result of ruminating on the past or future. Living your life in the present as much as possible eliminates these negative emotions and allows you to enjoy life to its fullest.

The same ability to think about thinking, which gives your verbal self the useful ability to direct change and plan for the future, can also contribute significantly to attitude decline. Many 'used to's' are caused by nothing more than a single bad experience followed by a lot of rumination. Activities that you really enjoyed gradually become converted in your memory into unpleasant memories. Your verbal self is often a mere spectator to your actions – and a biased spectator at that. Because of the cautious nature of verbal thinking, it often never quite buys into the enjoyment and good feelings your behavioural side felt – particularly in regard to activities that are somewhat risky or involve getting dirty or wet. Your verbal self never liked them in the first place because they violated its rules of cleanliness. It is therefore only too happy to see them stop and rearrange its rationalizations accordingly. Even though you had great fun playing in the rain and getting muddy, you may find it difficult to make plans to repeat the experience.

TURNING PANIC INTO ADVENTURE

Just about everybody likes a good adventure film or book. The best ones will actually get your heart pumping from the excitement.[14] When real life produces the same physical reaction, many people panic or find it unpleasant. This attitude towards challenge can rob the joy from life and make you live fearfully. People who live life boldly **enjoy** adventures.

Your attitude towards your body's visceral response to danger is a learned response that can be changed with practice. The same physical response that triggers a panic attack in some people is fondly sought after by people who love adventure. Your verbal self's assessment of visceral responses can be changed. Remember the experiment described in Chapter 2, where people were tricked into interpreting the effects of adrenaline injections as either euphoria or anger depending upon how another person in the room reacted? This shows just how easily our reactions can be changed. One of the goals of attitude jogging is to teach you to *enjoy* challenges. You already know how to enjoy sweaty palms brought on by an exciting film, now your goal should be to learn to enjoy them in real life.

One useful trick for changing your attitude about challenges that now make you panicky or scared is to switch your attitude to the same fantasy-pretend mode you use when reading a book or watching a film. Enjoy the challenges that real life brings you by treating them like adventure stories that are happening to you. Enjoy the thought of retelling them to your friends. Maybe you can't make yourself into an adrenaline junkie like the sky divers and mountain climbers, but you can at least learn to enjoy the unavoidable challenges that life throws your way.

Exercise One

1. Make a list of things that you avoid because they scare you.
2. Pick one that is relatively easy to overcome and attack it as a phobia by following the steps above.

3. If you fail, subdivide the problem into several smaller steps, each of which will bring you one bit closer to success.
4. Each time you succeed, move down the list to a harder goal.

Exercise Two

1. Think about the last time you did each of the things on your 'used to' list.
2. Can you think of a bad experience that caused you to withdraw?
3. Did that bad experience make you even more hesitant the next time?
   Is it now a little like a minor phobia that could be cured in the same way as a phobia would be treated?

Exercise Three

1. Think of a challenging real-world adventure that will stretch your comfort zone.
2. Think briefly about the worst that could happen, and your escape route. Write them down.
3. Enjoy the adventure as you would an exciting film, actually delighting in the difficulties you encounter and keeping very cool and confident as you deal with them. If your heart pounds, enjoy the feeling and say to yourself, 'I can handle this.'
4. Plan something even more challenging.

Exercise Four

Try to spend a whole day enjoying the present. Don't talk about or think about future plans. Don't compare anything to past memories or expectations for the future. Let your internal talk go quiet and try to experience your day like an animal would. To succeed you will probably need something non-verbal to focus your attention on, like a walk or a project of some kind.

CHAPTER SUMMARY

1. Phobias are extremely common and are often not diagnosed in older people because they are dismissed as 'normal ageing'.
2. They develop as a result of the self-reinforcing nature of atti tudes, often starting with a first-time bad experience.
3. Most phobics *incorrectly* interpret their normal anxiety response as something dangerous and go into a panic.
4. Learning to function in spite of feelings of fear or anxiety is called courage. It can be strengthened with practice.
5. Agoraphobia is fear of going out. Cognitive-behavioural thera pists have achieved an 80 per cent cure rate treating it.
6. Facing and conquering fear in its normal context by taking gradually more and more difficult steps reconditions behaviour.
7. Cognitive therapy consists of explaining the true meaning of the physical reactions and teaching tricks to stay in the present.
8. Rumination is a bad cognitive habit which often worsens depression and phobias. Thinking too much magnifies things.
9. Thinking over the worst outcomes and escape routes before doing something scary often makes it easier to control panic.
10. You can teach yourself to enjoy conquering fear just by mak ing it a game. Shift your mind into 'adventure film mode'.

CHAPTER
9

CHANGING HOPELESS SITUATIONS

Hopelessness can kill you. Just as animals separated from the herd often quickly die of disease, humans who feel chronic hopelessness are extremely vulnerable to disease. Experiments have shown that your immune system is significantly weakened by helpless reactions to stress, yet can actually be strengthened by stress which is dealt with successfully.[1]

This effect can be demonstrated experimentally on rats using an ingenious apparatus to induce the feelings of helplessness. Yes, rats can feel helpless just like we do when they are given an unpleasant stress which they have no power to control. The apparatus used consists of special pairs of cages, wired to give the rat in each cage identical random shocks through its feet. One of the rats has control of the shocks because he has a bar in his cage that stops the shocks in both cages when he presses it. The helpless rat receives exactly the same shocks but the bar in his cage does nothing to stop them. When a cancerous tumour is implanted under the rats' skins, only 27 per cent of the helpless rats can reject it compared to 63 per cent of the rats with control. Rats receiving no shocks at all reject the tumour 54 per cent of the time.[2]

Experiments on humans are necessarily much less direct, but they confirm that evolution has given us the same tendency for our immune response to give up when we experience feelings of helplessness.[3] Helplessness even slows the healing of wounds. In a 1995 *Lancet* article, Kiecolt-Glaser compared the rate of healing of wounds of long-term caregivers with normal controls. The caregivers were people who had spent years of their lives caring for relatives suffering with dementia. The feeling of helplessness resulting from their situation showed its effects in significantly slower healing of their (punch biopsy) wounds. After six weeks, *55 per cent* of the wounds of the control subjects were healed, versus only *17 per cent* for the caregivers.[4]

AN ANTIDOTE TO HELPLESSNESS

In Chapter 1 we showed how a test measuring feelings of pleasure and well-being could predict good health 21 years later with amazing accuracy. The link between emotions and good health is thus strongly established, but what good is that if you have no way of controlling your emotions? Feelings of joy or helplessness depend partly on *other people* and factors over which we seem to have little control. Some people seem to have all the luck and some seem always to lose. Yet 'lucky' people have certain identifiable attitudes, as do people who always seem to lose out.

People with a victim mentality feel that other people are the cause of their grief and fall quickly and habitually into feelings of hopelessness. Yet there are people who are able to take control of their lives and make things happen in spite of difficulties thrown in their path. Dr Grossarth-Maticek's *Self-regulation Index* was developed to measure this important ability. (You will find the complete test in Appendix II of this book.)

In 1972, his student-interviewers gave the test to almost 6,000 40 – 66-year-old residents of Heidelberg, Germany. Fifteen years later, when he compared the interviewees' health status to their earlier test scores, the results were amazing. *Only 1.6 per cent of the people who had scored below 2 on the test were still alive and well, compared to **81 per cent** of the people with scores above 5.* (The maximum possible score was 6.) Death rates from cancer, coronary heart disease and virtually all other causes varied directly with the self-regulation score.[5] The figure right shows a plot of the results.

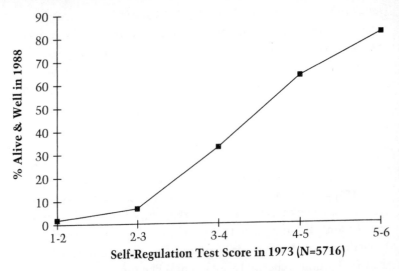

Self-regulation is the ability to continually adjust your behaviour to maximize your long-term feelings of pleasure and well-being. The graph above shows the results of a 1973 experiment where 5,716 elderly people took a test designed to measure self-regulation (Appendix II). As the graph shows, only 1.6 per cent of the people with scores of 2 or less were still alive and well in 1973, rising steadily to 81 per cent of the people with scores of 5 or better. With practice, self-regulation can be improved significantly.

How could a skill like self-regulation make such an amazing difference in future health? The answer is almost certainly that people with good self-regulation remain in control of their lives and therefore avoid falling into the kind of long-lasting stressful and helpless situations that lead to bad health. When your life is together, your immune system and cardiovascular systems run smoothly and efficiently. Germs, viruses, cancer cells and other challenges to your health are dealt with routinely by normal body defences when your basic emotional needs are well met.[6]

In Chapter 1 we saw similar results from another massive prospective study that used a test measuring feelings of pleasure and well-being to predict future good health. The subjects of that study were also given the self-regulation test; the scores on the two tests turned out to correlate almost perfectly: People with high pleasure and well-being scores also scored high in self-regulation. The reason is almost certainly a matter of cause and effect: Good self-regulation allows you to keep your life in order so that you experience more feelings of pleasure and well-being. This positive mental state goes hand in hand with excellent immune system function, which results in general good health. The cause-and-effect thus looks like this:

Self-regulation → Feelings of Pleasure and Well-being → Good Health

WHAT IS SELF-REGULATION?

The temperature of some homes and offices is *regulated* by a thermostat. The thermostat senses the temperature and turns on the heat only if the temperature dips below a certain pre-set level. If the thermostat breaks, this regulation breaks down and the building may become unbearably hot or cold. The thermostat monitors results and uses the information to *regulate* the heating effort.

Self-regulation is similarly based on paying attention to the results (of your own behaviour) and making corrections. When self-regulation breaks down, habitual behaviours which have been producing poor results are simply repeated endlessly. The result of such behavioural ruts is as disastrous as when a thermostat breaks. In both cases, failure to regulate the response based on results causes things to get worse and worse.

People with good self-regulation use their verbal self to recognize negative behaviour patterns and think about how they can be changed. Your love, parental and job relationships, career, and even body weight all have a tendency to get steadily worse if you don't pay attention. All regulation is based on sensing results and reacting to them. Habitual behaviour is like a heater that keeps running even when the room is already too hot. When feedback is ignored, catastrophic disregulation results – in heating your home or in living your life.

THE EXPERIMENTER APPROACH

The principle behind self-regulation is the same powerful way of thinking that has produced the breathtaking progress of modern technology. Research scientists and engineers tackle seemingly unsolvable problems, like going to the moon or curing polio, by breaking them up into small, manageable steps. They approach each step as an experiment which may succeed or fail. Failures are considered a normal part of the process because they provide the useful insights which eventually lead to a successful solution. The power of this systematic approach to problem-solving is everywhere evident in the amazing explosion of scientific progress we have experienced since this way of thinking was discovered.

Self-regulation is based on applying this same experimental approach to continual re-evaluation and development of your own behaviour. The goal is not going to the moon but rather maximizing long-term pleasure and satisfaction in your own life. This magical process is illustrated below:

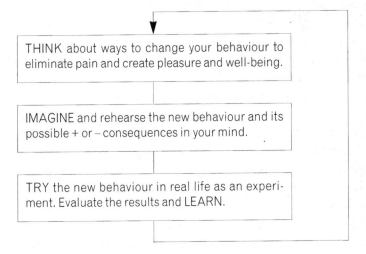

THINK about ways to change your behaviour to eliminate pain and create pleasure and well-being.

IMAGINE and rehearse the new behaviour and its possible + or – consequences in your mind.

TRY the new behaviour in real life as an experiment. Evaluate the results and LEARN.

Some of your experiments will fail and some will succeed, but each one will teach you something that will move you closer to your final goal of long-term maximum pleasure and well-being. By chipping away at the solution to seemingly impossible problems in manageably small steps, a workable solution gradually evolves. It is important always to remember that failure is a normal and expected part of the process, but try to take small enough steps that each attempt has a good chance of succeeding.

Many of life's problems which *seem* to be caused by other people and therefore seem beyond your control can actually be solved by changes in your own behaviour. This works surprisingly well because other people's behaviour towards you consists largely of reactions to your behaviour. You can discover these magical behaviour changes by using this trial-and-error, experimental process. One important principle to keep in mind is that achieving long-term pleasure and well-being often requires actions which are *less* pleasant in the short term. We often remain locked in to destructive behaviours because we fear the short-term discomfort and risk of change.

Generally there are three approaches to change to be considered in the first (THINK) stage of the process:

1. *Behavioural change*, which attempts to alter the situation.
2. *Avoidance*, by letting go of people or situations you can't change.
3. *Attitude change*, so that the situation no longer disturbs you.

The emphasis of this book so far has been on attitude change, which is only one of the three possible options. Though going with the flow is often the easiest option, there are many situations where it can lead you into disaster in the long run. Your relations with other significant people in your life such as parents, children, lovers and bosses are typical examples. These relationships must be carefully nurtured or they can turn sour and produce what feels like a helpless situation. People with good self-regulation are never victims because they are always THINKing and experimenting to develop their important relationships in a positive direction.

If you find yourself in a relationship that has deteriorated to a point where it seems hopeless, don't despair. The amazing thing about the experimenter approach is that it is tailor-made for approaching seemingly impossible problems. Other people may *seem* to be completely responsible for the problem, but the fact is that *their behaviour is strongly affected by your behaviour towards them*. The problem to be solved by experimentation thus boils down to finding changes in *your own* behaviour which can change the situation.

Each time you THINK and then experiment with a change in your behaviour, it either succeeds or fails to change things, but either way you LEARN things which will improve your chances for success in the long run. In the meantime you have feelings of hope and control instead of unhealthy feelings of hopelessness.

Thomas Edison, who invented movies, records and light bulbs, understood the experimenter approach well. He had to try thousands of different materials and construction techniques before he finally had a light bulb that produced adequate light and worked for more than a few minutes. These thousands of 'unsuccessful' experiments finally led him to the winning solution. By chipping away in tiny steps, he could confidently tackle virtually any difficult problem.

The IMAGINE step is what any scientist does with a new idea before actually going to the TRY stage. If an idea doesn't work on paper, there is no point in wasting the time and effort actually trying it, so they just go back to the THINK stage. Since you want to maximize your chances of success, rehearsing in your mind can improve your chances by eliminating unnecessary failures. Trying things out in your mind is much faster and less risky than trying them in real life.

Equally important, imagining possible setbacks can significantly improve your ability to handle them when you actually TRY them in real life. With a well-thought-out fallback plan, you can often turn failure into at least limited success. Rehearsing contingencies also increases your confidence because you avoid surprises. It is important to keep the experimenter attitude even in the face of failure. At the very least you will LEARN what *doesn't* work and that knowledge will increase your chances of THINKing of a successful experiment in the future.

OBSTACLES TO SELF-REGULATION

Though self-regulation is based on a simple principle, many people have basic beliefs and habits that stand in the way of beginning the process of change. Here are seven examples:

1. *The Victim Mentality*: A false belief that you are a victim and that you have no control of the situation. Other people may seem to be treating you unfairly, but remember that the way people act towards you is

strongly affected by your behaviour towards them. Try to chip away at their behavioural problems by changing your own behaviour in ways that may modify theirs. If they are critical of you, try unilaterally changing your behaviour so that criticism becomes impossible. Try being extra nice to someone who hates or ignores you. Discover and control obnoxious habits that other people may find annoying. If a co-dependent game has developed, break the vicious circle by altering your side of the pattern. Change the approach you have been using to achieve success. Don't be discouraged if such changes don't work at first. Consider them experiments and LEARN from the results.

2. *A lack of autonomy*: If your self-worth is based on the opinions of others rather than your own knowledge and values, you will tend to be drawn into dependent relationships where your need for the approval of others puts you into helpless situations. To recondition your own behaviour towards self-actualization, you should try to set up experiences where you accomplish things simply to please *yourself*. Pick something that really interests *you alone* and pursue it only for your own satisfaction. If you have been tending to live only to please others, you may find that you have been choosing goals, hobbies, etc. just because you thought they would please your parents, spouse or others. Pick things that will make *you* proud of yourself. Autonomy is such an important part of self-regulation that the two terms are sometimes used interchangeably. In fact, training designed to improve self-regulation is called 'autonomy training'.

3. *Blocked feelings*: Living only to please others often results in a disconnection of your behaviour from your feelings. Your basic emotions such as feelings of pleasure and well-being are messages from the same primitive parts of your brain that interact strongly with your immune system. If you ignore these messages because you have a misguided belief that you shouldn't bother others with your feelings, your health will be seriously affected. Be particularly cautious if the basis of your happiness is overly rational. Your gut feelings that are difficult to put into words should be listened to. If your logic tells you that you *should* be happy but your gut tells you otherwise, listen to your gut. The THINK and LEARN stages of the experimenter process should be directed at satisfying your long-term primitive needs, which are revealed to you only as feelings which may be difficult to put into words.

4. *A false belief* that you must achieve some goal at all cost. The goal may be gaining someone's love or approval or achieving success in some career goal. Knowing when to quit is sometimes difficult, but no goal is worth ruining your health and living a life of helplessness and frustration. Sometimes it is time to simply move on to other more achievable goals. If your father/lover, etc. is never going to love you, it's not the end of the world. You may as well let go of that goal and get back to enjoying your life.

5. *A lack of creative effort*: Scientists don't just jump into experiments without working hard to think of an idea that might work: You have to brainstorm for ideas. Most problems with people get better sometimes, worse at others. Try to remember what kind of things were going on when the problem seemed better and also what kind of things were going on when the problem was worse. Ask friends for ideas. Mentally go back in time to just before things went bad and think about what changed. Think about how you have solved similar problems in the past. Try breaking the problem up into smaller sub-problems.

6. *Lack of patience*: Your behaviour and the behaviour of others has been conditioned over a long period of time. Each time a new behaviour succeeds, the experience acts to recondition your behaviour and the behaviour of the person you are dealing with. However, remember that only *repeated* good experiences will gradually recondition behaviour. Breakthrough insights can change your verbal self's attitudes instantly, but behaviour will change only *gradually* through the conditioning of repeated success experiences. Remember that your verbal self is like the animal trainer that holds up the hoops for behaviour to jump through.

7. *An unwillingness to sacrifice* comfort in the present for future rewards. Change requires effort and the reward often takes some time to become apparent. This is actually what we called self-control. Self-regulation is quite different from self-control but cannot succeed without it. As we discussed in Chapter 5, if you lack self-control it can be built up gradually in a process similar to building up your muscles. Just keep your experiments within the current limits of your self-control and the success you achieve will make it stronger and strengthen your ability to try more ambitious experiments in the future. The important thing is to start some kind of experiment now.

CAN SELF-REGULATION BE IMPROVED?

Is it possible to improve your own prospects for health and longevity by improving your self-regulation? Happily, the answer is a definite yes. Dr Grossarth-Maticek, creator of the Self-regulation Test, also did several other experiments which proved that self-regulation can be improved by training. In his intervention studies his assistants taught self-regulation to middle-aged people who had been found by attitude tests to be at high risk for bad health. He then compared their health status over a decade later with that of a matched control group. In one such study, 600 people were given self-regulation training while 600 people, randomly assigned to a control group, received no training. When the health status of the two groups was checked 13 years later, *409 of the people given the training were still alive versus only 97 of the untreated control group!*[7]

The most amazing thing is that the training which gave this impressive improvement in health consisted of *only six one-hour sessions* spread over a one-year period! The principles of self-regulation are actually quite simple and are so effective that, once people experience their power, they become enthusiasts for life.

The trainees were given a pamphlet outlining the principles of self-regulation so that they could study it at home while they put its principles into practice in their lives. The complete pamphlet is translated and reproduced in full below so that you can do the same. Study it carefully since it could save your life, just as it saved the lives of many people in the study.

HOW TO ACHIEVE EMOTIONAL INDEPENDENCE AND A HEALTHY PERSONALITY

All human beings have the ability to alter their behaviour, and that of those around them, in such a way that they can attack their problems more successfully and achieve a complete solution.

I HOW DO PROBLEMS DEVELOP WHICH ARE IN PART DUE TO YOUR OWN ACTIONS?

Problems arise because you continue with a certain course of action, or maintain certain views and attitudes, which result in consequences that are negative, harmful and unpleasant. Possibly you expect positive, pleasant, agreeable consequences, such as the affection or love of somebody who is important to you, and suffer because this acceptable state of affairs is not realized.

II WHAT CAN YOU DO IN ORDER TO SOLVE THE PROBLEM AND OVERCOME DIFFICULTIES?

In principle, there are three things to be done:

(1) You can change your behaviour in such a way that conditions (e.g. your interpersonal relations) are changed in such a way that you are placed in a better position (e.g. lose weight, smoke less, improve your interpersonal relations).
(2) You withdraw from situations which do nothing for you in the long run, and avoid conditions which are likely to do you harm.
(3) Change your mental attitudes and values, and in that way improve your general adjustment.

In these three ways you have a better chance to solve problems which before gave you difficulties.

III WHAT ARE THE IMPORTANT VARIABLES TO CONSIDER IF YOU WANT TO CHANGE YOUR BEHAVIOUR AND YOUR ATTITUDES IN ORDER TO SOLVE YOUR PROBLEMS?

(A) You have to observe yourself carefully and try to answer the following questions:

(1) What are the conditions which produce distinctly negative, unde sirable effects for you?

(2) Why can't you change these conditions? Is it possible that you may expect positive effects although usually the effects are negative?

(3) What new, alternative activities are there which would enable you to produce more positive consequences, and get rid of the negative ones?

(B) The first thing to do is to imagine new, alternative varieties of behaviour. These activities may complement your usual type of behaviour, or may completely change it. Next go on to try out the consequences of these new activities, both in your thoughts and emotionally. When you anticipate positive consequences from this new type of behaviour, try it out in your everyday life.

(C) Always try to gain some insight into yourself, remember that your own needs and wishes are important, and that you should not always give way to others in order to preserve the peace.

IV WHAT CAN YOU DO WHEN THINGS DO NOT WORK OUT?

Failure should always be regarded as the reason for trying out new types of behaviour and activity. It should never be the cause of depression, but merely serve to enrich your range of experiences. Your principles should be geared to 'trial and error'; when some new type of activity does not lead to the expected success, abandon it and try something else. In doing so you may of course suffer sadness and despair, and express these emotions, but you should always try to act in such a way that your behaviour leads to better and more acceptable consequences.

V WHAT CAN YOU DO WHEN YOU HAVE NO IDEA WHAT ELSE YOU CAN DO?

You can only accept that state of affairs, but continue to observe your own behaviour in order to discover the conditions which prevent you from achieving satisfaction and happiness.

VI THE MOST IMPORTANT AIMS OF AUTONOMOUS SELF-ACTIVATION

(1) Your aim should always be to produce conditions which make it possible for you to lead a happy and contented life.
(2) To increase the positive consequences of your behaviour, and to reduce the negative consequences – go for what makes you happy, abandon what makes you unhappy.

VII WHAT IS THE ROLE OF OTHER PEOPLE IN HELPING TO SOLVE YOUR PROBLEMS?

The aim of autonomy training is not to be a completely independent person, but someone who is able to create the possible conditions which lead to pleasure and contentment. You will often find that the support and help of other people can be of great assistance. Consequently, it is usually important to enlist the help and assistance of other people. When you have a problem, such as giving up alcohol or reducing weight, then try to enter into a contract with another person who will hold you to your promises. When you cannot solve the problem by yourself, it is very helpful to have an obligation to another person to stand by the rules you have agreed on, such as not to eat more than 1,000 calories per day.

VIII HOW DO YOU ACHIEVE AUTONOMOUS SELF-REGULATION?

You are in a state of autonomous self-regulation when you succeed through your own activities, e.g. sport or jogging, refreshing
sleep, production of good interpersonal relations, to achieve an
inner equilibrium and contentment and respond appropriately to
deviations from this equilibrium. You will avoid dependence on
other people and conditions which produce dissatisfaction and
unhappiness, and you will also avoid too great dependence on
such things as coffee, alcohol or drugs. It is important to observe
your own behaviour and mental activity in order to identify those
people and objects on which you are too dependent and which
produce undesirable consequences. For instance you may be
drinking too much coffee, which in turn produces great excitement and prevents you from sleeping properly. In such conditions
it is necessary to engage in some alternative form of behaviour,
such as ceasing to drink coffee, or altering your behaviour vis-à-
vis a particular person, etc. When through your activities you
achieve more autonomous self-regulation, then you will feel that
you are very much better off. If this does not happen, you must
not despair, but go on looking for an improvement in the situation in which you find yourself.

Remember that no matter how much you study this pamphlet, it will directly affect only the attitudes of your verbal self.
However, as the results of the study show, this is just fine
because self-regulation is a logical, verbal concept. The self-regulation test in Appendix II, *like all written tests, tests only your
verbal self's version of your attitudes.* An important part of self-
regulation is a logical understanding by your verbal self that your
own basic needs, feelings and intuitions are important. Your verbal self must also understand how to push behaviour in healthy
directions at critical moments.

You can improve your understanding of self-regulation by
repeatedly reading the pamphlet above and, more important,
practising applying these principles to specific problems in your
life. If you retake the test in Appendix II every two months you
will find that your score will improve each time. When you truly
understand and practise self-regulation, you will have a perfect

score of 6 on the test – and the vibrant health that goes with it.

Some aspects of self-regulation require lots of practice to improve because they involve your habitual relationship between your feelings/behaviour and your verbal self. If you have a long-standing bad habit of ignoring your feelings, only repeated practice will correct it. Since the average age of the 1,200 people in the experiment was 58, it is clearly never too late to change.

Your Attitude Journal is a perfect place to set your goals and put your THINK, IMAGINE and LEARN steps on paper. You may have noticed that the experimenter process is actually identical to the one we used to deal with phobias and 'used-to's'. The only difference is that the problems are somewhat more complex because you are dealing with two-way interactions with other people rather than just your own reactions to things. The steps used in treating phobias are exactly the same as those used in the experimenter approach. In both cases problems are broken into manageable steps, goals are set, and results are anticipated and analysed. Another common principle is the need to set up repeated conditioning experiences so that your behaviour is gradually changed by positive experiences.

TAKING CARE OF YOUR NEEDS

Many people have been taught since childhood to ignore their own feelings and always do the logically correct thing. When this becomes a habit, basic feelings are effectively blocked and self-regulation can be misdirected at 'doing the right thing' even when that means ignoring your own needs and feelings. This pattern of behaviour is extremely unhealthy as it leads to bottled-up feelings of helplessness of which you may not even be aware.

Way back in 1965, as part of one of his early studies which led to his theories on self-regulation, Dr Grossarth-Maticek's interviewers questioned 1,341 elderly residents of Crvenka, Yugoslavia about their personality, health habits and attitudes. In 1976, when they checked the people's health status, they found that 11 of the questions relating to *rational and anti-emotional behaviour* had been amazingly predictive of future ill-health. In fact, 158 of the 166 cancer deaths were among those people who had answered yes to 10 or all 11 of the questions below:[8]

1. Do you always try to do what is reasonable and logical?
2. Do you always try to understand people and their behaviour, so that you seldom respond emotionally?
3. Do you try to act rationally in all interpersonal situations?
4. Do you try to overcome all interpersonal conflicts by intelligence and reason, trying hard not to show any emotional response?
5. If someone deeply hurts your feelings, do you nevertheless try to treat him rationally and to understand his way of behaving (so that you hardly ever attack and deprecate him or treat him purely emotionally)?
6. Do you succeed in avoiding most interpersonal conflicts by relying on your reason and logic (often contrary to your feelings)?
7. If someone acts against your needs and desires, do you nevertheless try to understand him?
8. Do you behave in almost all life situations so rationally that only very rarely your behaviour is influenced by emotions only?
9. Is your behaviour frequently influenced by emotions to such a degree that from a purely rational point of view it would have to be regarded as nonsensical or detrimental?
10. Do you try to understand others even if you do not like them?
11. Does your rationality prevent you from attacking others, even if there are sufficient reasons for doing so?

The people who answered yes to 10 or 11 of these questions were also 10 times more likely to die of heart attacks or strokes. Completely ignoring your own needs and feelings appears to be a very unhealthy habit. Logical thinking is extremely powerful, but like many powerful things it is capable of doing serious damage when used improperly. Notice that bad health came only to those who carried rationality to the extreme. Considering other people's feelings to some degree is healthy because your happiness is increased when people like you. A balance between taking care of your own feelings and considering others results in a 'middle' score. The really destructive pattern seems to be when you *never* consider your own feelings. Self-regulation should be directed at maximizing your *long-term feelings* of pleasure and well-being. It should not be directed at logical goals which ignore your own feelings and needs. You have every right to consider your own emotional needs because failing to do so can destroy your health.

Childhood experiences, such as trying to keep peace in a chaotic family, often start people down a path where they learn to suppress their own feelings. Good health requires that your verbal self learns to trust and act on the important feedback from your feelings. It must nurture them and respond to them, not suppress them. Decisive but minimal use of self-control can direct your life towards happiness and satisfaction which you will feel in your gut, not with your logic. Good health requires that your verbal self learns its proper place in the teamwork of your mind.

KNOWING WHEN TO QUIT

Sometimes people's upbringing is *too* effective at instilling values of hard work and determination, and the result is a life of helplessness and unhappiness. Yes you should try hard to succeed, but it is also important to learn when to quit. The idea that anyone can accomplish *anything* if they just try hard enough is simply not true. You can drive yourself crazy and ruin your health if you don't learn to realize your own limitations. There is a certain delight in quitting which is appreciated only too well by lazy irresponsible people, but too poorly by others. Unattainable goals give you a feeling of helplessness, while attainable goals give you feelings of pleasure, well-being and power.

Many hopeless situations are hopeless only because of unrealistic expectations and a refusal to give up on obsessive, fixed goals. Often the driving assumptions which draw people into helpless situations are inherently false. For example, after a loved one dies a false belief such as 'If I let go of his memory I am betraying him' can be the cause of years of hopelessness. Sticking with a hopeless career goal may be based on a false belief such as, 'If I fail at this my life is a complete failure.' Often taking THINK time to really re-examine your assumptions will make it clear that they are false and that quitting is the wisest thing to TRY.

Another kind of obsessive goal often starts when a wonderfully successful love or job situation comes to an end. Hopelessness and disease can follow if you spend the rest of your life trying to regain *that* situation. The solution is simple: get on with living life in the present and allow *something else* that is wonderful to happen to you.

Letting go of obsessive but impossible goals is possible only if you can live in the present and break the habit of ruminating on the future and the past. Spoiling your enjoyment of the present by comparing it to idealized hopes for the future or memories of the past is a sure way to block the normal development of new happy situations. If you focus on enjoying what is good about the present and grabbing the opportunities that present themselves, you remain open to new and unexpected kinds of happiness.

The THINK, IMAGINE and LEARN stages of the experimenter approach are all times for constructive reflection by your verbal self. When it comes to TRYing the new behaviour, self-control should be used only briefly and decisively during critical moments. You must teach your behaviour the new pattern by setting up an experience. Just as a good rider leads the horse to the hurdle but lets the horse do the actual jumps, self-control must nurture the new behaviour without taking too much control. A good rider controls her horse by brief jerks on the reins and stirrups at crucial times to keep it on track. Overcontrol makes real learning and development of behavioural competence impossible.

EVEN BAD EMOTIONS ARE HEALTHY

All emotions are useful feedback from the lower parts of the brain. Emotions were developed by evolution as a way to drive our behaviour in directions that will satisfy our instinctive needs. The newer, verbal parts of the brain add an ability to analyse this feedback further and either act on it or ignore it based on logical reasons and plans. Learned cognitive concepts and beliefs which are misguided can thus frustrate the satisfaction of important needs.

Though we have shown that positive feelings go with good immune function, it is extremely important to understand that negative feelings are also important and useful messages which must not be ignored or suppressed. Good health demands that you pay attention to all of your emotions. *Ignoring or suppressing negative emotions is extremely unhealthy* because they are important signals that changes are needed in your life.[9]

Good self-regulation must be based on acknowledging and responding to both positive and negative emotions. Negative emotions are avoided by *taking action* to correct the conditions that caused them, not by blocking them. If the conditions are truly uncontrollable, the cause of them should be avoided. Maximizing long-term pleasure and well-being is impossible if you ignore your negative emotions, because they are the only way you have of identifying the problems that need attention.

Ups and downs of emotion are a normal part of life and not bad for your health. Feel them and respond to them. When somebody gives you a bad feeling, it's time to THINK about what to do. If it's just a rude waiter in a restaurant, relax, make the best of it, and cross that restaurant off of your list. However, if the problem is more serious and has happened many times before, you must put your creativity to work to think of an experimental change in your own behaviour that will work towards a solution of the problem. The important thing is to avoid getting stuck in behavioural ruts which give you a *chronic* feeling of helplessness. The only bad emotion is a stuck emotion.

WORKING FROM BOTH SIDES

The self-regulation process normally assumes that other people's behaviour is beyond your direct control so that all change must come from *your own* behaviour. Since other people's behaviour is a reaction to your behaviour, this turns out to be surprisingly effective. The experimenter approach is even more powerful if it can be simultaneously applied from both sides of the problem. If both parties THINK together about behavioural changes that may fix it, and then both IMAGINE and discuss how the experiment might work, they can then jointly TRY the new behaviour and LEARN from the results.

Couples, parents and children, and bosses and employees can all use this technique to work on their relationship problems. By working from both sides of the problem, the power to fix the problem is increased dramatically. Breaking up negative ruts in behavioural interactions is much easier when both sides are really trying and paying attention. People in such a co-commitment situation can also help by reminding each other of commitments at crucial times.

In another controlled experiment, Grossarth-Maticek trained sports teams to use this technique to improve relations between the coach and players and between players. Eighteen football teams were divided into two matched groups with nine teams receiving training and nine used as a control. At the end of the season, the group receiving training had 104 wins while the control group had only 64.[10]

The basic problem-solving power of the experimenter approach is a relatively new invention for humanity which is still unknown within many tribal cultures. Often relatively simple changes in long-standing traditional behaviour can greatly increase food supply, improve health conditions or make a difficult existence much easier. The London branch of a world-wide organization called *Plan International*[11] has given valuable aid to 35,000 families in the villages of Burkina Faso in West Africa. Rather than tell people what to do, they hire local villagers and help them to define their own problems and opportunities and then help them to come up with their own solutions. Teaching these powerful problem-solving skills locally leaves the villagers empowered to help themselves make further improvements and solve future problems.

Once you really harness the power of the experimenter approach in living your own life, you will find that your power to control your own happiness will grow steadily, just as technology has grown steadily using the same principles. That same feeling of *progress* that drives scientific development can apply to the development of happiness and satisfaction in your own life. The opposite of feeling helpless, active experimentation and development of your personal life makes an exciting lifelong project.

Exercise One

IMPORTANT!
If you follow the steps below you will be giving yourself an autonomy training programme similar to the one that saved the lives of
more than half of the 600 elderly people treated in Grossarth-
Maticek's amazing intervention experiment. (*Note: If you have
access to the world-wide web see the chapter on the Attitude
Factor Web Site, beginning on page 208, for how to get computerized help in doing this exercise.*)
    Here are the steps:

1. Take the self-regulation test in Appendix II. Be careful to avoid
   rationalization and answer the questions with complete frankness
   and honesty.
2. Calculate your score by adding up the numbers you have circled
   and dividing by 105.
3. Look up your score in the figure on page 95. Notice the potential
   improvement in your health prospects that an improvement in
   your score could produce. For example, if your score was 4 you are
   in the group that was 22 per cent alive and well at the end of the
   study. If you could just increase your score by one point to 5, you
   would move up to the 62 per cent alive-and-well group. Almost
   tripling your chances of being alive and well at 70 is certainly
   worth some effort.
4. Think about and write down a list of things in your life that give
   you the most feelings of pleasure and well-being. Now do the
   same for things that give you the worst feelings of helplessness
   and stress. Pick a manageable problem from this list to attack by
   using the experimenter approach.
5. Read very carefully the self-regulation pamphlet reproduced on
   pages 195–205. As you read, THINK about how it can be applied
   to the problem you have chosen. Keep it next to your bed and
   reread it often.
6. Apply what you have learned by going through the experimenter's
   THINK, IMAGINE, TRY and LEARN steps (*see page 97*) as many
   times as it takes to improve the problem significantly.
7. Use your Attitude Journal to re-attack the problem regularly or

move on to another problem. Make a note on your calendar if you want to take a little rest between experiments. Make a contract with a friend with good self-control to discuss your progress every month or two for a year. Put it on your calendar. Long-term follow-ups for a year are extremely important to make self-regulation into a lifelong habit.

8. Retest yourself with the self-regulation test every couple of months. As you learn self-regulation by practising it, your score should steadily increase.

Exercise Two

1. Answer the 11 rationality/anti-emotionality questions on page 108.
2. If you score above 8, you should seriously work on your assertiveness and learn to value your own needs and feelings. It will take lots of practice to learn to recognize your real emotional needs and not just obnoxiously assert yourself because you logically think you should. Feel your emotions and value them.

Exercise Three

Whenever you feel a negative emotion from one of your significant relationships, THINK about how you can experimentally change your behaviour to work towards correcting the situation.

Exercise Four

1. Make a list of your significant relationships in family, love and work.
2. Rate each of them on a scale of 1 – 10 for the happiness they bring you.
3. THINK about how you could improve any that rate below 5. Decide which of the three basic approaches to fixing the problem

is appropriate. If you have fallen into a long-standing negative pattern, you should either withdraw now and get on with your life or begin immediately to experimentally change your own behaviour to correct the problem.

CHAPTER SUMMARY

1. Self-regulation means that you take responsibility for making your life better and adjusting your behaviour as necessary to adapt to the challenges that fate hands you. It also means that you are aware of your own feelings and needs and are able to take action in your long-term best interests, even when such action means short-term discomfort.

2. The Experimenter approach is a way to take control of seemingly impossible situations by repeatedly trying experimental changes in your own behaviour to find a way of correcting the situation.

3. Learning to withdraw from hopeless situations when your best efforts to correct them have failed is extremely important. Hopeless attachment to people and goals is very bad for your health.

4. Your long-term relations with significant other people in your life require that you constantly pay attention to the results of your own behaviour and change it when needed. Simply ignoring such problems can be disastrous in the long run. It is called disregulation.

5. Negative emotions are important feedback that should drive you to correct problems in your important relationships. Feel them and respond to them.

6. People who ignore their own basic feelings and needs and instead always try to do the logical thing have a high incidence of cancer and cardiovascular disease.

7. Problems that seem to be caused by other people can often be corrected by changes in your own behaviour because their behaviour interacts with yours.

8. Health and longevity are strongly related to one's score on the self-regulation test (*see Appendix II*). Attitude jogging can improve that score.

9. Self-regulation can be learned late in life and can make a dramatic difference in your happiness, health and longevity. Controlled experiments have proven it. Note: The experiments had bi-monthly follow-ups for one year. If you want results you must do the same. Lifelong habits don't change overnight.

CHAPTER
10

BEING CAREFUL CAN KILL YOU

In a survey of elderly urban people in England, Clarke and Lewis[1] found that *66 per cent* of those interviewed were *afraid to go out after dark* for fear of victimization. Unfortunately, this has become a common pattern. Many middle-aged and elderly people have become so frightened of life that it could probably qualify as a phobia, but we instead dismiss it as 'normal ageing'. Some people would explain this fear by saying that old people are easier victims, but the facts say otherwise. Actual crime statistics tell us that *elderly people are the least likely to be victimized.* Young people in their early twenties don't hesitate to go out at night even though they are *seven times more likely to suffer personal crimes than people over 65.* Personal crime rates actually fall off steadily above age 25.[2]

One of the most disabling effects of ageing is the attitude change that causes many old people's caution to increase to irrational levels. Teenagers are noted for being somewhat foolhardy with their personal safety, but as people mature the trend is often towards becoming more and more cautious and conservative about their own safety. Often the attitude change begins with parenthood. As parents we feel an extra obligation to protect our own safety and set a good example for our children. Unfortunately, long after the children have grown up these habits often live on. Since feelings of helplessness also weaken the immune response, fearful living can not only ruin the quality of life but can ultimately shorten it.

THE DOWNWARD SPIRAL

For a large percentage of the ageing population the caution gets clearly out of hand at some point in their lives and begins to resemble a phobia. As with most phobias, the downward spiral often starts with a single bad experience. An accident or crime affecting you personally or affecting a close friend often leaves you feeling predisposed to seeing danger everywhere. Once this fearful mentality gets a foothold, it's easy to find frightening news stories to confirm your fears and drive them deeper down the spiral towards a feeling of hopelessness.

The basic self-reinforcing tendency of attitudes perpetuates the decline as normal experiences are more and more perceived negatively. A walk down a dark street becomes a terrifying experience even if absolutely nothing bad happens. A shadowy figure makes you swear never to walk there again, even though he may simply be on his way to the corner shop to buy cigarettes. Getting lost fills you with terror and makes you swear never to drive in the city at night again. As a youth, getting lost was possibly frustrating but never terrifying. Once you found your way it made you *more* confident to drive or walk at night.

The downward attitude spiral that takes hold of people as they age is seldom diagnosed as a phobia. They rarely seek treatment because rationalization convinces them that they are simply taking wise precautions. Children and grandchildren often notice the problem but are powerless to do anything. Often they think of it as an inevitable consequence of ageing. Friends and parents have often provided the model for fearful behaviour. Almost like an epidemic, fearful people spread their outlook to others in their social set. If your parents became housebound in their old age, you will tend to imitate the same pattern because it seems 'normal'. Today's news media also feeds the epidemic, because they have found that it sells.

AVOIDING RISK CAN BE RISKY

Fearful attitudes do more than just ruin your enjoyment of life. They can actually shorten it. The effect of hopeless attitudes on cancer survival has been confirmed by numerous studies. For example, a study begun in 1979 by Greer, Morris and Pettingale categorized 62 cancer patients' attitudes and then tracked their later survival. They found that only 20 per cent of their 'help-less/hopeless' group was still alive five years later, while 81 per cent of the patients with 'fighting spirit' survived.[3] Having a help-less attitude significantly weakens your immune system.

The health benefits of good self-regulation are partly derived from the feeling of control that comes from mastering the experi-menter approach. Living confidently with a feeling that you are in control of your life energizes your immune system and increas-es your real safety. Every time you boldly face a minor risk it builds your confidence and feelings of being in control. The end result is that you are actually safer because your immune system works at peak efficiency. Feeling like a helpless victim is much worse because it significantly weakens your immune system.

We are all suffering from a sexually-transmitted terminal ill-ness called life. Nobody gets out of it alive. Yet, since worrying about things we can't change is pointless, we all use denial to ignore the problem and live our lives. This is a useful defence mechanism but it causes many people to be much more cautious about life than they should be. Denial effectively hides the unavoidable risks of dying, but it leaves the optional ones fully visible. This gives us the false illusion that we can be *100 per cent safe* by simply avoiding all of the optional risks. Unfortunately these optional risks are usually insignificant compared to the ones we ignore with denial.

Cautious people avoid even tiny risks because it makes them *feel* 100 per cent safe. They are not. Most of the dangers that cause people to live fearfully are in fact, insignificant compared to the unavoidable risks of cancer, heart disease, accidents and communicable diseases. The fact is that fearful living actually *shortens* your life. Let's look at the numbers.

The insurance industry and safety engineers have developed extensive tables of the actual risks in your life. They can calculate your basic life expectancy from your age and the various risks in your life. A convenient way to make that calculation is by looking up the risks in your life in a *risk catalogue* like the one on page 121. Each risk statistically shortens your life expectancy by a certain number of days. The table shows the LLE (Loss of Life Expectancy) numbers for many common risks.[4]

Your calculated life expectancy can be determined by subtracting the LLE numbers for any risks in your life from your basic life expectancy as determined by your age and sex. For example, if you work in a coal mine your life expectancy is shortened by 167 days. If you also spend one year pursuing a hang-gliding hobby, take off another 25 days. These LLE numbers can be added together, so your life expectancy in this case would be reduced by 167 + 25, or 192 days in total.

Smoking, 2 pack/day men	3139	Skiing-racing	0.5
Smoking, 1 pack/day men	2409	Snowmobiling	2
women	1533	Bicycling	6
Passive smoke	50	Air pollution	77
Cardiovascular disease	2043	Pesticide residue, food	12
Cancer, all	1247	Hazardous wastes	4
Breast cancer	109	Contaminated drinking water	1.3
Pulmonary disease	164	AIDS	50
Pneumonia	103	Medical radiation	6
All accidents	366	Natural radiation	9
motor vehicle	207	Radon gas in homes	29
collisions	87	Hurricanes	0.3
pedestrians	36	Tornadoes	0.8
home	74	Excess heat	0.7
falls at home	13	Excess cold	1
Overweight 25%	1303	Lightning	1.1
per percentage point	52	Floods	0.4
Unemployment	500	Earthquakes	0.2
Air travel	3.7	Tsunami	0.15
Ocean travel	3.3	Weather-related accidents	1.8
Occupation (average)	60	Venomous plants, animals	0.5
Agriculture	320	snakes, lizards, spiders	0.08
Mine, quarry	167	hornets, wasps, bees	0.4
Construction	227	Dog bites	0.12
Manufacturing	40	Injury by animals	0.6
High-wire performance	100	Poor social ties	1642
Professional diving	500	Good social ties	-1642
Championship auto racing	100		
Sports/year of participation:		Pleasure score of 3	5000
Professional boxing	8	Pleasure score of 4	3760
Hang gliding	25	Pleasure score of 5	-1606
Mountain climbing, all	10	Pleasure score of 5.5	-2732
dedicated	110	Self-regulation score 2	2737
Mountain hiking	0.9	Self-regulation score 3	766
Parachuting	25	Self-regulation score 4	-803
Sail planing	9	Self-regulation score 5	-4781
SCUBA diving, amateur	7	(Appendix II. avg=3.5)	

This table can be very useful for comparing the various risks in your life and gaining an understanding of which ones really justify your concern.[5] Since most people worry a lot about the tiny risks and ignore the big ones, you should study the table carefully. Let's look at the big ones first: If cancer were cured tomorrow, your life expectancy would be increased by 1,247 days. The average loss of life expectancy from cancer is thus 1,247 days. Cardiovascular disease removes 2,043 days from your life expectancy. The combined effect of cancer and cardiovascular disease on your life expectancy is thus 1,247 + 2,043, or 3,290 days (9 years).

We have already seen (*see tables on pages 4 and 139*) that your susceptibility to these and other health risks can vary significantly as your immune system responds to positive and negative emotions. A score of 3 on the Pleasure and Well-being test is predictive of a 5,000-day (13.5 years) reduction in your life expectancy compared to a person with an average score (4.3). A score of 5 on the test raises your life expectancy by 1,606 days (4.4 years).[6] Living in fear of small risks brings with it a feeling of hopelessness which can significantly increase your risk of death from all diseases. If you decided tomorrow to begin living boldly and accepting the risks of living adventurously, you might overcome that hopelessness and this change in your attitude factor could add thousands of days to your life expectancy. Let's look at the risk per year of participating in a few of the adventure sports you might take up as part of this new lifestyle:

Ski racing	5 days
SCUBA diving	7 days
Snowmobiling	2 days
Weekend mountain climbing	10 days
Parachuting	25 days
Hang-gliding	25 days

All of these sports are thought of as highly risky, yet if we were to take up all of them for one year each as part of a bolder life style, the total impact on your life expectancy would be a measly 69.5 days – only 2 per cent of your 3,290-day risk of cancer and heart disease![7] A tiny shift in your self-regulation or pleasure scores could more than make up for this tiny added risk.

The real way to live a long life is not by being a frightened and cautious victim but by living boldly and accepting the idea of taking reasonable risks. The variation in risk of cancer, cardiovascular and other diseases with attitude is so much greater than any of the risks most people worry about, that the emotional side-effects of worry and fear probably kill many times more people than the risks themselves.[8]

BEING PENNY WISE AND POUND FOOLISH

If your fixed monthly expenses are £2,000, you would be foolish to deprive yourself of something you really enjoy just to avoid a £1 expense. Yet many people do just that every day when they miss out on the joy of life to avoid risks which are an insignificant part of their overall total risk. Even if your attitude improvement didn't improve your chances of avoiding cancer and heart disease it would still be foolish to deprive yourself of the fun of living boldly for the tiny impact it would have on your life expectancy. *Simply buying a smoke detector for your home adds nine days to your life expectancy – enough to offset the risk of taking up both SCUBA diving and snowmobiling for a year.* Many people are 'penny wise and pound foolish' when it comes to accepting minor risks.

As we get older, our unavoidable risks from cancer, heart attacks and disease get higher and higher. Above age 65 you have a 1.9 per cent chance each year of dying from heart disease and 1.1 per cent chance from cancer. When your age is 45–64, these risks are .28 per cent and .22 per cent respectively.[9] As people age, they really should be less and less concerned with the shrinking effect of the minor optional risks on their life expectancy. Yet attitude decline causes most people to do just the opposite. They get more and more cautious about small added risks as they age, even though the effect of those risks becomes less and less significant.

LONG-TERM EFFECTS VS. SHORT-TERM GOALS

Seeking short-term safety makes you less safe in the long run. You may find this ironic statement familiar. In Chapter 2 we discussed a similar paradox in seeking comfort: We showed that seeking short-term comfort made you less comfortable in the long run. Both of these surprising consequences are caused by the same tendency of behavioural attitudes to change very gradually and invisibly as a result of the conditioning provided by the choices we make in life. Often pursuing seemingly reasonable *short-term* goals produces *long-term* attitude changes that defeat your original purpose.

Just as we found that seeking comfort can make you less comfortable in the long run by narrowing your comfort zone, *seeking safety can make you **less** safe in the long run* by reducing your ability to handle stressful events. A fearful, helpless attitude significantly weakens the immune system. As we found before, only our verbal self has the ability to understand logically the long-term effects of our actions. Our only hope for preventing attitude decline therefore lies in using self-control. We must use self-control decisively to push through behavioural fear on well-chosen challenges which we know we can face successfully. As we do this, we will build mental strength and flexibility.

Just as we attacked 'used to's' by entering challenges in our Attitude Journal and then intentionally confronting them, we can use our journal to attack fears. This challenge format is actually adapted from methods used by cognitive-behavioural therapists to cure phobias. The first step is to decide carefully what your first, easily achievable, step should be. You may have to subdivide a major goal into manageable sub-goals. Even more important is learning to be alert for opportunities that naturally arise in the normal course of living. Be alert for excuses and rationalizations that create 'no' answers to opportunities, and try instead to develop a habit of saying 'yes.'

Whenever you confront a fear, it's important to do it with a confident, 'matador' attitude. Some people develop a bad habit of being 'hot reactors' which greatly increases their probability of developing cardiovascular disease. Every time you allow a panic reaction to take hold of you, the increased stress on your heart can do a little bit of permanent damage.[10] Practise functioning calmly in fear situations, like you have 'nerves of steel'. Give yourself time to calm down and methodically handle situations.

Courage is nothing more than acting in spite of fear. It can be developed using exercise principles. By practising on mild challenges you will develop strength to allow you to keep your cool during bigger challenges. As you develop a gutsy attitude you will find that, though you actually take more risks, you will feel fear less. Your cardiovascular system will thank you.

FEARING THE WRONG THINGS

There are some things that you **should** be afraid of, but most people waste their fear and worry on things that aren't really risky at all. The news media creates many of these fears by emphasizing certain stories which they have found can really frighten people. Fearful people love to be frightened, so these stories sell lots of newspapers and increase TV and radio ratings. A large part of the population is living in fear and looks at the news daily for confirmation of the dangers they sacrifice so much to avoid.

Sudden unexpected deaths seem to be the most appealing. As you look at or read these sensational stories it's easy to forget that 5,900 people die every day in the US alone. *Though 1,095 people die every day from smoking-related illness, 822 die from the effects of being overweight, and 119 die from automobile accidents, these are not newsworthy events.* Shark attacks make much better reading, so even if the result is nothing more than a bite out of a surfboard or a minor cut, the news media will run a full story and picture. The result is that many people are very worried about shark attacks and even avoid going to the seaside to avoid the danger. The fact is that only 10 of the 365 kinds of sharks ever attack people. The actual death rate from shark attacks is too small even to appear on the risk data. Dog bites, which are a much greater danger, do appear. They account for a measly .12 days.

Aeroplane crashes are another popular item. By covering all crashes world-wide this small source of danger is made to look much worse than it is. Somehow a shot of 300 bodies scattered on a small area of ground is more photogenic than the 1,095 dead bodies scattered widely in US hospital morgues *every day* as a result of smoking-related illnesses. Actually, if you fly an average amount (1,000 miles/year) flying reduces your life expectancy by only .4 days.[11] If you flew every day, it would take 26,000 years before you would be expected to die in a crash.

Hurricanes, tornadoes and earthquakes are another great source of disaster photo opportunities. Their actual effect on your life expectancy are only .3, .8, and .13 days respectively. News photos always show the one worst street in the city after such disasters, but generally the other 99.9 per cent of the city looks completely normal. Once you adopt the fearful mentality you don't care about the other 99.9 per cent , you're just glad you stayed safely home. Your mental picture is of an entire city devastated like the photograph. By staying safely home, you will never find out otherwise.

I lived in the San Francisco area during the earthquake of 1989 and also in Los Angeles during the 1994 quake. In both cases if I hadn't watched the TV news I might have dismissed them both as minor events. The death toll in those two earthquakes was 63 in San Francisco and 57 in Los Angeles. Within a month, a cold wave had killed 300 people in the East, yet travel to both California cities from the East was way down for years after the quakes because people were afraid of the danger.

Snake and spider bites also make good copy but their actual effect on your life expectancy is only .08 days. Bees, hornets and wasps are much more of a threat – .4 days. The nightly news is full of stories of murder, and murder does affect the average life expectancy by 80 days, but wait. Most murder is directed at inner-city drug dealers and gang members. Your own risk is a tiny fraction of the average.

AIDS statistically shortens the average life expectancy by 55 days, but if you don't share needles with others or engage in unsafe sex your danger is a tiny fraction of this figure. Less than 1 per cent of the AIDS cases in Los Angeles County in 1995 were non-injecting, heterosexual men. Just over 3 per cent were heterosexual women, but the study didn't determine whether they had engaged in unsafe sex. Sixty-eight per cent of women with AIDS contracted it through injected drug use.[12]

In February 1986 nearly two million Americans cancelled their holiday plans abroad because a single cruise ship was hijacked by terrorists. People tend to generalize local events to a whole continent if it's far enough away. We all love to sit snugly in the safety of our home and watch disasters that happened to other people, but remember that the news media will always seek out the one worst scene on the whole continent. A few terrorist bombs in Paris are not a sane reason to avoid the whole continent of Europe. Even if you visit a city during a wave of terrorist bombings, your chances of dying there from an automobile accident are generally much higher than of being a victim of terrorism. The bombing scene is simply much more photogenic than the normal auto accidents scattered throughout any large city every day.

I was visiting Thailand in 1993 when the military dissolved Parliament and declared the Constitution null and void. The news media managed to find some military shots, but where I was staying it was a non-event. The photogenic stuff you see on the news is carefully selected by the camera crew. Don't extrapolate it in your mind to a whole country or continent. Remember that *the real risks in your life are **not** on the news*. They are here to stay no matter how much you try to hide in the safety of your home. Clinging fearfully to life is like dying a thousand deaths. The joy of life is yours for the taking. Don't let fear ruin it.

ENVIRONMENTAL DANGERS

The environmental movement has done an excellent job of scaring us into controlling pollution of our air, food and water, which are certainly in danger as the population skyrockets. However, the public awareness campaigns which made us take action to control pollution have had a terrible side-effect in recent years. Some people have adopted an overly fearful attitude towards life and have totally lost perspective of the real degree of danger. A new 'environmental disease' is becoming more and more common. Its victims live in terror of risks which are amazingly insignificant compared to the unavoidable risks of life. Many people actually develop psychosomatic physical symptoms similar to allergies which are actually based entirely on an attitude of panic.

One of the basic misconceptions behind this fearful attitude is the belief that things have been getting much worse, making life today very dangerous. Many chemicals that cause cancer were released into the environment and a public uproar was necessary to put a stop to it, but the publicity has caused fearful people to panic. Thanks to that pressure, our environment is cleaner than it has been for decades. The fact is that *the death rate from all but one major kind of cancer has stayed the same or gone down.* The one exception is lung cancer, which has risen by a factor of 10 over the past 20 years. This rise may be due to the increased stress of modern life or possibly the result of the increased popularity of cigarette smoking.[13] The delayed rise of women's lung cancer rates confirms that the cause is not primarily the air we breathe. Both the stress of high-pressure jobs and the popularity of smoking came later for women.

Holding the line on cancer death rates is particularly impressive when you consider the fact that non-vehicular accidents are one fifth of what they were in 1930, automobile accident rates are one third less per mile than they were,[14] and most of the major communicable diseases are now under control. With many of the non-cancer causes of death eliminated, the longer life span which results would normally cause the cancer death rate to increase significantly. However, medical progress has prevented that.

One of the major environmental causes of cancer is actually radon gas in homes, produced by natural radioactive decay and emitted by natural brick and stone construction and from the ground in many basements. The effect of radon on our life expectancy is 29 days. Other man-made building materials we hear so much about such as formaldehyde, chlordane, asbestos, benzene and hundreds of others only lower life expectancy by two days.

Many of the food additives we hear so much about are similarly insignificant compared to natural substances. Aflatoxin, which appears naturally in peanuts, corn and milk, is worse than any of the artificial additives we hear so much about. Peanut butter and milk are each listed as 1-day risks. Nitrosamines, which occur naturally in beets, celery and lettuce, and carotatoxin, found in carrots, would never pass the test used for FDA approval. Many of the natural pesticides in plants are worse than the banned commercial ones. It is estimated that all of the 200 kinds of man-made pesticide residues have a combined effect on life expectancy of 12 days.

Bad enough to require more attention by regulators, but not significant enough to worry yourself sick over because, compared to your unavoidable risks, it is insignificant.[15]

MEDIA FEAR STORIES

The media loves to scare you, and fearful people enthusiastically seek out scare stories like sweets. Bad news is turned into headlines, but good news doesn't sell so you often never hear it. For example, in spite of what you may have heard, the hole in the ozone layer has not produced any measurable increases in ultraviolet on the earth's surface except in the Antarctic region – and then only during the few weeks of the year that the ozone hole opens up. This *could* have developed into a major disaster but, thanks to the Montreal Protocol, the ozone layer is expected to begin healing itself by the year 2000. The maximum effect at the peak will be an 8 per cent increase in ultraviolet in the temperate zones in mid-summer. Scientists calculate that the maximum effect in the year 2000 will be equivalent to driving south about 200 miles now.[16]

Another typical fear story is the idea that magnetic fields from power lines contribute to cancer. This started years ago with a Swedish study which has since been contradicted by the results of other studies. Fourteen scientists, including six Nobel prizewinners, have joined with the American Medical Association in filing briefs with the California Supreme Court on the subject.[17] The story may never die out in the popular press, however, because reinforcing the fearful mentality sells more papers.

Air quality has greatly improved in the past two decades. The famous Los Angeles smog is now back to 1963 levels. Still the estimated effect of carcinogens in air is 77 days of lost life expectancy. Don't forget that in the 'good old days' city streets were awash with tons of horse and human manure, and the smell and flies were horrendous. Chamber pots were emptied out the window into the street until the marvellous invention of the flush toilet made it possible to wash them directly into the same river used for drinking water. *Natural, organic* substances like typhus and cholera bacteria took an appalling toll.

Drinking water supplies today have greatly improved. Yes, chlorine is a carcinogen, but its effect on life expectancy in cities like Miami and New Orleans, which use it heavily, is estimated at only .5 days. The total impact of all hazardous waste is estimated at 4 days. We can improve the situation further, but it certainly doesn't justify feeling like a hopeless victim. Remember that the killer diseases were all caused by *natural* bacteria and viruses, and cured by *man-made* drugs. With technology we win some and we lose some, but the important thing is that we should feel good about it. We *are* making progress and we are in control in most areas. Feeling helpless is a toxic and unwarranted attitude in today's world. Don't let the fear-mongers steal your joy and shorten your life.

HEALTHY AND UNHEALTHY DRINKING

Good self-regulation puts you in control of your life, so people with high self-regulation scores also tend to have good health habits.[18] For example, only 5 per cent of the people with self-regulation scores above 5 are overweight, compared to 58 per cent of those with scores below 2. Lack of exercise, bad nutrition, smoking and drinking all similarly tend primarily to be problems of people with poor self-regulation.

Could the increased longevity of people with good self-regulation be simply a result of better health habits? Grossarth-Maticek did a study in 1973–93 which proved that the answer is clearly no. Almost 300 of the people in one of his massive studies had good scores on self-regulation but very *unhealthy* lifestyles. *In spite of their unhealthy lifestyles, they outlived a group with healthy lifestyles but poor self-regulation by **8.5 years.***

Clearly self-regulation has a health impact which is stronger than and goes much deeper than just health habits. Healthy lifestyle was defined in this experiment as *no* smoking or drinking, good diet and at least 1.5 hours of exercise a day. Unhealthy lifestyle meant *at least 10 years of smoking 20 or more cigarettes a day, drinking over 60 grams of alcohol, unhealthy diet and little exercise.*

Of course, if you have good self-regulation and a healthy lifestyle you have the longest life expectancy of all. *With an unhealthy lifestyle, good self-regulation adds 15 years to your life expectancy.*[19] With a healthy lifestyle, it adds 20 years.

Drinking alcohol has been recently found by many researchers actually to be *beneficial* to health. Countries where people routinely drink with meals have significantly higher life expectancy rates than those where drinking is rare. France, for example, has a female life expectancy second only to that of Japan. In another important experiment, Grossarth-Maticek showed that the *pleasure* brought by drinking probably explains its positive effect on health. He gave a simple test to almost 2,000 steady drinkers to determine whether they drank for pleasure or to drown their sorrows. The test listed 11 possible negative effects of drinking and 10 positive ones.[20] People who answered yes to at least one negative effect or no positive effects were classified as negative drinkers. The result was two approximately equal-sized groups:

1. Positive drinkers who drink for pleasure and find that alcohol actually *improves* their self-regulation by relaxing them and making them more communicative.
2. Negative drinkers who drink to drown their sorrows. They find that drinking makes them more isolated and depressed and lowers their self-regulation.

When the health records were checked 20 years later, it was found that the positive drinkers significantly outlived the negative drinkers. The results were particularly dramatic for smokers. Negative drinkers who smoked had *22 times higher death rate* than positive drinkers (whether they smoked or not)![21]

Abstaining from drinking entirely turns out to be a good idea only if you are a negative drinker. Generally, *positive drinkers as a group drank considerably more than the negative drinkers yet outlived them by a wide margin.* In fact, the group with the highest average alcohol consumption turned out to be the positive drinkers who were still alive and well at the end of the study. The negative drinkers showed the opposite pattern, with much less alcohol consumption in the alive-and-well group. Alcohol seems to be able to improve or ruin your health, depending upon how you respond to its effects.[22]

Since alcohol reduces activity of the cerebral cortex, it tends to weaken self-control and allow behaviour to express itself uncensored. The two different responses to drinking may thus be an indication of the kind of partnership the person has established between self-control and conditioned behaviour:

- Negative drinkers have bad conditioned behaviour that is held in check by self-control – until they start drinking.
- Positive drinkers enjoy letting go of their self-control because their underlying conditioned behaviour is well adjusted and socially competent.

The negative drinker's behaviour is like an unruly dog which must be kept firmly leashed and in check by its owner (self-control) to prevent it from doing damage. The positive drinker's behaviour is like a well-trained dog which can be safely unleashed and allowed to run and frolic sometimes.

The relationship between your self-control and your non-verbal behaviour is like that of a dog and its owner. An over-controlled dog never learns good behaviour, so the owner must keep it tightly leashed and muzzled to prevent bad behaviour. With a more nurturing owner, the dog develops civilized behaviour and can be safely unleashed and allowed to romp freely. If you have a healthy relationship between your verbal self and your conditioned behaviour, drinking, which weakens self-control, lets your behaviour have a healthy romp, which gives you pleasure and good health.

You can develop your own personality in this healthy direction by using your self-control only minimally – at critical moments.

This will keep behaviour on the right track, yet let it gain strength and competence by being in control most of the time.

WHAT YOU CAN CHANGE

If you smoke cigarettes or are overweight then the tiny risks we have been discussing should be of no concern to you. Smoking one pack a day reduces your life expectancy by 2,409 days for men, 1,533 days for women. Being overweight costs you about 52 days of life expectancy for every per cent you are overweight. If you are 15 per cent overweight this means you lose 777 days, 25 per cent costs you 1,303 days, 35 per cent costs 1,964 days and 45 per cent costs 3,276.[23] These are pretty significant numbers compared to the tiny risks we have been discussing. *Working as a high-wire performer is less risky than being 2 per cent overweight.* Working in a coal mine shortens your life expectancy by 167 days, about the same as being 3.1 per cent overweight. If you take up both hang-gliding and parachuting, it's less risky than being 1 per cent overweight!

The amazing thing is that being a smoker or being overweight doesn't seem to stop people from worrying about other tiny risks anyway. It seems that *denial can hide the dangers of these chronic problems*, but people try to make themselves feel safer by being extra vigilant in avoiding the remaining tiny risks that they *can* control.

Attitude jogging can't directly help you to lose weight or stop smoking, but it can strengthen your self-control. By practising quick, decisive self-control, and building up your confidence while exercising it on things you *can* accomplish, you may be able to strengthen your self-control enough to conquer these dangerous habits. As with any difficult goal, the idea is to split it up in a series of smaller, more manageable sub-goals. You can start with easier 'used to's' or other things you would like to change to build up your self-control. In the meantime relax, enjoy life, and stop kidding yourself by obsessing on the small stuff.

The worst thing you can do is to continue smoking or being overweight and just worry all the time about your helplessness in being unable to control them. Either decisively attack them as problems, or just relax and enjoy your life knowing that there are plenty of other risks anyway. Don't worry yourself to death.[24] The worst of all possible worlds is to continue these unhealthy behaviours *and* add helpless worrying as an additional risk factor. Self-control should be used briefly and decisively – not as a drawn-out source of nagging and guilt.

If you really want to improve your prospects for a long, healthy life, attitude jogging is a much more fruitful place to direct your efforts. The risk numbers clearly show that your attitude factor, as reflected by your scores on the two attitude tests, has a much greater potential for adding years of good health and happiness to your life than all of the tiny risks people worry themselves about put together.

Notice, for example, that good 'social connections' can make a 3,285-day (9-year) difference in your life expectancy. If avoiding second-hand smoke (50 days) is limiting your social life, you are certainly shortening your life by trying to lengthen it. Good social connections means that you have close friends, family, clubs, church and other supportive connections with other people. In fact just being married makes a 1,825-day (5-year) difference in your life expectancy. If you were offered a pill that would add five years to your life with no bad side-effects, wouldn't you take it without hesitation?

Unemployment shortens your life expectancy by 500 days. Apparently the worry and loss of confidence increases drinking, suicide, homicide and a host of other causes. Living in poverty has a 3,300-day impact whether you are white or non-white.

Learning to relax, staying in the present and calmly accepting the inevitable risks of life is extremely important. The tension of living fearfully and worrying about insignificant future risks can definitely kill you by increasing your risk of cardiovascular death. The hopelessness of living fearfully can finish you off by increasing your chances of dying of cancer. By living confidently, and boldly accepting the little risks of *really* participating in life, you will improve both the quality and the quantity of your life.

Changing your attitude towards life takes more than just a cognitive decision to change. Logically understanding the false security of fearful living is only a start. To really change your attitude you must develop a habit of using self-control at the critical moments when fear tempts you to retreat. Over the years you will gradually regain the confident joy of your youth. You may find, as many vital people have, that your later years are the best.

Exercise One

1. Look carefully at the table on page 121 for risk factors that apply to you.
2. Add them up to find the number of days of life expectancy you are losing due to risks.
3. How much could you improve this number if you improved your self-regulation score by 1 point?

Exercise Two

1. Think of a 'used to' that you stopped doing because it seemed too risky.
2. Could it be that the risk involved is really insignificant compared to the unavoidable risks in your life?
3. If so, commit yourself to an attitude jogging programme to overcome the fear, using same techniques discussed in Chapter 8 for curing phobias.

Exercise Three

1. Do you tend to avoid scary, suspenseful or exciting films?
2. If the answer is yes, try building up your tolerance by pushing yourself with manageably exciting movies. Gradually increase the degree of challenge till you overcome your fear of fear. Fear and excitement can be enjoyable experiences, unless you have conditioned yourself to hate them.

Exercise Four

1. Does drinking alcohol give you pleasure and improve your ability to communicate your feelings?
2. If the answer is no, you should think about the relationship you have developed between self-control and behaviour. Try when you are sober to retrain and nurture back to health the bad behavioural traits which show themselves when you drink.
3. If the answer is yes, pour yourself a drink and enjoy!

CHAPTER SUMMARY

1. Your chances of being a victim of personal crimes falls off steadily after age 25. At 65 it has fallen by a factor of seven.
2. The hopelessness engendered by fearful living is much riskier than the minor risks people so carefully avoid.
3. If fearful living doubles your chances of getting cancer or heart disease, it will reduce your life expectancy by 3,290 days.
4. The combined risk of taking up hang-gliding, parachuting, mountain climbing, snowmobiling, SCUBA diving and ski racing for one year each would reduce your life expectancy by only 69.5 days.
5. Living boldly and accepting some risks makes you live longer because your improved attitude reduces the risk of major disease.
6. If you can improve your self-regulation score from 4 to 5 you can increase your life expectancy by 3,978 days.
7. Working as a high-wire performer is less risky than being 2 per cent overweight. Working in a coal mine is safer than being 3.1 per cent overweight.
8. Drinking for pleasure actually lengthens your life and is healthier than not drinking liquor at all.
9. Disaster photos show the one worst part of the city. Often the other 99.9 per cent of the city looks quite normal.
10. Crime is down, cancer risk is down, pollution is down. Don't believe all of the negative things in the news. It could kill you.

CHAPTER
11

EXPANDING YOUR BOUNDARIES

Man is a social animal and has been throughout evolution. All of our ancestors lived in tribes or extended families, as the apes still do. One exception was the outcasts. In many animal and human societies certain weaker individuals are excluded from the social group. *The result is usually early death.*

Our society has been trying out a major lifestyle innovation since the turn of the 20th century. A new concept called **privacy** has become increasingly popular. After millions of years of living in tribes or extended families, in the late 1940s more and more people began to live in small nuclear families. More recently, even that social unit has broken down and living completely alone has become a trend. Households consisting of only one person rose from 3.7 per cent in 1790 to 9.3 per cent in 1950, 13.1 per cent in 1960, 18.3 per cent in 1973,[1] and 24 per cent in 1990.[2] While living alone is considered by our culture to be a desirable luxury made possible by affluence, its effect on health and longevity is frightening.

Objectively, good attitudes should have a positive effect on health and longevity. Using this objective criterion, being a self-contained loner is clearly an unhealthy attitude because it significantly increases your chances of bad health and early death. Just as the outcasts of aboriginal societies quickly sicken and die, people with poor social connections in our society have significantly worse life expectancies. Could our experiment with this new concept of privacy turn out to be a disastrous mistake that helps only the economy? Only time will tell.

CONNECTED PEOPLE LIVE LONGER

The toxic effects of loneliness are confirmed by insurance statistics and numerous scientific studies. For example, one study of 972 Johns Hopkins medical students used results of personality tests to classify the students into one of five types. Thirty years later when they checked health status, they found that students classified as 'loners' had *16 times* more cancer than people who vented their emotions to friends.[3] Study after study has shown that feeling connected with other people is extremely important for physical and mental health. Suicide, alcoholism and mental illness rates are much higher among people living alone.[4]

A massive study of 4,725 randomly selected residents of Alameda County in California found that those with the fewest close friends, relatives and social connections had mortality rates that were two to three times higher than those with high levels of social connectedness.[5] Also, life expectancy tables show a difference of *nine years* between people with very poor social connections and those with very good ones.

Any social animal has an instinctive craving for social connections. We long to be a part of something larger than ourselves. Yet in today's society that longing often goes unsatisfied. One third of all children in the US today are raised in a household with only one or neither of their biological parents present. In the Afro-American community this figure rises to two-thirds. Street gangs are a pathetic attempt by these unfortunate children to satisfy their urge to belong.

When we were young most of us formed many social connections in school. We felt an integral part of our school, our classroom and our family. After leaving school most people's social connections begin to narrow. Today it is common to take a job far away from home. Children used to provide a rapid substitute family connection, but today many people defer parenthood till much later so that they can enjoy their privacy for longer. When they do have children, the children in their turn often move far away when they reach adulthood, for privacy. Even neighbours who used to talk to each other on front porch swings or in front gardens are now isolated by fences and enclosed porches.

We all have a primitive need to feel that we are a part of something and that we are loved and supported by the rest of the herd. Do you have that feeling? Do you have close friends or family members with whom you discuss your innermost feelings? If the answer is no, your first attitude jogging goal should be to take some manageable step towards correcting the situation.

SOCIAL ISOLATION AND PLEASURE

In Chapter 1 we saw that scores on the pleasure and well-being test were strongly predictive of future good health. The more than 3,000 elderly subjects in that study were also asked questions about their social connections, such as whether they had good friends and family. When the results were plotted it was found that social isolation had an amazingly strong association with low scores on the test.

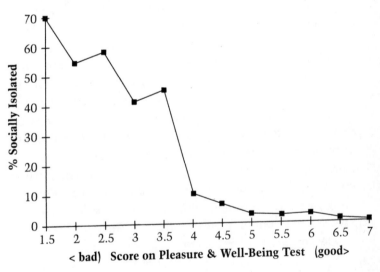

Seventy per cent of the people with scores below 1.5 were considered socially isolated, while *none* of the people with a perfect score of 7 was isolated. Generally anyone with a score of less than 3.5 had a high probability of being socially isolated.

Since self-regulation also correlates strongly with the pleasure score, the real cause and effect probably starts with bad self-regulation, which leads to social isolation, which leads to unhappiness and a low score on the pleasure and well-being test. The cause and effect thus looks like this:

Poor self-regulation → Social isolation → Low pleasure and well-being

AN EPIDEMIC OF DEPRESSION

A 1970 US Government-sponsored survey found that people born in the second half of the 20th century are *10 times more likely to suffer depression* than people born in the first half.[6] Could this epidemic of depression be a side-effect of our experiment in privacy? Though privacy may seem like a natural urge to us, it never occurred to people before the end of the 17th century.[7] Even kings and noblemen, who could certainly afford privacy, had servants or visitors in their rooms almost continually. The idea of having separate servants' quarters or even of individual dining chairs rather than benches are both·about a century old. Whole families often shared a single bed.

One of the purported benefits of living alone is that you don't have to compromise your taste or living habits at all. You can squeeze your toothpaste from whichever end you want. Another way of saying this is that *you can have zero flexibility and a very narrow comfort zone*. However, mental flexibility and the ability to adapt are both important qualities for happiness and good health. Humans have an amazing ability to adapt, as the tribes living in sweltering deserts and on arctic ice-fields prove. Creating your own no-compromise environment at home doesn't help when you go out in the real world and things don't go exactly the way you would like them to.

LIFE ABOARD A DESTROYER

In the 1950s I lived for three years aboard a US Navy destroyer, a warship only 19 feet wide. Our sleeping accommodations were called 'racks'. They consisted of a piece of canvas laced onto a rectangular pipe frame 2 foot by 6 foot, with a 1-inch thick mattress on it. These were stacked four high under an 8-foot ceiling, with four lockers, containing all of our belongings, on the floor below the bottom rack.

The racks were so close together that people had to be staggered according to weight, because an overweight person would cause the canvas to sag so much that a thin person had to be assigned to the rack below. If anyone wanted to get into his locker, the person on the bottom rack had to get up and fold his rack up so the cover on the locker could be raised.

Toilet facilities were upstairs through a hatch and through the mess hall. They consisted of a sort of stainless steel bathtub with continuous salt-water circulation and four pairs of boards across the top. The boards were shaped so that each pair served as a toilet seat. When someone defecated in the seat next to you, you would often be splashed as their excrement hit the water.

These living conditions may sound intolerable, but we all adapted quite nicely to them and they came to seem normal to us. There were many complaints about the quality of the food, but the living conditions were seldom mentioned. One of the reasons was that living so closely in a large group was a lot of fun. There was continual joking, teasing and deep discussions. It was never dull.

The important point is that there were hundreds of such ships in the Navy and virtually everybody quickly adapted to the living conditions. People left the Navy for many reasons, but these living conditions weren't among them. The fact is that *those living conditions were much closer to the ones our species experienced during millions of years of evolution than our present-day concept of private living.* Our ancestors clustered in caves or around campfires were happy to be together. Even in the wide open spaces, primitive people cluster closely together for mutual protection and warmth. They see themselves as a part of a group both day and night.

The Siriono Indians of eastern Bolivia sleep with as many as five family members in a single hammock. As many as 50 hammocks are hung in a 500 square foot hut.[8] They do this not because they are short on space, but out of preference. Their cultural tradition simply teaches them a different attitude towards privacy than ours. They would probably be as appalled by the loneliness of our separate bedrooms as we are by the crowding in their sleeping huts.

Any well-established cultural attitude seems to be obviously correct to the people raised with that attitude. This is why we must be wary of the seemingly 'obvious' benefits of privacy.

Self-contained living has been popular for less than 50 years, so we are just beginning to realize its long-term effects on our society. It seems logical that any new idea which can be experimentally shown to double the mortality rate should be carefully re-examined. Yet there are economic forces that discourage this re-examination.

PRIVATE LIVING AND ECONOMICS

Our economy is strongly affected by the number of people per household because this determines the number of houses we need. Private living doubles the need for cars, telephones, washing machines, TV sets, VCRs, stereos, computers, video games, CDs and tapes, books, living room furniture, barbecues, patio furniture, cookers, refrigerators, microwaves, answering machines, faxes, pots and pans, repairs, etc., etc. Could the rat race of modern life be a direct result of this privacy experiment?

The incredible increase in housing costs in the 1960s and 70s was much more than the result of inflation. Going from an average of four to a house to two means that *there must be twice as many housing units per population.* This generated a tremendous boom in the building industry, so supply and demand sent land prices skyrocketing. The result is that life today is a lot tougher than it used to be, not only because fewer people share their living expenses but also because the real cost of an average housing unit has doubled.

Advertising makes us want to own *things.* It very effectively manipulates us to buy products which are not necessarily good for us. Cigarette advertising is a perfect example. Here is a product that doubles your chances of dying of any of the major killers, yet millions of people have been tricked into buying it anyway. Could it be that getting your own private place to live and filling it with your own private furniture and appliances is a similar unhealthy con job?

Resisting the persuasive power of advertising and peer pressure is difficult, as the millions of people still smoking prove. But at least smokers now know the dangers of their habit. The dangers of self-contained living are a well-kept secret today. Is it really better for children to each have their own private bedroom? It wasn't thought to be when the generations who suffered one-tenth as much depression as we have today[9] were growing up. Learning to compromise and be flexible is easy for children but much more difficult later in life after habits are established.[10] Sharing feelings and secrets is the opposite of privacy.

The problem gets worse when children grow up and leave the home – often to take jobs in faraway places. Parents who were used to children as a primary source of social contact suddenly find themselves alone and without the social connections they might have developed had they not had children.

Jobs and children force people to practise flexibility. When children leave and retirement comes, people who live alone are left in a position where they can have exactly their own way in everything. Unfortunately this often means rapid attitude decline as they no longer push the limits of any comfort zone. Attitudes quickly shrivel and flexibility becomes a thing of the past. Their 'used to' list grows dramatically, and depression and illness often follow.

PERSONAL BOUNDARIES

Personal boundaries are the imaginary line between 'us' and 'them'. We all defend what is inside imaginary boundary and compete against what is outside. Through the ages all people, except for the occasional outcast, have included an extended family or tribe within their boundary. Today we have a new concept which has been called 'the empty self'.[11] Under this concept the self-boundaries stop at your own skin. All outsiders, including family members, are thought of as 'them' and are objects of competition.

. This mentality is great for the economy because it precludes sharing. In fact buying things, overeating, drinking and drugs are all popular ways to fill the void created when healthy social connections are eliminated. Shopping and eating essentially 'feed' the empty self. By buying a better house or car than our neighbours, the empty self hopes to build up self-esteem. Unfortunately this never works for long, because real self-esteem must come from inside.

Narcissism is another word for this self concept. Empathy and true interest in other people are signs of healthy attitudes. Attitude decline towards narcissism is a gradual process which develops the same way all other declines do: Your connections with other people atrophy without exercise. Taking the path of least resistance by watching telly or sleeping may feel restful in the short term but it lets your friendships and your ability to connect with friends atrophy.

Again self-control is your only defence because only your logical, verbal self can appreciate the long-term benefits of maintaining good social connections. Saying 'yes' to social invitations sometimes takes a second of self-control, but the payoff in keeping up social connections is significant.

Do you always prefer to be alone? If the answer is yes could it be that your comfort zone for socializing has shrivelled? Even people who like parties often force themselves to go when they feel 'tired' because they know that the energy of the people there will give them energy. If you've said no often enough your comfort zone for socializing may have narrowed to the point where you can no longer enjoy parties. If you find yourself in this position then you must start with something easier and work your way up to parties. Visiting with one good friend is a start. 'Acting as if' is often a useful way of getting yourself out of an antisocial mood. The short-term comfort of being a habitual loner is so provably unhealthy that it should not go unchallenged.

NARCISSISTIC CONVERSATIONS

The key to healthy socialization is developing a *true* interest in other people, not as listeners to what you have to say but as separate, interesting people. Narcissistic conversation always tries to turn the spotlight onto yourself. Here is an example to help you recognize it:

> Friend: 'I just got back from New Orleans and the seafood was great. You should see the size of the – (interrupted)'
> You: 'Yeah, isn't it amazing? I love to go down to the ... (the spotlight has been stolen and we will never hear the story).'

If you have a tendency to interrupt people, try watching yourself carefully. Are you doing it to shift the spotlight onto yourself? If the answer is yes, you may want to make narcissism an attitude jogging project. When someone else has the floor, use self-control to stop yourself from stealing the spotlight.[12]

Just keeping quiet is not enough; really *listen* carefully to what others say, even if it means you have to use the 'acting as if' trick. Focus your attention on what they are telling you. You may have had something even more interesting happen to you, but let them have the floor. A true conversationalist draws others out and makes them more interesting.

Your Attitude Journal can be a useful tool for this kind of work. Every time you have a conversation with someone, take some time to grade yourself afterwards on how good a listener you were. Write notes to yourself about what you will do next time and note interesting things you learned by letting the other person keep the spotlight. The ultimate key must be *really caring* about other people's experiences and feelings. The idea is to give yourself and your energy to the other person. The narcissist cares about nothing but his or her own self.

HELPING OTHERS

Interest in the news is a good indicator of your self-boundaries. If you don't care what is happening in your neighbourhood, your self-boundaries are small indeed. Caring about the city, the state, the country and the world indicates a larger and larger sphere of interest outside of your self. Many older people reach a point where their own bowel movements interest them more than whether a million Rwandans are massacred in genocide. Hypochondriacs are too aware of little aches and pains because their self-boundary stops at their own skin, so all attention is focused there.

Reading or watching the news with interest can be a start towards developing your focus on things outside of yourself. However, just watching the latest disaster on telly can be narcissistic if your focus is on nothing more than feeling glad that you weren't there. Try to expose yourself to quality newspapers or magazines that aren't just catering for self-absorbed people. Much telly news assumes that your only interest in news events is in how they relate to you personally. Real empathy is directed outside of your own skin.

If you want to work on expanding your boundaries try 'acting as if' you really care about others as you read or watch the news. Interest in events which don't directly affect you is healthy, but getting involved is even healthier. Working as a volunteer in politics or charities puts you in touch with people who really care about the world outside of their skin enough to try to improve things. The role models they provide can be a big help in widening your own self-boundaries.

Being interested in what friends say in conversation is a good start, but actually trying to help them is even more meaningful. Helping other people is a natural outgrowth of expanding your self-boundary to include others. When you help people you help yourself because you satisfy that primal urge to act in support of the tribe. If your urge to help others has atrophied over the years, you can make a project out of regaining it one step at a time.

Day-old infants already have an instinctive empathy which makes them cry when they hear another baby cry.[13] Many people form a protective shell as they grow up which is not really protective at all because it isolates them from the close social connections which are necessary for good health. Make an attitude jogging goal out of helping a friend with a project or a problem. Or volunteer for a charity or political party.

In San Francisco they have a foundation called Delancey Street which has helped many ex-prisoners and drug addicts to re-enter society and live normal lives. One of their basic principles is to 'act as if' they care about other people. This is a perfect example of self-control setting in motion an activity that reconditions behaviour. If it can work for hardened criminals, it can work for you.

KEEPING A JOURNAL

One of the reasons good social connections are so beneficial to your health is the therapeutic effect of being able to vent your feelings and discuss them with other people who really care about you.

A personal journal or diary is another way to vent your feelings which, if done properly, can provide another outlet. I encourage you to use your Attitude Journal sometimes to express and analyse your feelings and to direct and record the progress of your attitude jogging.

Journaling can also be a kind of mental masturbation, so let's cover a few cautions:

1. Don't do it *instead* of making friends. Real feedback and personal connection with a friend is far superior to talking to yourself in a journal.
2. Don't let it turn into an exercise in self-absorption. Narcissists are fascinated with themselves and a journal can encourage this focus.
3. Don't use a journal as a forum for uncensored complaining. Friends' comments can often be useful for keeping you in touch with reality.
4. Don't intellectualize or record minute details of your life.
5. Don't use a journal as a substitute for action.[14]

Journal entries should be constructive and action-orientated. They are an excellent place to practise seeing through your own rationalizations. Concentrate on getting in touch with your feelings rather than intellectualizing, and remain sceptical about the honesty of your own thoughts. A journal is a good place to be a devil's advocate about your own motivations. After recording an experience, do a critical analysis with suggestions about how you can improve your response next time.

If you have any important insights about yourself or life in general, mark them with a star or some other symbol. Going back and reviewing such insights later can be very interesting. Taking time to write about your thoughts can help you to organize them. Keep your list of attitude jogging challenges in a separate part of the journal so they don't get lost among the verbiage. Use a pencil on that part of your journal so you can change the challenges as you gain experience with the process.

Letter-writing or e-mail with a close friend can be an even better way to vent your emotions and make human connections at the same time. This is a good way to keep up old friendships where you are separated by large distances. Again, however, be careful this isn't a way to avoid real face-to-face human interaction, which is the best of all. Much of the subtle communications of feelings are through tone of voice, gestures, touching and body language. In fact, the best confidante of all is probably a lover, and the best human communication is pillow-talk.

Exercise One

1. Make a list of your current social connections. Include all the people you regularly express and discuss your inner feelings with and can depend upon for support.
2. If you can't think of at least two, make it an attitude jogging goal to find and develop some good connections. Use the Experimenter approach to find a way.

Exercise Two

1. Call your closest friend or relative and invite them for dinner, tea or drinks.
2. Make it a point to get the discussion onto important feelings. Ask them about their life and happiness and *really listen* to what they tell you. Be supportive rather than trying to give solutions. After you have listened carefully to their feelings, discuss your own deepest feelings.

Exercise Three

1. Are you currently living alone?
2. If the answer is yes, think about how you could share your accommodations with a good friend or relative. Look at the classified ads for 'shared accommodations' or 'flat share' and go look at a few – just as an experiment. Pick expensive ones that sound really nice and sit down for a cup of tea with the person running the ad. Remember, it's just an experiment that doesn't cost you anything. Think of it as window shopping for lifestyles. Let down your defences and just enjoy yourself in the present.

Exercise Four

1. If you don't already have a journal, buy one.
2. Start it off by examining what is good and bad about your present life from the point of view of your ability to have intense feelings of pleasure and well-being.
3. If you identify problems that are blocking your feelings of pleasure and well-being, THINK about some specific goals for experimentally changing your behaviour in ways that will work towards solving the problems.
4. Make regular entries in the journal about your progress towards these goals.

Exercise Five

1. If you are not currently reading a newspaper or otherwise keeping up with the news, start today. Take a real interest in things that are happening in the world which you may be able to do something about.
2. Volunteer to work on some kind of useful cause where you can directly help others – children or old people in the neighbourhood, for example.

CHAPTER SUMMARY

1. Man is a social animal. We have lived in extended families or tribal groups through the millennia of evolution.
2. Privacy is a new idea unique to Western industrial culture. It has increased drastically in the past 50 years.
3. Depression has become 10 times more common among women in the past 50 years.
4. Good social connections add about nine years to your life expectancy, compared to bad connections.
5. Marriage adds five years to your life expectancy.

6. Narcissism is an unhealthy focus on nothing but yourself. It's not only unhealthy – it's boring.
7. Privacy is very good for the economy but very expensive for you. It may well be the basis of the 'rat race' of modern life.
8. Helping others and taking interest in politics can expand your 'self-boundary'.
9. Keeping a journal can provide a healthy outlet for emotional expression but mustn't replace action or communications with friends.

CHAPTER

12

DEVELOPING OPTIMISM AND COMPLEXITY

An epidemic of depression has struck our society, making the antidepressant drug Prozac into a runaway best seller. But the difference between us and previous generations is not a chemical one. Changing attitudes and beliefs are the real cause of the epidemic. Cognitive therapists have identified certain bad mental habits which are the real cause of most depression. By teaching patients to change these habits, they have achieved a cure rate of about 70 per cent.[1] This is every bit as effective as the antidepressant drugs but has none of the bad side-effects and a much lower incidence of relapse.

The cognitive techniques that therapists teach to depressed people are the kind of healthy mental habits which everyone should be aware of. We can use attitude jogging techniques to develop these healthy habits to inoculate ourselves against depression and enhance our enjoyment of life.

EXPLAINING YOUR SETBACKS

Everyone has setbacks in life – failures, accidents, arguments – where things don't go as we would like them to. We each have a basic attitude towards setbacks which determines our habitual style of explaining them to ourselves and others. Your *explanatory style* can make a big difference in the impact setbacks have on your life and your health. Depressed people often have a *pessimistic style* which puts the worst possible interpretation on the cause and implications of any setback. Pessimists tend to turn minor bad events into major sources of strain and unhappiness. *Optimistic* people have a sunnier outlook. They tend to minimize the implications of setbacks and go cheerfully on with their lives.

We learn our explanatory style from parents and teachers, but just like so many other attitudes and habits, as adults we can learn to take control and use attitude jogging techniques to improve our attitude factor by guiding our own development in healthy directions.

The first step is to learn to recognize the characteristics of pessimism. Pessimists tend to see bad events as *Permanent, Pervasive* and *Personal*. The three P's of pessimism are all ways of making setbacks look worse. Let's look closer at what they mean:

- *Permanent* means that what may actually be an isolated event is projected out in time by the pessimist to become a permanent problem. Instead of saying, 'I really blew that interview,' a pessimist would say 'I am terrible at job interviews.' Notice that the healthy optimistic explanation is not unrealistic denial – pretending that the interview went well – but rather an honest recognition of the bad event without making it worse by projecting it both forwards and backwards in time.
- *Pervasive* means that the cause of the bad event is projected onto many other situations in your life. In this case 'My boss doesn't like me' gets changed to 'Nobody likes me.' An optimist recognizes problems without blowing them up into all-encompassing generalizations of inadequacy. Generally 'I am' statements should be changed to 'I did.'
- *Personal* means that the cause of the setback is put on yourself, even though it may have been externally caused. 'My boss was in a terrible mood today' can be changed by a pessimist to 'My boss hates me.' Combining Personal and Pervasive makes this one grow into 'Nobody likes me.' Or, if you use all of the three P's it becomes, 'I'm a loser.'

If you have a habitually pessimistic explanatory style, you are probably not aware of it – but you can develop an awareness by carefully analysing your explanations next time you experience a setback. Write down a description of the bad event in your

Attitude Journal, with your explanation right next to it. Carefully analyse your explanation for each of the three P's one at a time: first look for Permanence, then for Pervasiveness, and then for Personalization. If you find that you are guilty of any of the three distortions, rewrite the explanation from a more optimistic point of view. With lots of practice you can gradually change your habits and develop a more positive explanatory style. Tests which rate people's explanatory styles have been found to be predictive of success in business, freedom from depression, and even good health[2].

SELF-TALK AND AUTOMATIC THOUGHTS

Most of us try to be polite and sensitive in our remarks to others, yet many people don't hesitate to be mean and unfair in the things they say to themselves. Automatic thoughts, or self-talk, are the internal dialogue of your verbal self which does your future planning and adds a verbal spin to your emotions. Most automatic thoughts are brief and easy to miss if you don't pay attention, but they can lead to depression and low self-esteem. 'I am clumsy' is a typical automatic thought which you wouldn't think of saying to a good friend. 'That was a clumsy thing to do' eliminates the pervasive interpretation.

With practice you can learn to be aware of your automatic thoughts and test them for false assumptions and illogical conclusions. Depressed people often have habitually negative thoughts which are generally based on false assumptions which lead to illogical catastrophic conclusions. By paying attention to your self-talk, you can learn to recognize these bad patterns, challenge them, and break your bad habits.

If somebody else insults you, you tend to defend yourself and challenge the person doing the insulting, yet most depressed people are very bad at challenging their own insults. The important thing to realize is that, just as other people can be biased and wrong when they criticize us, we can also be biased and wrong in our own self-criticism. With practice you can develop the skill of catching your automatic thoughts and challenging them as you would an insult from somebody else. Don't blindly accept your own insults.

Look first of all for the bad assumptions. Often they begin with unrealistic expectations such as 'I must ...' and end with catastrophic results like 'I'm not worth while.' Here are some examples:

- 'Unless everything I do is perfect, I'm a failure.'
- 'Unless everybody likes me, I'm a failure.'
- 'Unless I always excel, I'm worthless.'
- 'Unless I'm the best at something, I'm a failure.'
- 'I must keep worrying if something seems dangerous.'
- 'Life should work out the way I want it to.'
- 'I can't live without being in love.'
- 'I can accomplish *anything* if I try hard enough.'
- 'If I visualize what I want, it will happen.'

Accepting imperfection in yourself and others is an extremely important ability which can be developed with practice. Being 95 per cent perfect is **a lot** easier than trying to be 100 per cent, and the results are just as good in most cases. One good trick for teaching yourself the fallacy of your false assumptions is to have a friend present your own self-talk to you as a criticism. For some reason we are much more likely to challenge other people's criticisms of us than we are our own. You can even do this yourself by writing your automatic thoughts down in your Attitude Journal and then reading them back to yourself, pretending they are someone else's comments.

Self-talk is your verbal self in action. It can be helpful if it is constructive – or disastrous if it is destructive. Some people develop a bad habit of endlessly recycling the same thoughts. In the case of negative thoughts this can make you really miserable because a bad feeling is reinforced by the resulting negative thought. If you keep repeating this process, the feelings get worse and worse each time you go round the vicious circle. Sometimes the best action is just to stop the thoughts and get back into the moment.

Feelings
Thoughts

Rumination is the endless repetition of self-talk that leads to depression, phobias and obsessions. The idea of minimal self-control we discussed in Chapter 7 also applies to self-talk. While a little bit at the right time is useful, it is important to avoid the habit of 'thinking too much' whether it is positive or negative thoughts. Stay in the moment most of the time and let your natural behaviour take control. Use your self-talk minimally and effectively only when it will really be helpful. Sometimes shutting up is the smartest thing your verbal self can do.

WELCOME TO REALITY

'Shit happens,' life isn't perfect, people die, true love is rare and we can't all be geniuses. Your attitude about these realities of life is extremely important to your happiness. If you can learn to accept life's setbacks as the inevitable *dues you must pay* for the pleasure of being alive, you can be happy in spite of adversity.

Many people have convinced themselves that we are living in terrible times, but if these are terrible times what would you call the times of the Black Death, when one quarter of the population of Europe died a horrible death from the plague? Or the almost continuous wars and crusades that used to ravage Europe? Even without an epidemic, the life expectancy in 17th-century Britain was only 32 years.[3]

At the other extreme, some people in the self-help field teach that you can accomplish *anything* if you just visualize the result you want and hold the picture in your mind. This is similar to doing the THINK and IMAGINE steps of self-regulation and then just stopping. It would be nice if life were that easy, but unfortunately others want the same things that you do and there is not enough to go around. Following through with the all-important TRY step is crucial if you really want to achieve your goals. If you can succeed the first time around the loop, you are lucky. In the real world, you may have to LEARN from your failures and go through the whole process again many times before you succeed.

The idea that you can accomplish *anything* if you just try hard enough is a cognitive error that causes much depression in this society. The problem is that there are other people in the world with the same goals and not everyone can be a film star or a Nobel prize winner. Our current epidemic of depression is largely the result of *unreasonable expectations*, rather than real misfortune. Often people miss important opportunities where unexpected good things could have happened to them because they are locked into an obsession with a specific goal that blinds them to other opportunities which present themselves. You *can* control your destiny to a large degree, but flexibility and persistence, not blind faith, is what works in the real world.[4]

FEELING GOOD VS DOING WELL

Optimism and positive thinking have the power to transform negative events into positive ones. But unbridled optimism can also be dangerous. Feeling good in the short term can make you miserable as a result of long-term side-effects. For example, if positive thinking prevents you from trying harder after your failures, it can lead you down the path to incompetence. Self-esteem comes from the satisfaction of successful accomplishment. Developing the ability to accomplish things often takes hard work, but why work hard if you are already such a wonderful person? Optimistically interpreting failures as successes doesn't build self-esteem in the long run, because the empty slogans and affirmations soon have a hollow ring if they aren't backed up by real accomplishments.

Again, the emphasis must be on energetically attacking the things you can change with the Experimenter approach and using your optimism to make the best of the things you can't change. Ignoring the fact that you will die some day is a healthy attitude as long as it doesn't keep you from seeing a doctor when you have dangerous symptoms. Once you have seen the doctor, optimism while you wait for the test results is also a healthy attitude. The goal is to *be as optimistic as you can be without missing the crucial times when tough-minded action is required*. Sometimes we must feel the disappointment of failure to give us the determination and understanding it takes to turn failure into success. Negative feelings are the driving force for change, so ignoring them can be disastrous in the long run. Even stress is a useful emotion when it pushes us to really perform.

Since the late 1960s many primary and secondary schools, especially in the US, have emphasized building self-esteem as a major goal of education.[5] The problem is they have tried to treat the symptom instead of the cause of the disease. Slogans and posters saying 'We applaud ourselves!' and 'Make loving yourself a habit' communicate the message that everyone is equally wonderful. Grade inflation ensured that nobody would feel inferior by getting F's or D's. Competition was discouraged because the losers would feel bad. Homework and minimum standards were relaxed in an attempt to reduce the dropout rate. The result has been a disaster. Kids graduate from secondary school full of slogans about how wonderful they are, but many are unable to do simple maths or read and write proper English. Their lack of ability in the real world causes crushing and depressing failure.

Low self-esteem and a high dropout rate are symptoms, not the disease. By treating the symptoms only, the schools have removed the incentive to work hard to overcome failure. Without real accomplishment, self-esteem collapses into depression[6] and the positive affirmations become as empty as insincere compliments.

Assertiveness is another thing that can't be changed by slogans or affirmations. It is based on self-esteem, which in turn is based on accomplishment. In attitude jogging we develop self-esteem and assertiveness by working on accomplishments. When you succeed at overcoming an attitude jogging challenge you have set for yourself, you don't need slogans or praise from other people. Your own feeling of satisfaction builds real self-esteem which in turn forms a basis for real assertiveness. It's simple cause and effect:

Accomplishment → Self-esteem → Assertiveness

COMPLEXITY

People who speak many languages can instantly switch from one to another. As they do this their manner of speaking, gesturing, and even attitudes towards other people also change to fit the context of the language. In different contexts we also switch our walk, our talk, our attitudes and our values. As a mother, a lover, a sports enthusiast or a business manager we instantly assume different roles. We can do this easily because our minds are organized like parallel computers. Separate specialized modules[7] self-organize and evolve as needed to handle different aspects of our lives. We all have many specialized sub-personalities which can instantly take control depending on the situation.

Each of our sub-personalities has its own developmental history. Each can grow in ability, or atrophy, depending upon how much and how well it is used. When you grow up the part of you that plays like a child can atrophy or continue growing depending upon how often you let it take control. Many men let their work personality stay in control most of their waking hours. The natural result is that it grows extremely powerful at the expense of all of the other sub-personalities.

One common mistake of workaholics is to use their work sub-personality for things that are better done by the specialist in childhood play. These people realize that they need to exercise to stay healthy, so they use their work sub-personality to begin some very intent, efficient and competitive exercises. A preferable approach is to use exercise as play. Letting your childhood play sub-personality do the job helps it to evolve rather than atrophy. Hobbies can also be ruined as sources of complexity by approaching them as work instead of play.

When people become parents they usually create a whole new sub-personality which uses their own parents' behaviour example as a starting point. As this evolves through life it can take on a great or minor importance depending on how much it is used. Many parents leave their Mummy or Daddy sub-personality in control too much, sometimes even during private time with their spouse. Don't let the lover in you die.

MULTIPLE SOURCES OF SELF-ESTEEM

Each of your separate sub-personalities is capable of becoming an independent basis for self-esteem. You can derive pleasure in life and take pride in yourself as a mother, a lover, a tennis player, a lawyer, an artist, a friend, or any number of separate roles. *Complexity* is a measure of how many unique roles you have developed as a basis of your self-esteem and how much they are independent from each other. If you have high complexity you are relatively immune to being thrown into depression by bad events because your self-esteem has a broad base. If you lose a job or your children move away, it isn't the end of your world because you haven't put all your eggs into one basket.

Complexity should be intentionally developed throughout your life to give you a rich and diverse basis for happiness. If all you care about is reading books, then losing your vision in old age is much more tragic than if you were also an avid music lover. If your children grow up and move away, it's much easier to adjust if you also took great pride in your artistic ability.

Work is often a great source of self-esteem, but if it is your only source you may find retirement a devastating experience. Men are much more inclined to let everything except their work sub-personality atrophy. Perhaps that is why men's suicide rate rises steadily with age, while the women's suicide rate falls after the age of 50. By the age of 85, men are 10 times more likely to commit suicide than women.[8]

Complexity has been found to reduce the amount of depression and illness. It can be numerically measured by analysing the amount of variation in personality traits between different contexts. A wide variation indicates well-developed, separate sub-personalities.[9] If your sports sub-personality is just an extension of the one you use at work, it won't be much help in keeping you happy after you retire. Most people have more complexity during their school and university years, but this complexity gradually narrows with age as the 'used to's' accumulate.

THE CHRISTMAS PRESENT TEST

When people's interests narrow, they seldom notice it them-selves. In fact people will often angrily deny it. Younger family members are often painfully aware of the decline but unable to do anything about it. Sometimes Christmas is when the decline becomes most painfully obvious. Children are easy to buy pre-sents for. They will excitedly explore any new gift they receive. On the other hand, as some people reach old age it becomes more and more difficult to find them an appropriate gift. Each 'used to' means one less gift that would excite their interest. Gifts that could awaken new experiences and interests are often thought of as unwelcome intrusions by people with severe attitude decline. They become convinced that they *want* to keep in their narrow rut. Is it becoming harder and harder for people to buy Christmas presents for you? If it is, maybe it's time you set some attitude jogging goals to expand your enthusiasm into new areas, or revive some old ones.

Exercise One

1. Use your Attitude Journal to write an explanation of a recent bad event in your life. Better yet, find a letter or journal entry where you have already done this.
2. Analyse your explanation for each of the three P's one at a time. Look for instances where you put a Permanent, Pervasive, or Personal spin on your explanation.
3. Rewrite the explanation from a more optimistic point of view.
4. If you have pessimistic habits, make it a practice to follow this procedure whenever something bad happens to you until you break the habit.

Exercise Two

1. Whenever something bad happens to you, watch yourself to see if you are giving it a pessimistic explanation.
2. If you are guilty of any of the three P's, try restating your explanation in a more optimistic way.

Exercise Three

1. Examine your automatic thoughts for false assumptions like the ones listed on page 154.
2. Try substituting a sounder assumption and see how it changes your feelings about yourself.

Exercise Four

1. Do you have fixed goals which may be blocking you from recognizing unexpected opportunities that present themselves?
2. Make a list of recent opportunities that you may have missed because you were focused on these goals.
3. Resolve to be more flexible in the future by living in the present and being open to good things you might never have expected or wished for.

Exercise Five

1. Do you have good self-esteem which is based on real accomplishments that you are proud of?
2. If not, set yourself an achievable goal and begin using the Experimenter approach to achieve it.

Exercise Six

1. Make a list of as many *separate* things or activities you can think of that bring you intense feelings of pleasure.
2. If your list is a short one, set yourself some attitude jogging goals to expand your list. Variety is important, so try to develop interests which are totally different from your occupation. They should cover both mental and physical pleasures.

CHAPTER SUMMARY

1. Bad cognitive habits can cause depression. Correcting them is as effective as Prozac and has less relapses and no side-effects.
2. Your habitual style of explaining bad events and setbacks can interfere with your success and cause depression.
3. A pessimistic explanatory style makes things seem worse by making them *Permanent*, *Pervasive* and *Personal*.
4. If you write down your explanation of a bad event, you can examine it for the three P's of pessimism, one at a time.
5. Automatic thoughts can cause depression by applying unrealistic expectations then coming to catastrophic conclusions.
6. If you read back your own self-talk as though somebody else has said it to you, you may be able to see the flaws and defend yourself.
7. Self-esteem building can defeat itself by forgiving bad performance. The resulting incompetence *lowers* self-esteem.
8. Both self-esteem and assertiveness cannot be built with slogans. They must be supported by accomplishments.
9. Complexity means having many independent and unique sub-personalities, each specialized to handle a different part of your life.
10. Complexity provides protection from major setbacks in life by giving you multiple sources of self-esteem.
11. Ask yourself if you are hard to buy Christmas presents for. If you are, you may need to work on your attitudes and complexity.

CHAPTER
13

SEX, SENSUALITY AND FOOD

A study of 100 women hospitalized for heart attack found that 65 per cent reported sexual dissatisfaction or frigidity.[1] In a control group of 100 women in hospital for non-cardiac problems, only 24 per cent had sexual difficulties. Another study of 40 women with breast cancer found that only 5 out of the 40 interviewed were freely capable of orgasm.[2] Twenty-five had never experienced orgasm and considered sex a distasteful wifely duty, five were still virgins, and five had orgasms only rarely.

Sex is certainly good medicine, but it is more likely that the real meaning of these findings is that unhealthy attitudes towards pleasure in general also ruin your sex life. People who are blocked for pleasure are bound to find sex an unpleasant intrusion. On the other hand, people who value and appreciate sensual pleasures tend also to have a good sex life. The strong correlation of scores on the pleasure and well-being test with later good health (*see page 4*) prove how vitally important attitudes towards pleasure are. One of the first youthful pleasures to hit the 'used to' lists is adventurous, imaginative sex, and with it go a whole list of other sensual pleasures.

But why should sensual pleasures be the first things to go when attitudes decline? The answer is probably that sensual pleasures and behaviour come from the most primitive parts of the brain. They are therefore the most thoroughly separated from verbal cognition of all behaviours. Sensuality is consequently the area where the difference between self-control and non-verbal behaviour becomes most obvious.

Quadriplegic men whose spinal cord has been severed in an accident are paralysed from the neck down. Though all spinal connections to their brain are broken, they are able to have erections and even orgasm if their penis is stimulated.[3] Because the connections are broken, they can't even tell if they have an erection unless they can see it. They can, however, feel the pleasurable surge of chemicals released into their bloodstream by orgasm. This separation of our verbal self from more primitive behaviour is an extreme example of the kind of decentralized control that goes on continually beyond our awareness as we live our lives. The only knowledge our verbal self has of many sensual pleasures is through the chemical effect of endorphins in the bloodstream released by lower-level structures.

Self-control can override most behaviour from other parts of the brain, but not from spinal reflexes. Though self-control can't produce an erection it can certainly override other behaviour that originates in the lower parts of the brain. Many sexual problems are a result of self-control interfering in areas where primitive behaviour is best left in control. Being self-conscious about sex, or any other sensual experience, is a sure way to ruin it. Many kinds of sexual dysfunction are a result of too much self-control resulting from ruminating about performance, or guilt. When people with sexual problems suddenly freeze up during sex, it is usually because self-control has just taken over in panic.

The split between the attitudes of the verbal self and more primitive behaviour becomes amazingly clear in dating. Sexual chemistry is clearly separate from the logical, rational judgements that tell you that you *should* be attracted to somebody. Often people are attracted to people they logically dislike, or are left cold by people who seem to be perfect when analysed logically. Welcome to the cognitive-behavioural dichotomy.

Sensual feelings originate in the lower parts of the brain and are therefore best enjoyed without the interference of self-control. But there is a problem: the short-term orientation of pure instinctive pleasure-seeking can lead to reduced pleasure in the long run. Conditioned behaviour always tends to take the path of least resistance. In making love with a particular partner, this means evolving a routine that gives orgasm with as little effort as possible. In the long term following your pure instinct will lead you into a rut where the same efficient love-making routine is repeated endlessly.

Kissing, caressing, oral sex and other foreplay are common early in a relationship, but all tend to be bypassed when a minimum-energy routine for sexual satisfaction is allowed to develop. Holding and cuddling to enjoy the 'afterglow' and feelings of closeness with your partner are also often dropped out of minimum-effort sex. Love is an abstract emotion based on romantic verbal concepts. It is reinforced by primitive bonding instincts which can greatly complement the good feelings of love-making. Sexual penetration is a true merging of physical boundaries, one inside of the other, which perfectly expresses the mental merging of self-boundaries.

Love is a perfect example of how cognition and primitive emotions can reinforce each other in a kind of endless circle. It can produce the ultimate ecstasy, but because of the unstable nature of self-reinforcement, it can also mislead us into painful mistakes. Many people become blocked for pleasure through fear of such mistakes. The ability to take reasonable risks is a basic part of being open to pleasure.

SEX AND SELF-CONTROL

Since only the logic of the verbal self can understand the long-term problem of keeping love and sensual pleasure alive, self-control is your only defence against slipping into ruts. However, since self-controlled sex tends to be sterile and unfeeling, self-control must be used judiciously, mainly to break out of ruts and start you off in different directions. Two seconds of self-control is all it takes to break a routine and start having intercourse in a new position. Primitive behaviour is quite capable of finishing the job once started down the new path. The result will be behavioural conditioning down a new path which will prevent a deep rut from becoming established.

Continuous self-control can turn love-making into a self-conscious intellectual exercise. Tantra yoga uses self-control to intentionally draw out the sex act by holding back at the edge of orgasm. With practice your behaviour can be trained by experience to remain in control with only an occasional lapse from self-control. Again, self-control is the animal trainer that keeps the animal inside you on the right path with an occasional crack of the whip. It takes practice to develop a kind of teamwork where your self-control intervenes just enough to alter your routine and keep things interesting, but not so much that it spoils the sensual experience.

Instinctive behaviour is always in the moment and unaware of long-term bad consequences. Without some self-control, promiscuous sex can ruin your close relationships, compromise your job and expose you to sexually-transmitted disease. The crucial thing is to develop a healthy relationship between your verbal self and your behaviour. Your self-control is like a chaperone: A bad one spoils all your fun, while a good one is a helpfully protective friend to your instinctive behaviour.

Feeling guilty after pleasure lowers your score on the pleasure and well-being test. Negative feelings of guilt offset the good effects of pleasure by bringing feelings of helplessness. Guilt is caused by indecisive use of self-control followed by rumination about the past. Both of these mental habits violate the basic principles of attitude jogging.

SEXUAL EXPECTATIONS

Expectations learned from your culture and your parents can make you act out a role as you age which may include a sexual decline which is well in advance of any actual physical decline. If your parents were overly discreet about their sexual activity, or just not interested in sex, you may unconsciously begin to play out that role when you become a parent and begin to imitate their role model.

Sex is a self-reinforcing activity in the short term because the pleasures you feel originate in lower parts of your brain. This is why sensual behaviour carries with it a short memory span. Long-term memory is based on words, so sensual sensations lose a lot in the translation to long-term memory. Just after a good orgasm, the sensual memory is vivid so you can easily motivate yourself to want some more, but as time passes the only memory that remains is your verbal long-term recall, which is much more abstract and less tempting.

A common experience after re-enjoying a sensual 'used-to' after a long hiatus is to say, 'Wow! Why didn't I do that before?' The reason is that after the real experience, you now have a fresh sensual memory to replace the much less vivid verbal long-term memory you were relying on before. Once you learn to recognize this phenomenon, you realize that it is often necessary to use self-control to force yourself to do things that don't really seem that great based on your long-term memory of them.

When you use self-control to push yourself into sensual experiences, you may have to force yourself even if only a week has elapsed because your sensual memory fades quickly. Your verbal self must compensate by realizing that it will be even better than you can remember once you get into it. People who have not had sex for an extended period often feel that they can easily do without it, until they actually have their sensual memory refreshed by a real experience. This is why it is common for people who stop sexual activity in middle age to feel that they don't even miss it.

The dual nature of memory is clearly demonstrated by infantile amnesia. Though you learn a lot in the first two years of your life, you can't recall it verbally because the newer verbal part of your brain wasn't yet fully developed at the time. As an adult you can verbally recall experiences for a long time, but the vividness of sensual memories fades quickly. When a long time has elapsed since you have had sex or any sensual pleasure, your memory of that pleasure becomes colder and more logical and you miss it less and less.

The menopause is another time where expectations learned from parents can steal the joy from your life. Women often unconsciously act out a decline in sexual desire which isn't really caused by biology. A negative attitude can be self-reinforcing if you don't push yourself to get out of the rut. Physical decline due to lack of exercise can aggravate the problem.

'Use it or lose it' is particularly true for women after the menopause because their vaginal walls tend to thin and dry up without exercise. Any woman who thinks her sex life is over owes it to herself to use some self-control, and a bit of lubricant, to push herself and find out what her true potential for sexual joy is – a perfect attitude jogging exercise which can easily be broken down into manageable steps.

ENJOYING SENSUALITY

Sensuality sounds like a bad word to some people but it is actually the source of the most intense joys in life. It includes much more than just sexual pleasure. The warmth of sunshine on your skin, the caress of a balmy tropical breeze, the bubbling of a cool stream, the feel and smell of moist earth and the smell of garlic being sautéed are all sensual pleasures. Your ability to enjoy these pleasures can fade as you age if you don't occasionally use your self-control to push yourself into situations which will keep them alive.

Your score on the pleasure and well-being test reflects your mental habits with regard to sensual experience of all kinds. Often parental training aimed at teaching us responsible behaviour is too effective. If you ignore your feelings of pleasure and live in a logical world of duty and obligation, you soon forget what you are missing. Keeping your awareness of sensual pleasures alive may require the occasional use of self-control to *not* do your duty so that you break unhealthy patterns which may be blocking your pleasure.

Many 'used to's' are a direct result of the fading of sensual memories. When it comes to planning holidays, picnics, skiing trips, days out to the seaside and other sources of sensual pleasure, you often need consciously to push yourself a bit to get out of comfortable, minimum-energy ruts. If it's been a long time since you took a real holiday, you may find that if you push yourself to go, once you get there you will like it a lot more than your long-term memory made you expect.

HABITUATION

Habituation is a useful characteristic of the mind which allows us to ignore repeated stimuli and pay attention only to things that are new. Even small babies will soon stop paying attention to things such as noises or movements which happen regularly and repeatedly. For small children almost everything is new and fascinating, but many people begin as early as 30 to carry the process too far and become 'hyper-habituated'.[4] They develop a bad habit of seeing everything as 'just like' something else. Meeting a new person, their reaction is, 'He reminds me a lot of ...' instead of being alert to what is unique about a new person. This tendency can grow with age and make life seem extremely boring.

The older you are the more things and types of people you have seen, but keeping vital means retaining the ability to appreciate what is new. The same natural tendency that leads to minimum-energy sex can ruin other sensual pleasures by making them routine. Listening to music – *really* listening – is quite common among young people. Yet many people's musical taste freezes at a certain point in their lives so that listening to music becomes more a trigger for bringing back nostalgic feelings of their youth than a true sensual experience.

Really listening to music means that you are stimulated by what is new and interesting. It means being open to discovering new sounds and ideas and really paying attention, not talking over everything you hear. If you have developed bad habits in this regard, it can be a good attitude jogging exercise to sit down, close your eyes, shut your mouth and really listen to something good that you haven't heard before. Forget about 'it's just like' and listen to what is unique in it. If you think that all new music today is trash, you need to open up your mind. A lot of beautiful and interesting things are happening.

Natural beauty is certainly something we have seen before, yet some people can see it fresh each time while others become habituated and don't even notice it. If self-control will just direct your attention, your own sensuality can finish the job without any help. Sometimes your sensual appreciation is helped by a little verbal knowledge. A little understanding of geology, for example, can make a rock or a mountain range much more interesting by focusing your attention. Your sensual appreciation follows if you let it. Studying sculpture greatly enhanced my own appreciation of shapes by giving me a new level of understanding about them.

You can develop the sensitivity of your senses by focusing on one sense at a time. A blind person has heightened senses of touch, hearing and smell. You can develop yours similarly by spending some time wearing a blindfold and focusing on *really* feeling or smelling things. When you are in nature, pay attention to the smells. Often we don't stop to smell the flowers because we think we are too busy. Take some time when you aren't busy and relearn how to use your senses.

THE JOY AND PAIN OF EATING

Eating is one of the most basic sensual pleasures. Yet it is a source of pain to many people because eating in excess makes you overweight. In the US, over one-third of the population are 20 per cent or more overweight. Carrying around extra weight wears out your joints and your heart and also makes you tired because everything you do takes a lot more effort. Our culture doesn't like fat, yet provides a fatal combination of labour-saving devices that do everything for us, and restaurant portions that virtually guarantee overweight.

Since conditioned behaviour always has a short-term orientation, self-control is your only defence against overeating. Your logical thinking can understand that maximum *long-term* pleasure sometimes means limiting your pleasure in the short term. The first bite always tastes the best, so focus on giving in to sensual enjoyment of the best part of the experience, which is tasting, enjoying and then moving on. Skip the later parts where you are just shovelling down more and more food and enjoying it less and less. Most important of all, don't clean up your plate. Throwing it in the bin is much healthier than throwing it into your stomach (which, incidentally, doesn't help starving children despite what your mother may have told you as a child).

Crash diets often work but have a 90 per cent relapse rate. Long-term conditioned behavioural changes of your normal eating habits are the only lasting way to lose weight. Starving yourself only makes your metabolism slow down and consume less energy, so you are better off eating regular meals but keeping the quantity down. If you eat in restaurants, try splitting meals with a friend or get a doggy bag and eat the second instalment tomorrow. Basic attitudes about food determine how much you enjoy it and how much you abuse it, so use attitude jogging to develop an emphasis on quality and break the habit of going for quantity.

As many people age, their ability to really enjoy food decreases. The food in most cafes popular with elderly people is bland and uninteresting. Music popular with elderly people is similarly bland. The reason is that attitude decline brings with it a tendency to avoid challenge, dissonance and excitement. This is another aspect of the tendency of behaviour to seek minimum-energy ways to satisfy basic needs. With self-control we can push ourselves to break out of ruts and try new and exciting things to keep life interesting.

Instead of routinely eating your food without even thinking about it, really pay attention to fine details – as a wine connoisseur does. Instead of simply gulping a wine down, a connoisseur first feels and smells the cork, swirls the wine in the glass and smells the bouquet of the wine, carefully notices and appreciates the colour of the wine. When he is finally ready for a taste, he lets the wine roll around his tongue to appreciate the full taste. This conscious attention to detail begins with self-control, but soon develops into a natural ritual which enhances the sensual pleasures of a glass of wine. Wine-tasting emphasizes enjoyment and attention, not drinking large quantities.

The same attention heightens your pleasure when eating food. Notice smells, visual presentation on the plate, colours and textures. When you are finally ready for your first bite, let your tongue feel the grains of rice and the textures of the food. By changing your focus to really experiencing the food sensually, you can eliminate the necessity for eating large quantities and keep your weight under control.

You can also direct your tastes away from meats, which are full of fat, to vegetables, which are mostly water and fibre. Taste preferences are a matter of habit and conditioning. You can gradually guide your tastes in a direction you know to be better for you simply by eating better foods. In the long run your tastes will be re-conditioned towards liking what you have been eating.

Be adventurous in trying things that push your comfort zone for exotic food. Raw oysters are an acquired taste which few people liked the first time they tried them. They grow on you partly because they are so bizarre at first glance. Dissonant notes in music are the ones that aren't sweet but, like hot salsa, add an interest and a challenge. Learn to welcome challenge in your sensual enjoyment, just as you do in the rest of your life. It's a basic goal of attitude jogging.

Exercise One

1. Increase your pleasure and well-being score by letting your sensual side really enjoy things whenever possible without long-term bad side-effects.
2. Use your self-control to set up a sensual evening of candlelit dinner and sex. Note: If you don't have a partner, no problem. Do it for yourself! Treat yourself to the same love and sensuality you would a lover.
3. Avoid minimum-effort patterns you may have developed. Use self-control just long enough to break the habitual pattern and make it a really special evening – then let your behaviour do the rest.

Exercise Two

1. Spend an evening really listening to music. Keep your mind and your mouth quiet for the entire evening and let the animal side of you respond directly to the beauty and emotions in the music.
2. Dance to the music with no thought of how you look. Just let your body naturally express its response to the music. Feel shapes in the air created by the music.

Exercise Three

Enjoy a small but delicious meal using the techniques of the wine connoisseur to enjoy it to the fullest, giving each of your senses full attention in its turn. Feast on the food with your eyes and sense of smell for a long time before you put any in your mouth. Feel the food with your tongue before you begin chewing. Take your time.

Exercise Four

Blindfold yourself and maintain silence for an hour as you focus entirely on exploring things with your other senses. Focus on the feel, smell, sound and taste of things. Try to experience them directly, as an animal without language would perceive them.

Exercise Five

Take a long walk in a beautiful place and maintain complete silence. Experience the ecstasy of being an integral part of nature. Pay attention to small details that you would normally miss – tiny plants and bugs, lichen on rocks, the structure of tiny seeds, the movements of flowing water, and cloud patterns. Urinate into the ground and feel your connection to the earth as the fluid from your body flows back to the earth.

CHAPTER SUMMARY

1. A poor sexual and sensual life often leads to major illness.
2. Sexual and sensual behaviour is the most primitive and therefore the most separated from cognition.
3. Behaviour is short-sighted and tends to get you into minimum-energy ruts unless self-control intervenes.

4. Sensual memories fade quickly and are replaced by verbal long-term memories which lose a lot in the translation.

5. It is often necessary to push yourself into activities because you know they will be better than long-term memory makes them seem.

6. Sexual decline in old age or after the menopause is often simply imitation of parental role models.

7. Habituation can make you see things as 'just like' other things, causing you to ignore their uniqueness.

8. Practice in paying attention can enhance your enjoyment of music, food, and other sensual pleasures.

9. Dieting doesn't work for long, but eating habits can be changed by learning to focus on initial appreciation rather than continued eating until the plate is clean. Split restaurant meals with a friend, or yourself (the next day).

10. Being adventurous and pushing the limits of your comfort zone for food and sensual experience makes life more interesting.

AGEING AND CULTURE

How old would you be if you didn't know how old you were? We are all like actors playing out roles we have learned from our parents and our culture. When it comes to ageing, we play our role so convincingly that we almost obscure the real biological basis. In rural Portugal women begin wearing shapeless black dresses as soon as they get married. The black dress is a costume for their role as a woman too old to be frivolous and gay. In Beverly Hills, people who are biologically the same age are likely to be wearing a pair of tight-fitting leopard-skin leggings for their evening out at the latest trendy dance club.

In Georgia, a southern republic in the former Soviet Union, it is quite common for people to continue working into their eighties. One survey of 15,000 Georgians over the age of 80 found that 60 per cent were still gainfully working, mostly on collective farms.[1] Another place noted for longevity is the Hunza valley in Pakistan. Respect for elders there is reflected in their custom of gathering the elders of each small village every morning to arbitrate disputes and make decisions for the village. At wedding parties and festivals, the first dance is customarily led by the oldest man present.

In ancient Greece and Rome men spoke in the public councils in order of age. In the College of Augurs, Cicero wrote, 'each has precedence in debate according to his age, and the oldest is preferred, not only to those of higher official rank, but even to those having imperium.'[2] Even the very word 'Senate' is derived from *senex*, which means aged. The word alderman is

derived from middle English for 'older man'. In spite of this her-
itage, our modern industrial society has downgraded the prestige
of age to a low point never before seen in history. Respect for age
has fallen so low that it has become quite common for people to
disguise their age by dyeing their hair and using plastic surgery.

Is this an inevitable result of modern industrial society?
Japan today is living proof that the answer is no. In Japan it is
common for people to use cosmetics and clothing actually to
emphasize their age.[3] They even have a custom of celebrating the
61st birthday, much as the 21st is observed here. They also have
the longest life-expectancy in the world.

THE DECLINE OF THE BODY

Yes, there is an inherent physical decline that goes with old age.
However, the only way to see its effect clearly is to look at people
who remain vital into old age. If you go to a seniors tennis tourna-
ment you will see healthy, good-looking people in their seventies
who still play tennis extremely well. The limitations of biological ageing force them to play somewhat differently than the
juniors, who can often beat them. They are forced to emphasize
elegance and style rather than youthful energy. They still do surprisingly well – and they look great!

Runners usually set their lifetime record by the age of 30 and
then their peak ability declines. Yet, a 69-year-old has recently
run a marathon in under three hours. That's 53 minutes longer
than the present world record, but actually *faster than the winning time in the 1908 Olympics.*[4]

The power of expectations to define physical performance is
clearly demonstrated by the way sports records are often deterz was
considered impossible until 1954. Over 50 medical journals had carried articles saying that it was humanly impossible. Then Roger
Bannister actually did it. Within a little more than a year, *four others had duplicated the feat.*[5] Today running a mile in four minutes
is a routine milestone for any serious competitor. Often what
seems like a physical barrier is really a mental one. Roger Bannister
was a role model who showed others what could be done.

There is a natural decline in oxygen-carrying capacity (VO_2max) with age, but it is relatively minor compared to the decline most people experience when they don't exercise. For example, at age 78 marathon runner Mavis Lindgren had a VO_2max measurement equivalent to that of a typical untrained woman in her early twenties.[6] One thing Georgia, Hunza, and all of the exotic places noted for vitality in old age have in common is hilly terrain and a lack of vehicular transport. Walking in hilly terrain forces people to keep in good physical shape.

FRAILTY IN OLD AGE

Frailty of muscles and bones is a classic symptom of old age which is often a direct result of a downward-spiralling attitude. If you think of yourself as frail, you carefully avoid stress and strain on your body. Since muscles and bones atrophy without stress, a vicious circle is created: The more you think of yourself as frail, the frailer you become. It becomes virtually impossible to determine which came first – the attitude or the physical decline. Certainly ageing does cause some physical deterioration, but your response can speed the decline or resist it. Bone mass has been proven to increase in direct proportion to the stress it undergoes. Athletes in contact sports such as rugby develop massive bones.

Space exploration has given us a large body of research and real experience on the effects of inactivity on the body. Living in space causes damage to many body systems because, in the weightlessness of space, bones and muscles atrophy quickly because they do not experience the stress of gravity. The *Skylab* astronauts lost 4 grams of calcium from their skeletons for each month in space. This bone loss would place a nine-month limit on space voyages if special precautions weren't implemented. The inactivity of space travel also affects blood pressure, cholesterol levels, sleep, temperature control and a person's mental state in ways which are virtually identical to what we consider the normal effects of ageing.[7]

Parental role models give us a 'script' for ageing which we unconsciously act out. If your family is known to have 'good ageing genes' it also means that you have good role models. You expect to retain your vitality so you automatically resist and minimize the effects of physical ageing. If your family 'normally' grows frail at a young age, you will tend to act out that script, which you unconsciously learned from your parents. Often genetics is given credit for vitality in families when *the real secret lies in the attitudes* passed down through the generations. If your family doesn't age well, don't despair – you may be able to use attitude jogging to be the first in your family really to enjoy your later years.

Since attitude tests can predict longevity better than tests that focus on family genetic background or health habits, it is clear that the attitude factor is even more important than good genes. The genetic factor looks much more powerful than it is because families also pass down attitudes. We learn from our parents' example the patterns which can lead to attitude decline, disease and shortened lifespan. Unhealthy attitudes, such as the tendency to suppress feelings, 'do the right thing' and live in chronic hopelessness, are learned from parents. These unhealthy attitudes are strongly associated with cancer and are passed down just as surely as the genetic defects which cause some cancer.

Physical ageing is a formidable opponent. You can stand tall and use your will to hold it back, or weakly cave in to its destructive power. Your habitual response to challenge will determine the result. You can enjoy your old age or be miserable in it – the power is yours.

Many old people get depressed and give up when they lose their eyesight or other important functions. Yet the millions of people who are born blind and go on to lead happy lives prove that there are still plenty of other ways to enjoy life if you keep a positive attitude. Stephen Hawking, author of *A Brief History of Time* and other best sellers, can talk only with an electronic gizmo and is almost completely paralysed, yet he has achieved distinction making use of the abilities he has left.

The ability to make the best of a bad situation is an ability that may save your life someday. It is important to start developing it now, when you are young, so that it has time to put its roots down deep into your soul.

WALKING LIKE A MATADOR

Bullfighters defeat the bull with nothing but a cape, a sword and lots of attitude. If you watch their walk, you will see that it is more of a cocky strut than a walk. Attitude is reflected in the way you bear yourself. More importantly, the reverse is true – the way you bear yourself affects your attitude. If you walk like a wimp, you'll feel like a wimp. Walking like an old person is worse. It not only makes you feel old and look old, it actually *makes you old* by weakening your muscles and bones. *Avoiding stress makes you more vulnerable to stress and accidents in the long run.*

As we age we all act out a part we learned from our parents. If you expect to be frail, you carry yourself like a frail person and avoid all stress. This causes your muscles and bones to atrophy. Walking proudly, with an erect back and a bounce in your step, puts healthy stress on bones and muscles, keeping them vital and strong.

One of the traditions of matadors and rodeo cowboys is always to walk proudly out of the ring no matter how seriously they are injured. This never-say-die attitude is the way you should face ageing. Physical decline is an unwelcome enemy that will win in the end, but by facing it like a matador you can have the satisfaction of a kind of proud moral victory of your own spirit – just like the matador.

CRITICAL MOMENTS AND FRAILTY

Often the long road to frailty begins with a seemingly innocent critical moment which turns the last healthy source of exercise into a 'used to'. For example, my friend George, an avid tennis player, missed his weekly game two weeks in a row due to a business trip. When he got back, he accepted a dinner invitation on his normal tennis night. Critical moment ... He never played tennis again.

Sometimes an accident or injury makes it temporarily impossible to exercise. The 'path of least resistance' orientation of behaviour makes it quite natural to stop physical activity at the slightest excuse. Only the long-term view of self-control is capable of rescuing you. *If you think you don't have enough time for exercise today, you will sooner or later have to find time for illness.*[8]

Sometimes an injury makes it necessary to stop playing a sport permanently. This is a critical moment where you should make every effort immediately to find some kind of replacement. Strenuous exercise which requires co-ordination and balance is best, but even dancing or vigorous walking is enough to prevent frailty. The important thing is to do something *with vigour*. Your chances of being injured in a fall are greatly reduced when you regularly make use of your ability to balance adaptively.

George Burns, the comedian, performed and even danced till he was 99 years old. Yes, he ultimately had a fall which made him frail, but who knows how many years of vitality he added by having the spirit of a matador. Many old people give in to frailty prematurely because they are too vain to carry a cane. It's much healthier to walk vigorously with a cane than to sit home because you are afraid of what people will think. At some point in your life a cane becomes the perfect prop for the feisty image of a person who is staying in the fight to the end.

MENTAL DECLINE

The same 'use it or lose it' principle applies to mental functioning. If you have heard studies about IQ declining after the age of

30, take heart. Most of those studies have been discredited today because they had serious flaws. First of all, IQs have been rising steadily, so people who are old today had lower IQs to begin with.

An even worse flaw applies to all generalizations about old people. Our society has such a poor attitude about ageing that the majority of old people today have allowed themselves to fall well below their real potential. Many of the people tested were living in the deprived environment of an old people's home, or alone and cut off from society. It's a bit like trying to determine the characteristics of a plant type when most of your samples were grown in parched, rocky soil. Any generalizations based on testing elderly people who have been allowed to atrophy in our current society's unhealthy environment will certainly show significant decline.

If we look instead at people who are treated with honour in their old age and are following a tradition of vitality, we get an entirely different picture. Take musicians, for example: Arthur Rubinstein gave a triumphant Carnegie Hall concert at 89. Meiczyslaw Horszowski celebrated his 100th birthday with a concert at Carnegie Hall. Toscanini, Horowitz and Serkin all performed in their eighties and nineties. Verdi wrote the opera *Falstaff* at 80, *Te Deum* at 85. John Cage was still active 82. The jazz musician Benny Carter gave a sell-out concert at the Hollywood Bowl at the age of 87. His lifelong pal Doc Cheatham, who is 90, also got raves.

Could it be that music keeps people young? A much more probable explanation is that musicians and other artists are playing out a different role than people in professions where 50 is considered over the hill. There is a tradition of working and staying vital which defies our normal tradition of putting people out to pasture at a young age. The fact that musicians and other artists love their work, feel really appreciated, do physical exercise as part of their work and get emotionally high whenever they perform certainly helps. Getting your emotional juices flowing and feeling extreme pleasure regularly may be an important factor. The important point is that artists are genetically the same as the rest of us, so if they can do it, so can we.

Picasso still worked long hours on his paintings at the age of 91. Michelangelo started designing St Peter's Cathedral at 72 and continued working on it while he painted and sculpted till he died at the age of 89. Marc Chagall did the murals at New York's Metropolitan Opera at 79. Claude Monet did 19 huge water lily paintings at 73 and continued working till he died at the age of 86. Georgia O'Keeffe decided to change from painting to sculpture when her vision failed at 96, and she was still going strong at 100. Grandma Moses didn't really *start* her painting career until she was 78, well after the age many people today give up on life. She continued till her death at 101. Artists must be in touch with their deepest feelings and must feel pleasure intensely. Their score on the pleasure and well-being test is surely high.

These exceptional artistic subcultures show us what is biologically possible. One important thing about any subculture is that it can set expectations and attitudes that are different from those of the mainstream culture. If you were lucky enough to have been born into a family which traditionally retains their youthful vitality, curiosity and energy, spend lots of time with them. They will make it seem natural for you to do as they did. If you're not so lucky, try to find friends who will set a good example for you. If you don't have children nearby, find some friends who are younger than you. Enrol in college courses. You will meet both young people and vital older people. Make friends with them. Create your own little subculture of people with vitality. Their youthfulness will keep you young.

Exercise One

1. Does your family tend to retain youthful vitality into old age?
2. If the answer is no, try to find one that does and spend lots of time with them. You can learn by their example.

Exercise Two

1. Observe your own walk as you walk down the street. Does it have the confident bounce of youth?
2. If not, practise 'the matador walk'. Hold your shoulders erect

and take your steps with confidence and authority. Watch John Travolta in the opening scene of *Saturday Night Fever* for a good example.

Exercise Three

1. Do you regularly get your juices flowing and feel extreme pleasure doing something you enjoy?
2. If the answer is no, use your self-control to force yourself into something which can open up that part of you. Try a night class in something which you could potentially get passionate about – art, sculpture or music, for example.

Exercise Four

1. Do you regularly get some kind of vigorous exercise that includes mild shocks to your bones to keep them strong, and some practice balancing?
2. If the answer is no, begin taking long vigorous walks, playing a sport or dancing. If you are already frail, build up gradually, starting with non-vigorous walks. Use your self-control to force yourself, because the long-term consequences of inactivity are depression, poor health and premature death.

CHAPTER SUMMARY

1. Your culture and family role models give you a script which you unconsciously act out as you age.
2. A study found that 60 per cent of people over the age of 80 in the Republic of Georgia were still gainfully employed.
3. Expectations often determine physical performance. Running a mile in four minutes was thought to be impossible until Roger Bannister did it in 1954.

4. Thinking you are frail makes you frail because muscles and bones atrophy when you protect them from stress.
5. *Skylab* astronauts lost 4 grams of calcium from their bones each day because of lack of physical stress.
6. Avoiding physical stress makes you more vulnerable to stress and accidents in the long run.
7. Many studies showing decline with age exaggerate the decline because they test subjects who have given in to the vicious circle of decline expected by our society.
8. Musicians and artists better demonstrate our real potential because their subculture gives them more positive expectations about ageing.
9. Surround yourself with vital, happy role models. This will extend your years of happy living.

CHAPTER

15

PRINCIPLES OF RUT-BUSTING

Ruts are predictable, comfortable behaviour patterns which evolve from seeking minimum-energy living. They are like dangerous drugs because they provide short-term comfort while causing serious long-term damage. Loss of energy, depression, and mental and physical decline are all inevitable by-products. Vital people who avoid ruts retain their energy, joy and enthusiasm because challenge, variety and surprise are stimulating.

Escaping from a rut can be the ultimate test of will-power because the lethargic urge to stay in your familiar rut feels so strong. If you are deeply in a rut the pain of breaking out is not unlike the pain of a drug addict quitting 'cold turkey'. All of your powers of rationalization will be marshalled to defend the status quo. Yet when people do successfully escape, they always look back in amazement at the dullness of their previous existence. 'Why didn't I do this years ago?' is a typical reaction.

The reason ruts feel so comfortable is that they are so predictable. The fact that they eliminate challenge and surprise is both the source of their attraction and the reason they are so bad for you in the long run. We have already seen many examples where seeking short-term comfort causes long-term misery. The supreme test of your self-control can be breaking out of a comfortable rut. As a lifelong attitude jogger, I would like to share a few tricks I have learned which may help you to break out of any boring ruts you may currently find yourself trapped in. Perhaps a good start is to tell you how I recently broke free.

MOVING TO AUSTRALIA

As I began to write this book in my comfortable home in Santa Monica, California, one of the books I read for my research was an inspiring one called *Breaking Patterns* by Cathrine Chapman Pacheco. In it she describes how she and her husband sold their home and moved aboard a 38-foot sailboat. They travelled the world, had adventures and met fascinating people. I suddenly realized that I couldn't in good conscience write a book about attitude jogging from the predictable comfort of my own nest.

One critical-moment phone call to an estate agent and I had my flat put up for rent, completely furnished. The first person who saw it signed a six-month lease, so I packed my suitcase and went to live with a writer friend in northern California. The companionship of living with a friend with minimal possessions of my own was exhilarating. After decades of being loaded down with truckloads of possessions which had to be moved, repaired, stored and otherwise worried about, I felt really free.

As November approached, I decided to go one step further and trade the California winter for a summer in Australia. I had originally planned to stop off at my flat to get more clothes and things for the long stay, but I found to my surprise that I *liked* having only a few clothes. The ones I had left behind were the ones I never really wore. They were the ones that stare back at you when you look in your cupboard full of clothes and can't find a thing to wear. My one suitcase had only the clothes I really liked to wear.

When I arrived in Australia, I didn't know a soul. I hired a car at the airport and got a newspaper so I could begin looking for a place to live. A large 'shared accommodations' section in the classifieds pointed me in the right direction. I began calling some of the ads from the airport, and used a map to go look at a few places that said they had fantastic views.

After interviewing many nice people who each showed me around their place and then invited me to sit down for tea and conversation, I finally fell in love with a place right on the sand at Freshwater beach for only £100 per week. The place was completely furnished and my three flatmates were all pleasant professionals in their thirties. Three days in Australia and I already had three friends, a place to live and my own car, which I bought through an ad in the paper.

Yes it was challenging at times trying to find my way around while driving on the left-hand side of the street, but I kept my cool and enjoyed the excitement of the challenge. I now have lots of friends and find that my writing is going better than ever in this stimulating environment. I recently extended the lease on my flat back in California and brought my laptop to Europe, where the adventure continues.

If things hadn't worked out so well I could have simply returned to my flat, which still has all my stuff waiting for me in it. Having been away for over a year, I now realize how nice it is *not* to have all those things holding me down. Will the furniture be damaged or dirty when I eventually return? I am amazed at how little this matters to me now that I have been away from it for so long. I have always had a very strong nesting instinct and have taken great pride in decorating and fixing my place up, but after this rut-busting exercise I realize that there are other things in life much more important.

HOW ABOUT SOMETHING EASIER?

Moving to Australia was just the right challenge for me, but I have been attitude jogging for a while. If you don't feel ready for anything so major, don't feel bad. You can start with something much easier and build up your strength a little at a time. The important thing is to be spiralling upward and outward. Many people spiral downward as they age and the spiral gets smaller and smaller as they reach the bottom.

Before you are old you should begin working towards expanding your flexibility and daring so that you will be able to *enjoy* your old age. Many people end their lives huddled alone inside a house they have become too attached to only because it is familiar and predictable. Most people put great effort into saving money for their old age, yet ignore the even more important preparations they could be making to ensure that their attitudes will allow them to enjoy their old age in happiness and good health.

Holidays and sabbaticals are classic rut-busters on which many people tend to short-change themselves. Some people are in the habit of wasting their holiday opportunities doing unimaginative chores around the house or going to the same place every year. Holidays are a golden opportunity to do some serious attitude jogging and to break cleanly out of your comfortable routines. By disrupting the comfort of your rut, a holiday can often help you to see the real possibilities in life much more clearly. Life is a banquet, but most people are starving to death. A good time to make some really dramatic long-term rut-busting plans is just after the end of your holiday, while your head is clear.

Guided tours, cruises and luxury hotels are better than no holiday at all, but the stress-free environment they provide is more designed to let your comfort zones shrink than stretch. The more you can open yourself to challenge, the more effective a trip will be at freeing you from living for short-term comfort. A holiday that alternates between challenge and restful recovery is an ideal compromise which is in accord with sound exercise principles. Take a great adventure and *then* lie on the beach and think about it. Adventure holidays, which emphasize stretching your comfort zones, are available at all travel agents.[1] Of course the best adventures of all, if you're up to it, are the ones you do without a tour operator.

OUTWARD BOUND

During the Second World War, many British merchant ships were sunk by German U-boat torpedoes. Most of the casualties were younger sailors who drowned even though they were more physically fit than the old salts who survived many sinkings. A training programme was set up to build up the sailors' inner strength and tenacity. Over half a century later that programme still exists as a world-wide non-profit organization called *Outward Bound*.[2] Over 12,000 people go through their rigorous courses every year.

All US Peace Corps volunteers undergo the course before reporting for overseas duty.

The Outward Bound courses are all intensive crash courses in self-esteem based on accomplishment. Rock climbing, dog sledging, winter backpacking, whitewater rafting and ocean kayaking provide the challenge. Some courses even end with an individual wilderness survival experience. They have special courses for women only and for parent and child, but they discourage you from taking the course with a friend. They feel that, since the idea is to learn a new way of seeing yourself, a friend will only remind you of your old self.

Military boot camp is another kind of crash course in mental and physical toughness. It is interesting that, though verbally belittling recruits is part of the programme, people come out of boot camp with significantly *greater* self-esteem. Accomplishing things you thought you couldn't do is the best possible medicine for self-esteem. Contrast the good results of boot camp with the ineffective, easy-compliment-based self-esteem programmes in many schools.

The kind of toughness built in boot camp or Outward Bound is perhaps something many of us have always thought of as 'a man's job'. Women have been taught to be delicate rather than tough, and the result is that women are several times more likely to suffer depression than men and also much more likely to have problems with assertiveness. Abseiling down the face of a cliff is not something many women can visualize themselves doing, but having done it certainly changes their self-image fast. Peak experiences like this affect your basic attitude towards challenge itself. Though one experience cannot change your life by itself, it can be a critical moment which affects your approach to the thousands of difficult challenges that still lie ahead. The sum total of all of these experiences can truly change you into a different person. You simply have to use your self-control occasionally to keep the spark alive.

SECOND CHANCES

If at first you don't succeed, try, try again. When you start to get the feeling of power that comes from mastering things you thought you couldn't do, enjoy building on it by attacking the things you always thought of as your weak points.

Public speaking is a source of fear for many people, but an international organization called Toastmasters[3] has helped thousands of people to overcome their fear and feel good about themselves. Whenever you take action on a problem, you also gain the opportunity to meet people like yourself who are really trying rather than staying home in their comfortable rut. Friends can drag you down or pull you out of your ruts, so try to spend your time with people who set a good example.

I was a late bloomer who was an uncoordinated nerd in secondary school. At the age of 38 a friend dragged me up to the ski slopes and taught me to ski. It turned out to be one of the critical moments in my life because for the first time I was really good at a sport. That one experience totally changed my life because it led to my discovery of the right side of my brain. I had been approaching sports with my intellect, which is great for some things, but terrible for sports. I was so excited about my discovery that I wrote my first non-technical book, *The Right Brain* (Doubleday, 1980).

My discovery of the powers of non-verbal thinking gave me a second chance at a whole range of activities which had always made me feel inadequate. I found that dancing was easy now and my tennis game got much better. Encouraged by these successes, I took a course in sculpture and found that it also had become easy. I had always been terrible at art because I was using my verbal, logical thinking too much. By letting the non-verbal part of my brain have control, I went from being an inept klutz to being an artist.

I'm sure there are many people who would be just as excited to discover their verbal, logical side and then use that knowledge to conquer all of the things they failed at before. If computers and other technical things have always been a mystery to you, take a course to see if you can break through and open up that side of yourself. As you grow older you learn how to work on difficult things more effectively, so things you failed at before can suddenly become easy. One way to find out what you can do is to take night courses in things you did badly at when you were young. Once you get that feeling that you can do anything you set your mind to, this confidence itself can steer you through any difficulties.

SOME REALLY WILD POSSIBILITIES

The rat race and the ruts that we get into often seem like they are beyond our control, but this is only an illusion created by our own rationalizations. The fact is that you can write your own life story. Children and money are two common excuses for remaining trapped, so let's look first at the children excuse.

In 1980 I got a job in Europe with International Telephone and Telegraph. They paid the way for my wife and two children. The children loved it. They went to the American school, where classes were taught in English and filled with expatriate children from all over the world. They made good friends with children in our neighbourhood and learned some priceless lessons about the diversity of the world's cultures. We often took weekend breaks all over Europe. The experience for the children would have been worth the trouble, even if my wife and I hadn't both loved it too. Your biggest gift to your children may be showing them that life has rich possibilities if you just take them.

Now let's talk about money. During the six months I lived in Australia to write this book, my living expenses were about one-third of what they were in California and much lower than in my current home in London. Part of the reason is the fact that my housing costs were only one-fourth of what they were when I had my own private place because I was sharing the rent with three flatmates. But there were other savings: utilities, telephone, maid service, repairs, food, TV, and the miscellaneous stuff you always seem to need, were all almost divided by four. My car was an old one but it ran fine. Were any of these things real sacrifices when they made such an experience possible? I think not. One of my flatmates has lived in shared houses and flats all over Europe for over a decade. By getting out of the materialistic rat race you can gain freedom to live wherever you want to. Once you enter that world you find that there are lots of other people doing it too.

If you're really adventurous, contact Volunteer Services Overseas[4] for information on doing overseas volunteer work. They train you and pay expenses plus a tiny salary for going to third world countries and teaching or helping them create jobs and simple infrastructures. They place about 1,000 people aged 20 – 70 every year. Couples are welcome. The pay isn't great but the payoff of a new lease on life and a vastly improved attitude factor is worth much more than money.

The possibilities are endless, but the important thing is that the worst that can happen is that you end up coming home with some good stories. If you don't break out of your rut you will never know what you could have done. Having a dream and carrying it out is in itself an empowering experience. The important thing is to *try*. If you let fear stop you, you may miss out on what could be the best part of your life.

THE PLEASURE AND WELL-BEING TEST

Instructions: Answer each of the following questions by circling one of the seven numbers. Answer with complete honesty and with a long-term focus. Try to ignore your present mood and answer the questions honestly based on your usual feelings over the years and, in particular, the past 12 months:

1. How intensely do you feel pleasure? (For example, from love, contentment, sexual pleasure, foods, sports, nature, music, etc.).
   Slight   1   2   3   4   5   6   7   Intense

2. How long do your feelings of pleasure last when they do occur?
   Seconds 1   2 (minutes)   3   4 (hours)   5   6 (all day)   7   Days

3. How often do you get a feeling of pleasure? (while doing sports, sleeping, having sex, listening to music, working, joyfully fulfilling your needs, etc.)
   Almost never   1   2 (monthly)   3   4 (weekly)   5   6   7 Daily

4. Do you sacrifice your short-term pleasure when necessary to avoid negative consequences or improve your prospects for pleasure in the long-term?
   Never   1   2   3   4   5   6   7   Always

5. Are you afraid of your own feelings of pleasure, particularly in areas of great emotional importance such as love?
   Total fear 1   2   3   4   5   6   7   No fear

6. How certain are you that you will feel pleasure in the future?

    Impossible   1   2   3   4   5   6   7   Certain

7. Do you believe that the highest peak of pleasure you have felt in your life will ever be equalled or surpassed in the future?

    Unlikely   1   2   3   4   5   6   7   Certain

8. When you feel a sense of well-being, how strong is the feeling?

    Blocked   1   2   3   4   5   6   7   Powerful

9. How long do your feelings of well-being last when they occur?

    Seconds   1   2 (minutes)   3   4 (hours)   5   6 (days)   7   Almost continuously

10. How frequently do you experience a feeling of well-being?

    Almost never 1   2 (monthly)   3   4 (weekly)   5   6 (daily)   7   Many times a day

11. Do you sacrifice your short-term well-being when necessary to avoid negative consequences or improve your prospects for well-being in the long term?

    Never   1   2   3   4   5   6   7   Always

12. When a feeling of well-being occurs, do you sometimes act in ways that destroy it?

    Almost always   1   2   3   4   5   6   7   Almost never

13. How strong is your feeling of security that you will experience well-being in the future?

    Unlikely   1   2   3   4   5   6   7   Certain

14. Do you believe that the strongest feelings of well-being that you have experienced in the past will be felt again in the future?

    Unlikely   1   2   3   4   5   6   7   Certain

15. After you have experienced pleasure do you often have negative feelings such as guilt, bad conscience, depression or physical symptoms?

    Almost always   1   2   3   4   5   6   7   Almost never

(Scoring: Divide total of all numbers circled by 15. See the figure on page 4 for interpretation.)

THE SELF-REGULATION QUESTIONNAIR

Circle one of the six numbers after each question. Ignore the numbers themselves but position your circle between the extremes of the answers at each end to indicate your answer. Be brutally honest and avoid rationalizations or wishful thinking. Try to ignore recent events and make your answer fit your usual habits over the past 12 months.

[1] I try for one or more aims which are very important to me.
How true is this of you?
Not very   1   2   3   4   5   6   Very much

[2] I discuss my personal problems and needs with other people.
How frequently?
Very rarely   1   2   3   4   5   6   Very frequently

[3] I always feel very inhibited when it comes to making requests and demands for myself.
No   6   5   4   3   2   1   Yes

[4] I am active in a way that suits me, i.e. in any job or profession, in sport, in my personal relationships.
Very rarely   1   2   3   4   5   6   Very frequently

[5] I can keep my independence in dealing with people who are emotionally important to me.
Very poorly   1   2   3   4   5   6   Very well

[6] I get a feeling of well-being through the way I act towards myself and towards others.

Very seldom   1   2   3   4   5   6   Very often

[7] I would rather go along with others than make demands for myself.

No   6   5   4   3   2   1   Yes

[8] My hopes for the future are:

Very low   1   2   3   4   5   6   Very high

[9] In general, my will to live is:

Very weak   1   2   3   4   5   6   Very strong

[10] In general, the expression and satisfaction of my emotionally most important wishes and needs are:

Very weak   1   2   3   4   5   6   Very strong

[11] I do things in order to fulfil the expectations of people close to me, rather than trying to please myself.

No   6   5   4   3   2   1   Yes

[12] When I am feeling very low and my mental equilibrium is disturbed, I engage in activities that restore my equilibrium and make me feel better.

Very seldom   1   2   3   4   5   6   Very often

[13] When I have problems in dealing with other people, I engage in various activities until I have got a grip on my problems.

Very rarely   1   2   3   4   5   6   Very frequently

[14] I prefer to keep up harmonious relations with other people rather than please myself.

No   6   5   4   3   2   1   Yes

[15] I alter my behaviour until I am successful in getting what I want.

Very rarely   1   2   3   4   5   6   Very often

[16] My way of acting and behaving enables me to deal with other people satisfactorily.
No   1   2   3   4   5   6   Yes

[17] Usually I manage to avoid psychological or physical demands that are too taxing.
No   1   2   3   4   5   6   Yes

[18] I have always found it difficult to give expression to my most important feelings and needs towards other people.
No   6   5   4   3   2   1   Yes

[19] I believe that I can influence my state of health positively through my own activities.
No   1   2   3   4   5   6   Yes

[20] I always pay close attention to my physical state of health.
No   1   2   3   4   5   6   Yes

[21] I pray to God to help me overcome my problems
Never   1   2   3   4   5   6   Very often

[22] Certain people have always been the cause of my unhappiness.
No   6   5   4   3   2   1   Yes

[23] People who are emotionally important to me help me to overcome my problems.
Rarely   1   2   3   4   5   6   Very frequently

[24] When I am really tired, I am always ready and willing to do what is necessary in order to recover (e.g. sleep or go for a walk).
Seldom   1   2   3   4   5   6   Nearly always

[25] I try to get away from people who constantly thwart my emotional expectations.
Seldom   1   2   3   4   5   6   Nearly always

[26] I can express and satisfy my emotional needs without inner inhibitions.
Hardly ever   1   2   3   4   5   6   Nearly always

[27] I am certain that I am of importance to someone.

Not certain   1   2   3   4   5   6   Very certain

[28] I have a high opinion of myself.

Not really   1   2   3   4   5   6   Certainly

[29] There are parts of my life where I am really important.

Hardly any   1   2   3   4   5   6   Many

[30] For years now I have tolerated conditions without protest which are in fact harmful to me.

No   6   5   4   3   2   1   Yes

[31] I exert some influence on what is happening in my life.

No   1   2   3   4   5   6   Yes

[32] My life has meaning, and is directed towards a goal.

No   1   2   3   4   5   6   Yes

[33] I arrange my eating habits in such a way that I feel well.

No   1   2   3   4   5   6   Yes

[34] I find it very difficult to express negative feelings such as anger, hatred or aggression overtly.

No   6   5   4   3   2   1   Yes

[35] I exercise my body in such a way that I feel well.

No   1   2   3   4   5   6   Yes

[36] As far as religion is concerned, I am comfortable in my beliefs.

No   1   2   3   4   5   6   Yes

[37] I usually succeed in getting away from events and conditions that do me no good in the long run.

No   1   2   3   4   5   6   Yes

[38] Certain people keep disturbing me and making my personal development difficult.
No   6   5   4   3   2   1   Yes

[39] I change any ways of behaving and reacting which do me no good in the long run.
No   1   2   3   4   5   6   Yes

[40] I arrange my daily life in such a way that I can always relax.
No   1   2   3   4   5   6   Yes

[41] When I am feeling unhappy and dissatisfied, I don't just give in but try to get active in ways that get me over these feelings.
No   1   2   3   4   5   6   Yes

[42] When I am annoyed and excited, I try to do things that help me develop a mental equilibrium which takes me out of the situation.
No   1   2   3   4   5   6   Yes

[43] I cannot do anything about the causes of my constant excitement and tension because they are due to the behaviour of other people.
No   6   5   4   3   2   1   Yes

[44] I behave in such a way that my needs are satisfied and other people can benefit.
No   1   2   3   4   5   6   Yes

[45] In all my activities I always respect the independence of other people.
No   1   2   3   4   5   6   Yes

[46] I can always recognize and take into account positive as well as negative characteristics of other people.
No   1   2   3   4   5   6   Yes

[47] I tend not to show overtly any emotional shocks or stresses that I may be suffering.
No   6   5   4   3   2   1   Yes

[48] I try to act in such a way that positive results can be achieved in the long run.

No   1   2   3   4   5   6   Yes

[49] I give up ways of acting and behaving that lead to negative consequences in the long run.

No   1   2   3   4   5   6   Yes

[50] I always try to achieve long-lasting well-being in the various aspects of my life (work, eating, exercise, relations with partner, etc.)

No   1   2   3   4   5   6   Yes

[51] When my emotional expectations are disappointed, I feel very inhibited and paralysed.

No   6   5   4   3   2   1   Yes

[52] I always keep an eye on my physical state of health.

No   1   2   3   4   5   6   Yes

[53] I always keep an eye on my emotional state of health.

No   1   2   3   4   5   6   Yes

[54] I always pay attention to the way my actions affect myself and other people.

Seldom   1   2   3   4   5   6   Always

[55] Certain conditions disturb and make difficult my personal development.

No   6   5   4   3   2   1   Yes

[56] In my imagination I try out various ways of acting which I can adopt if my present behaviour is not successful.

Seldom   1   2   3   4   5   6   Always

[57] I adjust my behaviour according to the consequences – abandoning ways of acting that lead to negative consequences, and carrying on with ways of acting that lead to positive consequences.

Seldom   1   2   3   4   5   6   Nearly always

[58] When I experience a severe failure, I don't get upset but try to learn from my mistakes.
Seldom   1   2   3   4   5   6   Nearly always

[59] When some emotional catastrophe happens to me, such as the death of a loved one, or a separation, I feel unable to give expression to my feelings and wishes.
No   6   5   4   3   2   1   Yes

[60] Every day I indulge in various activities that are good for me and complement each other.
Seldom   1   2   3   4   5   6   Nearly always

[61] I always live my own life, doing what is advantageous for me.
Seldom   1   2   3   4   5   6   Nearly always

[62] When I can't establish close contact with someone who is emotionally important to me, I prefer to leave that person.
Seldom   1   2   3   4   5   6   Nearly always

[63] Certain conditions have always been the most important causes of my unhappiness.
No   6   5   4   3   2   1   Yes

[64] I can live in contentment and relaxation with or without a person who is emotionally important to me.
No   1   2   3   4   5   6   Yes

[65] I always try to discover new points of view and ways of acting to achieve surprising and agreeable solutions to problems.
Rarely   1   2   3   4   5   6   Nearly always

[66] I am self-reliant and independent, relying on nobody for any length of time in a way that would be to my disadvantage.
No   1   2   3   4   5   6   Yes

[67] I manage to feel good through the way I act.
No   1   2   3   4   5   6   Yes

[68] I very rarely experience boredom, monotony or lack of excitement.

Often   1   2   3   4   5   6   Rarely

[69] I have many pleasant and enjoyable things happening to me all the time.

No   1   2   3   4   5   6   Yes

[70] I often succeed through my activities to reach a stage of very pleasant contentment.

No   1   2   3   4   5   6   Yes

[71] I always rely on my intuition.

No   1   2   3   4   5   6   Yes

[72] I have been protesting for years about conditions I find harmful, but am not able to change them.

No   6   5   4   3   2   1   Yes

[73] When something I do leads to failure, I don't carry on in the same way but rather try something different.

No   1   2   3   4   5   6   Yes

[74] I reach inner contentment through my activities.

No   1   2   3   4   5   6   Yes

[75] I often get an emotional 'buzz' through my actions.

Hardly ever   1   2   3   4   5   6   Very often

[76] When somebody threatens me or annoys me, I can respond with appropriate aggression.

No   1   2   3   4   5   6   Yes

[77] I feel helpless in relation to hostile people or aggravating circumstances, because I can't do anything to change them.

No   6   5   4   3   2   1   Yes

[78] When somebody attacks me without justification, I can change my reaction in such a way that I can ultimately defend myself successfully.

No   1   2   3   4   5   6   Yes

[79] When anybody criticizes me justly, I try to change my behaviour accordingly.
Hardly ever   1   2   3   4   5   6   Nearly always

[80] I am always on the look-out for people or situations that increase my well-being.
Hardly ever   1   2   3   4   5   6   Nearly always

[81] I don't stick with people or situations that are not doing me any good; sooner or later I try to get away.
Hardly ever   1   2   3   4   5   6   Nearly always

[82] I abandon ways of thinking and acting that inhibit me.
Hardly ever   1   2   3   4   5   6   Nearly always

[83] I always seem to encounter the negative aspects of certain people.
No   6   5   4   3   2   1   Yes

[84] I abandon ways of thinking and acting that lead to anger and annoyance.
No   1   2   3   4   5   6   Yes

[85] I am always on the look-out for ways of acting that will have good consequences for me and others as well.
No   1   2   3   4   5   6   Yes

[86] When I am not in a position to distance myself from people or conditions that are harmful, I nevertheless try to satisfy my needs and desires.
Seldom   1   2   3   4   5   6   Nearly always

[87] When I have personal problems, I admit their existence to myself and others.
Seldom   1   2   3   4   5   6   Nearly always

[88] I admit my good points as well as my bad points.
Nor really   1   2   3   4   5   6   Definitely

[89] Although certain bodily physical conditions, such as overweight, worry me, I am unable to change them.
No   6   5   4   3   2   1   Yes

[90] When I have problems, I don't hesitate to ask others for help.

No   1   2   3   4   5   6   Yes

[91] When things go wrong, I know that I must change my behaviour.

No   1   2   3   4   5   6   Yes

[92] I don't carry on with activities that constantly lead to failure.

I do   1   2   3   4   5   6   Definitely

[93] I don't believe in feeling guilty.

I can't   1   2   3   4   5   6   Definitely

[94] When I feel guilty about somebody, I try to avoid that person and get my kicks elsewhere (e.g. an extra-marital affair).

I'm not like that   1   2   3   4   5   6   Definitely

[95] I sometimes talk about my intentions and aims, but feel completely unable to put them into practice because of external conditions.

No   6   5   4   3   2   1   Yes

[96] I only tolerate my weaknesses until I succeed in overcoming them.

No   1   2   3   4   5   6   Yes

[97] I try to solve my personal problems, to obtain a maximum of pleasure and well-being.

No   1   2   3   4   5   6   Yes

[98] I don't hold grudges, and forgive easily.

No   1   2   3   4   5   6   Yes

[99] I constantly monitor what is happening in my body, in order to discover what is of benefit to me.

Hardly ever   1   2   3   4   5   6   Nearly always

[100] I am unable to change my relations with certain people although the outcome is negative.

No   6   5   4   3   2   1   Yes

[101] I constantly watch my relations with other people, with the aim of developing the best possible way of dealing with them.
Hardly ever   1   2   3   4   5   6   Nearly always

[102] When I feel inhibited about expressing my wishes and expectations, I start doing things that will hopefully make the inhibitions disappear.
Hardly ever   1   2   3   4   5   6   Nearly always

[103] When I am upset or annoyed, I start doing things that will hopefully resolve the situation.
Hardly ever   1   2   3   4   5   6   Nearly always

[104] When things aren't going too well, I try to discover the reasons and make an effort to change the situation.
Hardly ever   1   2   3   4   5   6   Nearly always

[105] I cannot do anything about the cause of my constant excitement and tension because they are due to certain situations which I cannot change.
No   6   5   4   3   2   1   Yes

(Scoring: Add up answers and divide by 105. See figure on page 95 for interpretation.)

ABOUT DR GROSSARTH-MATICEK

Dr Ronald Grossarth-Maticek has been doing research on the relationship between personality and attitude factors and health for over 30 years. The Bibliography includes a selection of his most important technical papers from a list of over 70 published.

His first research was done in Yugoslavia in the early 1960s. He identified a personality pattern which was strongly associated with cancer, and another pattern associated with cardiovascular disease. He also defined a healthy personality which formed the basis of the later work I have used in this book. His staff of interviewers questioned over 10,000 elderly residents of Heidelberg, Germany in 1972–3. The figures on pages 4, 95 and 139 tabulate some of the important results. Appendices I and II are translations of the questions used in that study, and are reproduced with his kind permission.

In 1996 I spent a month in Heidelberg and spoke to several of Dr Grossarth-Maticek's former interviewers, as well as to some of his collaborators and critics, to verify the reliability of his data. Dr Grossarth-Maticek plans to publish two books and a computerized expert system in the spring of 1998. All will eventually be translated into English, but here are the German titles of the two upcoming books:

Ronald Grossarth-Maticek, *Gesundsein lernen – Versorge und Genesung durch Selbstregulation* [Self-regulation, Well-being and Health] (Köln: Kiepenheuer & Witsch)

Ronald Grossarth-Maticek and Helm Stierlin, *Gesund-heitsverhalten und Krebserkrankungen – Therrien, Methoden und Ergebnisse Auer Verlag, Heidelberg.*

He is also working on another, more technical book called *Synergistic epidemiology and preventative behavioural Medicine of chronic diseases*, which should be completed late in 1998.

THE ATTITUDE FACTOR WEB SITE

WHAT IS A WEB SITE?

If you haven't experienced the world-wide web, I can heartily recommend that you make it an attitude jogging goal to do it soon. If you're afraid of computers, you will find that the web is much easier to use once you're on it than any computer. The best way to learn is to let a friend get you onto our site (www.attitudefactor.com) and then stay with you for a while in case you get stuck.

The next best way is to go to a cyber-café and let them help you. Cyber-cafés have sprung up all over the world to provide a fun place to learn about and use the world-wide web without having to buy a computer and modem or pay a monthly connection charge. They are simply cafés full of computers connected to the world-wide web. They will charge you by the hour for your usage, give you lots of hand-holding and even sell you some coffee and pastry if you like.

If you are a computer user, you can get one-month free connection from CompuServe, America On-line, Microsoft Network or hundreds of other Internet providers (the web is a part of the Internet). After that it costs about £10 a month.

THE PURPOSES OF THE WEB SITE

The *Attitude Factor* web site will automatically administer and score the tests in this book for you and also analyse the meaning of your answers. It will compute your current life-expectancy based on the experimental data and also give you suggestions for how you can change unhealthy attitudes uncovered by the tests. By printing these suggestions and reading them every day you can relearn your bad habits for a longer, healthier life.

The site will also help you to go through the steps of the Experimenter approach as described in Chapter 9. This important tool for solving problems in your life is a very important part of self-regulation because it allows you to avoid situations that lead to helplessness and maximize the feelings of pleasure and well-being in your life. The programme will lead you through the following steps:

1. Help you to identify the worst problems in your life.
2. Help you THINK of possible solutions. Makes suggestions.
3. Help you to decide between changing, adapting or quitting.
4. Help you to subdivide the goal into manageable steps.
5. Help you IMAGINE the results and rehearse.
6. Record your specific goal for the next experiment. You should print out and keep this with you.
7. Send you a timed e-mail reminder asking you to log in and close the loop at a time you specify.
8. Prompt you to think about what you have learned from the experiment and what to do next. (Then returns you to step 1 or 2.)
9. Periodically it will ask you to repeat the tests to assess your progress.

When fully developed, a one-year subscription to this training programme can be purchased for a nominal price to cover the cost of maintaining the site. People who stay with the programme for one year will receive a diploma. All other features of the web site will be free.

The site also presents information on other research showing the strong effect of attitudes on health prospects. The results of several important experiments by Grossarth-Maticek, Denolet, Fernandez-Ballesteros and Andas are summarized, with full text available by faxback. A discussion group allows people to make comments and debate the material presented.

Virtually all of the experiments replicating the results of Grossarth-Maticek's work are on a much smaller scale than his. It is sad that such important work has not been repeated because of the cost of large-scale prospective studies. I intend to change all that by using the web site to gather data for a massive replication study.

Questionnaire results from the site will be coded and kept confidential and will be archived in a safe place. In 5 and 10 years' time I plan to check the health status of older users against public records. I expect to find a strong correlation between test scores and longevity, and also a significant improvement in longevity for people who stayed with the programme for one year. Reading and enjoying *The Attitude Factor* is also expected to result in longer lifespans.[1]

When you have finished reading this book, please log in to the web site and give us your rating and your feedback. If you need more books for your friends, parents or loved ones, you will be able to order them directly through the site.

SELECTED BIBLIOGRAPHY

Ader, Robert, Cohen, N. and Felten, D., 'Psychoneuroimmunology: Interactions Between the Nervous System and the Immune System', *Lancet* 345 (1995): 99–103

Baars, Bernard J., 'Why Volition is a Foundation Problem for Psychology', *Consciousness and Cognition* 2 (1993): 281–309

Bacon, C., Remeker, R. and Ertler, M., 'A psychosomatic survey of cancer of the breast', *Psychosomatic Medicine* 14 (1952): 453–60

Barton, Scott, 'Chaos, Self-Organization, and Psychology', *American Psychologist* 49.1 (Jan 1994): 5–14

Berkman, Lisa F. and Syme, Leonard, 'Social Networks, Host Resistance, and Mortality: A Nine-Year Follow-Up Study of Alameda County Residents', *American Journal of Epidemiology* 109.2 (1979): 186–203

Blakeslee, Thomas R., *The Right Brain* (New York: Doubleday, 1980)

–, *Beyond the Conscious Mind: Unlocking the Secrets of the Self* (New York: Plenum Press, 1996).

Butz, Michael, 'The Fractal Nature of the Development of the Self', *Psychological Reports* 71 (1992): 1043–63

Chapman Pacheco, Cathrine, *Breaking Patterns* (Kansas City, MO: Andrews and McNeel, 1989). *Excellent personal story of a rut-busting couple.*

Cohen, Bernard, 'Catalog of Risks Extended and Updated', *Health Physics* 61.3 (1991): 317–35. *An excellent discussion of risks with many calculated risk factors.*

–, 'How to Assess the Risks You Face', *Consumer's Research* 75 (June 1992): 11–16

Cohen, Sheldon, Tyrrell, David and Smith, Andrew P., 'Psychological Stress and Susceptibility to the Common Cold', *The New England Journal of*

Medicine 325.9 (1991): 606–11

Cowley, Geoffrey and Springen, Karen, 'Critical Mass', *Newsweek* September 25, 1995: 66–7. *A new study of 100,000 nurses which relates longevity to overweight.*

Cushman, Phillip, 'Why the Self is Empty: Toward a Historically Situated Psychology', *American Psychologist* 45.5 (May 1990): 599–611

Darnay, Arsen (ed), *Statistical Record of Older Americans* (Detroit, MI: Gale Research, 1994)

Desharnais, Raymond *et al.*, 'Aerobic Exercise and the Placebo Effect: A Controlled Study', *Psychosomatic Medicine*, 55 (1993): 149–54

Deutscher, Irwin, *What We Say/What We Do* (Glenview: Scott Foresman, 1973)

Dienstbier, Richard A., 'Arousal and Physiological Toughness: Implications for Mental and Physical Health', *Psychological Review* 96.1 (1989): 84–100

Dienstbier, Richard A., LaGuardia, Robert and Wilcox, Noreen, 'The Relationship of Temperament to Tolerance of Cold and Heat: Beyond "Cold Hands-Warm Heart"', *Motivation and Emotion* 11.3 (1987): 269–95

Elliot, Robert S., *From Stress to Strength* (New York: Bantam, 1994). *Describes how 'hot reaction' to stress causes permanent heart damage.*

Everson, Susan A. *et al.*, 'Hopelessness and Risk of Mortality and Incidence of Myocardial Infarction and Cancer', *Psychosomatic Medicine* 58: 113 (1996). *(2428 men tested for hopelessness. 6 years later 3 times as many dead.)*

Eysenck, H. J., *Smoking, Personality and Stress* (New York: Springer-Verlag, 1991b)

–, 'Cancer, Personality and Stress: Prediction and Prevention', *Advances in Behavior Research and Therapy* 16 (1994): 167–215. *An excellent review of all of the literature.*

Eysenck, H. J. and Grossarth-Maticek 'Creative Novation Behavior Therapy as a Prophylactic Treatment for Cancer and Coronary Heart Disease: Part II – Effects of Treatment', *Behavior Research and Therapy* 29.1 (1991): 17–31. *(See above)*

Eysenck, H. J. and Wilson, G. D., *A Textbook of Human Psychology* (Lancaster: MTP Press, 1976)

Eysenck, Michael W., *The Blackwell Dictionary of Cognitive Psychology* (Cambridge: Blackwell Publishers, 1990)

Fernandez-Ballesteros, Rocio, Zamarron, Ruiz, Sabastian and Spielberger, 'Assessing Emotional Expression: Spanish adaptation of the Rationality/

Emotional Defensiveness Scale', in *Personality and Individual Differences* 22(5): 719–729, 1997

Friedan, Betty, *The Fountain of Age* (Simon and Schuster, 1993)

Gleik, James, *Chaos* (Viking, 1987). *A good introduction to mathematical chaos theory.*

Gove, Walter R. and Hughes, Michael, 'Reexamining the Ecological Fallacy: A Study in Which Aggregate Data Are Critical in Investigating the Pathological Effects of Living Alone', *Social Forces* 58.4 (1980): 1157–77

Greer, S. and Morris, Tina, 'Psychological Attributes of Women Who Develop Breast Cancer: A Controlled Study', *Journal of Psychosomatic Research* 19 (1975): 147-–53

Greer, S., Morris, T. and Pettingale, K. W., 'Psychological Response to Cancer: Effect on Outcome', *Lancet* October 13 1979: 785–7; also see 15-year follow up in *Lancet* 335 (1990): 49–50

Grossarth-Maticek, Ronald, and Boyle, G. J. 'Alcohol Consumption and Health: Synergistic Interaction with Personality', *Psychological Reports* 77(2):675–687 (1995b)

Grossarth-Maticek, R. and Eysenck, H. J, 'Creative Novation Behaviour Therapy as a Prophylactic Treatment for Cancer and Coronary Heart Disease: Part I – Description of Treatment', *Behaviour Research and Therapy* 29.1 (1991): 1–16. *Tells how they reduced mortality rate by a factor of 4.3 in high-risk people over 40.*

–, 'Is Media Information that Smoking Causes Illness a Self-Fulfilling Prophecy?', *Psychological Reports* 65 (1989): 177–8

Grossarth-Maticek, R. and Eysenck, H. J. 'Prediction of Cancer and Coronary Heart Disease as a Function of Method of Questionnaire Administration', *Psychological Reports* 73 (1993): 943–59

Grossarth-Maticek, R. and Eysenck, H. J. (1995) 'Self-regulation and mortality from cancer, coronary heart disease, and other causes: A prospective study Personality and Individual Differences" 19(6):781-795. *Very important report of the self-regulation experiment.*

Grossarth-Maticek, R., Eysenck, H. J., and Vetter, H., 'Personality Type, Smoking Habit and Their Interaction as Predictors of Cancer and Coronary Heart Disease', *Personality and Individual Differences* 9.2 (1988): 479–95. *Complete review of the amazing results of early Yugoslav and Heidelberg studies of four personality types and mortality.*

Grossarth-Maticek, Ronald, Bastiaans, Jan and Kanazir, Dusan, 'Psychosocial Factors as Strong Predictors of Mortality from Cancer, Ischaemic Heart

Disease and Stroke: The Yugoslav Prospective study', *Journal of Psychosomatic Research* 29.2 (1985): 167–76. *About the significance of the 11 rationality questions.*

Grossarth-Maticek, Ronald, Eysenck, Hans, Reider, Hermann and Racik, Lyobasa, 'Psychological Factors as Determinants of Success in Football and Boxing: The Effects of Behaviour Therapy', *Int Journal of Sports Psychology* 21 (1990a): 237–55

Guisinger, Shan and Blatt, Sidney J., 'Individuality and Relatedness', *American Psychologist* 49.2 (1994): 104–11

Heimberg, Richard and Becker, Robert, 'Cognitive Behavioral Group Treatment for Social Phobia: Comparison with a Credible Placebo Control', *Cognitive Therapy and Research* 14.1 (1990): 1–23

House, James S., Landis, Karl R., and Umberson, Debra, 'Social Relationships and Health', *Science* 29 (1988): 540–5

Jeffers, Susan, *Feel the Fear and Do It Anyway* (New York: Ballantine, 1987). *An excellent book on overcoming your fears.*

Johnson, T. E., Lithgow, G. J. and Murakami, S., 'Hypothesis: interventions that increase the response to stress offer the potential for effective life prolongation and increased health', *Journal of Gerontology: Biological Science Medical Science* 51.6 (1996): B392–395. *Pollution may be good for you!*

Keeney, Ralph, 'Facts of Life About Risks', *New England Journal of Medicine* 331 (1994): 189–90

Kiecolt-Glaser *et al.*, 'Slowing of Wound Healing by Psychological Stress', *Lancet* 346 (1995): 1194–6. *Slower healing of punch biopsy wounds in caregivers.*

Kimmel, Douglas C., *Adulthood and Aging* (New York: Wiley, 1974)

Klerman, Gerald L. and Weissman, Myrna M., 'Increasing Rates of Depression', *JAMA* 261.15 (1989): 2229–35

Koestler, Arthur, *The Ghost in the Machine* (New York: Macmillan, 1967. *An excellent book on self-organization.*

Lang, Frieder R. and Carstensen, Laura L., 'Close Emotional Relationships in Late Life: Further Support for Proactive Aging in the Social Domain', *Psychology and Aging* 9.2 (1994): 315–24

Laudenslager, M. L., Ryan, S. M., Drugan, R. C., Hyson, R. L. and Maier, S. F., 'Coping and immunosuppression: Inescapable but not escapable shock suppresses lymphocyte proliferation. *Science*, 221 (1983): 568–70

Le Doux, Joseph E., 'Cognitive-Emotional Interactions in the Brain', *Cognition and Emotion* 3.4 (1989): 267–89

Leaf, Alexander, *Youth in Old Age* (New York: McGraw Hill, 1975)

Lew, Edward A. and Garfinkel, Lawrence, 'Variations in Mortality by Weight Among 750,000 Men and Women', *Journal of Chronic Disease* 32 (1979): 563–76

Lewin, Roger, *Complexity* (Macmillan, 1992)

Linville, Patricia W., 'Self-Complexity as a Cognitive Buffer Against Stress-Related Illness and Depression', *Journal of Personality and Social Psychology* 52.4 (1987): 663–76

Locke, Steven *et al.*, 'Life Change Stress, Psychiatric Symptoms, and Natural Killer Activity', *Psychosomatic Medicine* 46.5 (1984): 441–53

Loehr, James, *Toughness Training for Life* (Plume, 1993). *Excellent. Written by a famous sports trainer.*

London, Perry, and Klerman, Gerald L., 'Evaluating Psychotherapy', *American Journal of Psychiatry* 139.6 (June 1982): 709–17

Luborsky, Lester, Singer, Barton, and Luborsky, Lise, 'Comparative Studies of Psychotherapies: Is it true that everyone has won and all must have prizes?', *Archives of General Psychiatry* 32 (Aug 1975): 995–1008

McCraty, Rollin, Atkinson, Mike, Rein, Glen and Watkins, Alan, 'Music Enhances the Effect of Positive Emotional States on Salivary IgA' *Stress Medicine* 12 (1996): 167–75

McHugh, Paul R., 'Psychiatric Misadventures', *American Scholar* 61.4 (Autumn 1992): 497–510

Manson, Joann E. *et al.*, 'Body Weight and Mortality Among Women', *New England Journal of Medicine* 333.11 (1995): 677–84

Masters and Johnson, *Sex and Human Loving* (Boston: Little Brown, 1982)

Mathews, P. M., Froelich, C. J., Sibbitt, W. L. Jr.and Bankhurst, A. D., 'Enhancement of Natural Cytotoxicity by B-endorphin', *Journal of Immunology* 130 (1983): 1658–62

Meyer and Haggerty, 'Streptococcal infection in families: factors altering susceptibility', *Pediatrics* 29 (1962): 539–49

Meyers, David, *The Pursuit of Happiness* (New York: Morrow, 1992)

Money, John, *Love Maps* (New York: Irvington, 1986)

Murray, Linda, 'Bedroom Healing', *Longevity* December 1994: 28

Nesbit, Richard and Wilson, Timothy, 'Telling More Than We Can Know: Verbal Reports on Mental Processes', *Psychological Review* May 84.3 (1977): 231–65

Ornstein, Robert and Sobel, Danial, *The Healing Brain* (Simon and Schuster, 1987)

Ortony, A, Clore, G. and Collins, A., *The Cognitive Structure of Emotions* (Cambridge University Press, 1988)

Palmblad, Jan, 'Stress and Human Immunilogic Competence', in Guillemin, R. (ed), *Neural Modulation of Immunity* (New York: Raven Press, 1985)

Pennebaker, James W., *Opening Up* (New York: Avon, 1990)

Pert, Candace, Ruff, Michael, Weber, Richard and Herkenham, Miles, 'Neuropeptides and their receptors: A psychosomatic Network' *The Journal of Immunology* 135.2 (1985): 820–6

Peterson, Christopher, 'Explanatory Style as a Risk Factor for Illness', *Cognitive Therapy and Research* 12.2 (1988): 119–32

Prigogine, Ilya and Stenses, Isabelle, *Order Out of Chaos* (New York: Bantam, 1984)

Prioleau, Leslie, Murdock, Martha and Brody, Nathan, 'An analysis of psychotherapy verses placebo studies', *The Behavioral and Brain Sciences* 6 (1983): 275–310. *Recommended. Includes peer review discussion.*

Quander-Blaznik, Jutta, 'Personality as a Predictor of Lung Cancer: A Replication', *Personality and Individual Differences* 12.2 (1991): 125–30. *A small-scale replication of Grossarth-Maticek's work.*

Radner, Dasie and Radner, Michael, *Animal Consciousness* (New York: Promethius, 1989)

Rainer, Tristine, *The New Diary* (Los Angeles: Tarcher, 1978). *Journaling techniques.*

Ross, Jerilyn, *Triumph Over Fear* (New York: Bantam, 1994). *An excellent book about treatment of phobias.*

Rossi, Ernest L., *The Psychobiology of Mind-Body Healing* (New York: Norton, 1986)

Sampson, Edward E., 'The Decentralization of Identity', *American Psychologist* 49.11 (Nov 1985): 1203–11

–, 'The Debate on Individualism: Indigenous Psychologies of the Individual and Their Role in Personal and Societal Functioning', *American Psychologist* 43.1 (Jan 1988): 15–22

Schaffer, John W., Graves, Pirkko, Swank, Robert and Pearson, Thomas, 'Clustering of Personality Traits in Youth and the Subsequent Development of Cancer Among Physicians', *Journal of Behavioral Medicine* 10.5 (1987): 441–7

Schieve, William C. and Allyn, Peter M. (eds), *Self-Organization and Dissipative Structures: Applications in the Physical and Social Sciences* (Austin: University of Texas, 1982)

Schmitz, Paul G., 'Personality, Stress Reactions and Disease', *Personality and Individual Differences* 6 (1992): 683–91

Schneider, Allen and Tarshis, Barry, *An Introduction to Psychology* (New York: McGraw-Hill, 1986)

Schoeman, Ferdinand David, *Privacy and Social Freedom* (Cambridge University Press, 1992)

Seligman, Martin E. P., *Learned Optimism* (Oxford University Press, 1993)

–, *The Optimistic Child* (Random House, 1995)

–, *What You Can Change ... And What You Can't* (New York: Fawcett Columbine, 1993)

Sipski, M. L., Alexander, C. J. and Rosen, R. C., 'Orgasm in women with spinal cord injuries: a laboratory-based assessment', *Arch Phys Med Rehabil* 76.12 (Dec 1995): 1097–102

Smith, Mary Lee, and Glass, Gene V., 'Meta-Analysis of Psychotherapy Outcome Studies', *American Psychologist* September 1977: 752–60

Solomon, Robert C., *The Passions* (New York: Doubleday, 1976). *An excellent book on the logic of emotions and the meaning in life.*

Stone, Arthur A., Reed, Bruce R. and Neale, John M., 'Changes in Daily Event Frequency Precede Episodes of Physical Symptoms', *Journal of Human Stress* 13 (1987): 70–4

Taylor, Robert, *Health Fact, Health Fiction* (Dallas: Taylor Publishing, 1990)

Thorpe, Susan J. and Salkovskis, Paul M., 'Phobic Beliefs: Do Cognitive Factors Play a Role in Specific Phobias?' *Behavior Research and Therapy* 33.7 (1995): 805–16

Urquhart, John and Heilman, Klaus, *Risk Watch* (New York: Facts on File, 1984)

Vaillant, George, *Adaptation to Life* (Boston: Little Brown, 1977)

Velmans, Max, 'Is Human Information Processing Conscious?', *Behavioral and Brain Sciences* 14 (1991): 651–726. See also commentary in *Behavioral and Brain Sciences* 16.2 (1993): 404–15

Veltman, Dirk J., Van Zijderveld, Gudo and Van Dyck, Richard, 'Fear of Fear, Trait Anxiety and Aerobic Fitness in Relation to State Anxiety During Adrenalin Provocation', *Anxiety, Stress and Coping* 7 (1994): 279–89

Visintainer, Madelon, Volpicelli, Joseph and Seligman, Martin, 1982, 'Tumor Rejection in Rats After Inescapable or Escapable Shock' *Science* 216.23 (1982): 437–8

Waldrop, Mitchell, *Complexity* (Simon and Schuster, 1992)

NOTES AND REFERENCES

CHAPTER 1   KEEPING YOUR YOUTHFUL JOY

1.   The mind-body connection is amazingly powerful. Take for example the voodoo curse. The victim often dies in a short time with no other cause than his belief that he has been cursed. Pointing a bone or sticking pins into a voodoo doll is all that it takes to kill a believer.

One large-scale study in Finland examined the extensive national health records of 96,000 widowed people and found that **their probability of dying was actually doubled** in the week after losing their mate. (See Meyers 1992, p. 144.) Religious faith-healers have the opposite effect. By simply laying their hands on the sick and the lame they often restore good health merely by changing the recipients' attitudes and expectations. An extreme example of the placebo effect.

2.   See Blakeslee 1997 for a complete description of this experiment. In 1996 I spent several weeks in Heidelberg, Germany, visiting Dr Grossarth-Maticek and interviewing both his supporters and his critics. His critics' main problem seems to be that his results are too good to be true. My conclusion was that he is a prolific genius who has done an incredible volume of work which deserves a Nobel prize. In Chapter 9 I discuss some of Dr Grossarth-Maticek's other important experiments which show how other mental habits can affect the immune system and general health.

3.   A high score (7 = max) means that the person has very intense feelings of pleasure and well-being which last for a long time, happen very often and are not followed by feelings of guilt. In addition, the person is able to forego short-term pleasure when necessary to avoid long-term consequences. Low scores indicate that feelings of pleasure and well-being are very rare or completely blocked and ruined by guilt. Deaths of those taking

the test were also strongly correlated with the score, varying from only 5 per cent still alive of those with the lowest scores to 78.4 per cent for those who scored highest. Social isolation was an amazing 70 per cent for those with the lowest scores, varying to 2.3 per cent for those with a score of 5, and 0 per cent for those with the lowest score.

There are no other studies of the massive scale and duration of Grossarth-Maticek's work, but one long-term study which extended over 30 years was done by George Vaillant of Harvard University (Vaillant, 1977). He extensively interviewed 268 second-year students from the classes of 1939 to 1944 and judged the quality of their adjustment to life by the defence mechanisms they habitually used. Good adult adjustment meant that the subject used mature defence mechanisms such as *altruism, humour, suppression, anticipation* and *sublimation*. Bad adjustment meant they used immature, neurotic or psychotic mechanisms such as repression or projection. Thirty years after the original interviews, in 1975, the subjects were interviewed again and their relative success was compared to their placement on the adult adjustment scale.

Amazingly strong correlations were found to their level of happiness and also to their mental and physical health. ***Only one of the top 30 scorers had a chronic illness, while half of the 30 worst outcomes were either dead or suffering from chronic illness***. Here was *a 15 to one variation in good health predicted by a test on habitual defence mechanisms*. Healthy defence mechanisms lead to good physical health, while unhealthy ones can kill you. Another strong correlation to good health was found when the subject's ability to love and form close human connections was considered. Forty-six per cent of the men classified as 'lonely' had chronic physical illnesses by age 52, while only 4 per cent of the 'friendly' men had such problems.

4.   Thorpe 1995, p. 808.

5.   Please note that this is very approximate and based on the fact that the average age of the people in the study which produced the graph was 58. Since the final health status was checked 21 years later, the average age at that point would be 79.

CHAPTER 2   WHY ATTITUDES DECLINE

1.   To make matters worse, we all have many different behaviours and attitudes that have developed as we play different roles in life. For example, as a mother, a father or a boss you will show completely different attitudes than you would on a romantic holiday with your lover. We all thus

have many different attitudes within us which take control in different contexts. These attitudes may not agree at all with the logically arrived-at version of our attitudes we discuss and use to exercise self-control. My previous book *Beyond the Conscious Mind* (Plenum, 1996) develops this idea of separate thinking modules in much more detail.

2. Daryl Bem developed his self-perception theory of attitudes in 1965. He convincingly argues that our verbal attitudes are based on observing our own behaviour (see Lippa 1990, p. 240).

3. In this classic experiment by Schachter and Singer, some of the subjects were given a clear explanation of what the drug would do to them physiologically so they would not think they were having an emotional reaction. These subjects were not fooled by the accomplices since they already had a satisfactory cognitive explanation of the effects. We use the more commonly understood term 'adrenaline', though the authors used 'epinephrine'. See *Psychological Revue* 69 (1962): 379, or the summary in Schneider (1986), pp. 445–6.

4. Our facial expressions for euphoria and anger are also identical. Here is another example: If you are taking a walk in the woods and a bear startles you, it is your behavioural self which makes you run away. The fear you feel is triggered more by the act of seeing yourself running away than by the bear itself. Our verbal explanations are often after-the-fact rationalizations based on observations of our own behaviour.

Our emotional reactions have been shown to be separate from cognition by experiments in shape preference. People prefer shapes they have seen before, though they don't consciously remember seeing them (see Le Doux 1989, p. 279).

5. Experiments have shown that people's verbal description of their attitudes as measured by tests can be changed by setting them up to observe their own conflicting behaviour. For example, in one study (Gazzaniga 1985, p. 139) students were given a test about their attitude towards cheating. Later they were given an important exam where the teacher left the room so that cheating would be very easy. The students didn't know it but the experimenters were carefully monitoring them for cheating. Later they were tested again for their attitude about cheating. The students who had disapproved of cheating before but had cheated changed their answers on the second attitude test towards approval of cheating. The students who had previously condoned cheating on the attitude test yet who didn't cheat on the exam were much more critical of cheating on the second attitude test. People

often change the cognitive version of their attitudes to agree with their own observed behaviour.

In another experiment (Lippa 1990, p. 241) students changed their previously tested attitudes on ecology after being given a test about their conservation habits which intentionally elicited pro-ecology answers. After seeing their own answers the students readjusted the verbal version of their attitude to match their own observed behaviour.

6.   Notice that we can use *cognition*, *you* and *your verbal* self almost interchangeably in this context. Actually *you* are the sum total of your non-verbal behaviour and many specialized verbal behaviour modules, but since your verbal self is the specialist in talking about and acting as a spokesperson for all of them, we can say *you* in the traditional context and it really means your verbal self. For a better understanding of this see Blakeslee 1996.

CHAPTER 3 CHAOS AND ATTITUDE DEVELOPMENT

1.   The self-reinforcing nature of attitudes is an example of *positive feedback* in the engineering sense. (Not in the sense that means encouragement, which is another meaning entirely.) In engineering, **negative feedback** is an important way to achieve stability. The thermostat in a home or office uses negative feedback to stabilize the temperature by turning on the heat when it is too cold or the air-conditioning when it is too hot. If you swap the heating and the cooling connections on a thermostat you will change the negative feedback into **positive feedback**: If the office is too hot the heat will come on and make things worse, likewise if the office is initially too cold the reversed thermostat will make things worse by turning on the air-conditioning. Positive feedback generally produces disastrous and unstable results.

We all have a built-in positive feedback mechanism in our mind because our perception is strongly biased by our attitudes and beliefs. The result is that once we start seeing things in a certain way, our biased perception will always tend to confirm our initial bias. We can eliminate the bad effects of this positive feedback by using the negative feedback of our logical thinking to try to see through our own rationalizations.

2.   See Prigogine 1984, Sampson 1985, and Gleik 1987 for more on these ideas.

3.   As the reliability of weather forecasting demonstrates, the theories of complexity and chaos theory are far from being able to solve these complex problems, but they have provided some useful insights by observing some of the common characteristics of these problems.

CHAPTER 4   PAIN, PLEASURE AND PLACEBOS

1.   See Gazzaniga 1988, p. 19.

2.   The experiment was done by Ronald and T. H. Scott at McGill University in Canada (see Kerr 1981, p. 12 for more details of this experiment).

3.   In fact the emotional response to anxiety seems to have evolved from primitive mechanisms for reacting to cold. The physical reactions we have to cold are identical to the ones we have to emotional stress, so toughening the temperature-adjustment system can reduce fear and anxiety. Finland and Norway are the only two industrialized countries that don't have the high incidence of depression in females which all other industrialized countries have. Could this be a result of their sauna custom? (See Dienstbier 1987, p. 292.)

4.   See Ornstein 1987, p. 97.

5.   Many surgical procedures were thought to be 90 per cent effective until controlled experiments showed that placebo surgery was equally effective.

6.   Roberts, Alan H., Kewman, Donald G., Mercier, Lisa and Hovell, Mel, 'The Power of Non-specific Effects in Healing: Implications for Psychosocial and Biological Treatments', *Clinical Psychology Review* 13 (1993): 375–91. Excellent discussion of super-placebo effect.

7.   Double-blind testing is the foundation of conventional medicine. It is extremely expensive but necessary to separate truly effective treatments from ineffective ones. It is interesting that many doctors reject the idea that mental factors can affect health, yet accept the need for double-blind testing. If mental factors didn't affect health we could save billions of pounds a year by eliminating this expensive testing. We can't because the mind *does* affect health strongly.

8.   Many test laboratories will give you saliva test samples and run the tests for you for about £2.

9.   See McCraty 1996 for the experiment. The CD is called *Heart Zones* by Lew Childre on the Planitary Productions label. It is available through record stores or by ringing the US on 00-1-408-338-2161. A training videotape and book on the technique is available from HeartMath in California (00-1-408-338-8727).

10.   Classical, rock and new-age music were tested and found to be ineffective (McCraty 1996).

11.   See Pert 1985. In all there are 60 – 70 different peptides, many of which are known to communicate emotional responses.

12.   Mathews 1983 found a 30 per cent increase in activity and a 170 per cent increase in maximal effector-cell recycling capability.

13.   See Cohen 1991 for details, including a graph of colds vs test scores.

14.   See Meyers 1992, p. 144.

CHAPTER 5   THE PRINCIPLES OF EXERCISE

1.   *Toughness Training for Life* by sports trainer James Loehr (Plume 1993) presents a generalization of the principles he has used to train many famous sports stars.

CHAPTER 6   EXPANDING YOUR COMFORT ZONES

1.   Conditioning yourself to cold water actually builds up your body's system for responding to mental stress also. Experiments have shown that people who are conditioned to temperature extremes are calmer under mental stress (Dienstbier 1989, p. 96; also Dienstbier 1987). The immune system can also be toughened by challenge, or weakened by protecting it too much. North Americans often get sick when they go to Mexico because comparatively excellent sanitation has protected their immune system from challenge so much that their immune defences shrivel. Children who are allowed out in all weathers often get fewer colds than the ones whose mothers are always fussing over them and making sure they wear a jumper. The thymus gland is a proving ground for immature immune cells. It must be exposed to a certain level of stress for proper development to take place. Animals raised in a germ-free environment live for only a short time when they are removed from it. Their thymus glands were found by experimenters to be severely undeveloped (see Loehr 1993, p. 202).

2.   Experiments have shown that swimming in cold water has a toughening effect which is associated with lower emotionality and less depressed mood (see Dienstbier 1989, p. 91 and Deinstbeir 1987).

CHAPTER 8   NEW CURES FOR PHOBIAS

1.   The Duke Epidemiologic Catchment Area Community Sample, quoted in Coffey 1994, p. 281. The lifetime figures were 18.11 per cent for simple phobia, 3.18 per cent for social phobia, and 9.4 per cent for Agoraphobia. Lifetime means experiencing the symptoms at any time in your life, whereas the six-month figures mean you have experienced symptoms within the past six months.

Another study, the National Comorbidity Survey, found that one in every four respondents had experienced at least one anxiety disorder (see Ross 1994, p. xvii).

2. See Seligman 1993, p. 61, or Coffey 1994, p. 283. Other chemicals which produce physical reactions also produce the same results. People prone to panic attacks will often even react to the feeling produced by breathing into a paper bag. Even reading aloud word pairs such as 'breathlessness-suffocation' and 'palpitations-dying' can trigger the attacks (Seligman 1993, p.64).

Fully one-third of the people going to casualty for heart attacks are actually having a panic attack (Ross 1994, p. 28).

3. Even a placebo is capable of producing a panic reaction in some people. In one experiment the effects of the placebo injection was about half as strong as that produced by adrenaline (see Veltman 1994, p. 284).

4. Thorpe 1995, p. 806.

5. Seligman 1993, p. 81.

6. See Ross 1994, p. xiv.

7. See Ross 1994.

8. For more on this, see Blakeslee 1996.

9. Addresses of the various branches of this organization can be found in the back of Ms Ross's excellent book, but here is the address and phone number of the parent organization:

ADAA, P.O. Box 96505, Washington, DC, 20077-7140.

Their phone number is (301) 231-9350.

10. See my earlier book *Beyond the Conscious Mind* (Plenum 1996), chapter 8 for a further discussion of the sorry state of this profession. Smith 1977 in *American Psychologist* compared results of nearly 400 psychotherapy outcome studies and concluded, 'Despite volumes devoted to theoretical differences among different schools of psychotherapy, the results of research demonstrate negligible differences in the effects produced by different therapy types.'

See also Prioleau 1983 for an excellent review and peer discussion of the problem. In their summary they said, 'After about 500 outcome studies have been reviewed – we are still not aware of a single convincing demonstration that the benefits of psychotherapy exceed those of placebos for real patients.' Note that there are now recent studies of cognitive-behavioural therapy with significant results. See, for example, Heimberg 1990. Also see Smith 1977.

11. See Seligman 1993, p. 73. This book has an excellent discussion of which kinds of therapy work and which don't. Cognitive-behavioural therapy is very effective against phobias and depression.

12. See Salkovskis 1989, p. 51. For more on this exciting new therapy, see Scott 1989 and Ross 1994.

13. See Seligman 1993, p. 66.

14.   If you don't currently like adventure movies, I suggest you use them as a first step toward enjoying challenge. They condition you almost as well as real-life experiences do because they cause the same physical fear reactions as real danger. Work up from easy ones to toughen yourself. If you can learn to enjoy the really scary ones, you will be ready to graduate to trying real-life adventures.

CHAPTER 9 CHANGING HOPELESS SITUATIONS

1.   Cancer cells result from damage to the genetic codes in the strands of DNA in your cells. Some of these errors occur when the DNA strand is replicated when cells divide. Such errors are bound to happen occasionally in the billions of cell divisions in a lifetime. Radiation, carcinogenic chemicals and other environmental factors cause the errors, but our immune system usually attacks and immobilizes the resulting bad cells. Cancer cells damage the mechanism which normally limits cell division to normal controlled growth and repair. Experts have estimated that cancer cells appear in the average person's circulatory system 10 or more times in a lifetime (see Elliot 1994, pp. 42–3.)

Normally these damaged cells are destroyed by your immune system, but if they come at a time when your immune system is weakened they can get a foothold and begin their uncontrolled division. Cancer is what happens when these cells get the upper hand and multiply out of control. AIDS, colds, pneumonia and other diseases likewise often get a foothold when the immune system is weakened by stress.

Diseases are based on complex probabilities so it is not possible to say that somebody got cancer because of a bad attitude or even because of smoking. What we can say is that both attitude and environmental factors interact in a complex way. You can reduce your probability of getting cancer by reducing your exposure to carcinogens and radiation and also by developing healthy attitudes which will prevent stress from weakening your immune system. The strong results of these experimental studies certainly indicates that diligent attitude jogging effort could extend your life considerably.

2.   See Visintainer 1982. It seems that stress which can be controlled may actually energize the immune system, but stress which we are helpless to control significantly weakens it. Another experiment (Laudenslager 1983) used a similar paired-cage apparatus but actually measured the immune response (lymphocyte proliferation) of the rats. The measurements were 48 for the rat in control of the shocks, 18 for the helplessly shocked rat, and 36 for the rat receiving no shocks.

3.   One important part of your body's immune system is the *natural killer cells*. These amazing fighting units have the ability to recognize and selectively kill both cancer cells and virus-infected cells. Experimenters have actually measured variations in natural killer cell activity based on interactions between stress and attitude. For example, Dr Steven Locke at Harvard Medical School questioned subjects about stressful events in their lives and also about their psychiatric symptoms of distress. He then took blood samples and used them to measure their natural killer cell activity. The subjects were sorted into four equal-sized groups according to the level of their stress and the degree of their symptoms. The median killer cell activities measured for the four groups were as follows:

Group	Killer cell activity
Good coping (high stress/low symptoms)	22.5
Lucky (low stress/low symptoms)	15.1
Neurotic (low stress/high symptoms)	10.6
Bad coping (high stress/high symptoms)	7.5

The killer cell activity level of the group with high stress and low symptoms was three times higher than those with high stress and high symptoms (Locke 1984, p. 448). Clearly the goal of attitude jogging is to get you into the top group by improving your ability to cope with stress. This group has low symptoms in spite of high stress because they have a wide comfort zone and a well-developed ability to face challenges successfully. It is interesting that the good coping (high stress/low symptoms) group had one-third greater killer cell activity than the lucky (low stress/low symptoms) group which was not even challenged by stressful events. This is consistent with other research which shows that overcoming reasonable stress results in better health than having no stress at all. The emotional buzz of overcoming a challenge actually stimulates your immune system.

    The low stress/high symptoms group demonstrates what we would call a fearful or neurotic attitude. In spite of low stress they had high symptoms anyway, indicating that they got upset unnecessarily. It is interesting that, in spite of their low external stress, their immune activity was less than half that of the group that was successfully coping with high stress. A hopeless, fearful attitude can thus weaken your immune system, while learning to handle stress in a healthy way strengthens it and protects you against the unavoidable setbacks of life. Another good test of your immune system's resistance to viral infections is your resistance to the common cold. Have you ever noticed that you seem to get colds a few days after something bad happens to you? Well, it isn't just your imagination. Dr Arthur Stone of the State University of New York (Stone 1987) did an experiment where 79 adult subjects kept daily logs of good and bad life events and also their health status. Colds were found significantly to follow bad events by three to five days.

Another study in the *New England Journal of Medicine* (Cohen 1991) gave psychological stress questionnaires to 394 healthy subjects and then gave them nose drops containing several types of cold virus. The chances of getting cold symptoms turned out to vary linearly with the stress index over almost a two-to-one range (*see figure, page 1*). Their stress index included measures of helplessness and negative emotions, which as we will see later can significantly weaken the immune system.

Hopelessness and stressful events were also linked to strep throat infections in a similar study by Meyer and Haggerty (1962). Parents kept a diary of events while their children were regularly checked for the throat infection. In this case the lag time between bad events and infection turned out to be about two weeks.

4.   Kiecolt-Glaser *et al.* 1995.

5.   See Eysenck 1994, p. 181. Interestingly, the average self-regulation score for women is 4, compared to only 3 for men. Better expression of emotions could be the reason. This difference is just enough to account for the normal difference in longevity between men and women.

6.   Another study by Grossarth-Maticek of 621 cancer patients found that their survival time correlated strongly with their self-regulation scores (Eysenck 1994, p. 182).

Survival Time group	1–2 years	6–9 years	18–27 years
Average self-regulation score	2.2	3.7	5.1

7.   The training was done by two interviewers who visited the subjects in their homes. Only subjects who had been found to be high-risk by a previous personality questionnaire were used in the study. The interviewer spent about an hour discussing the best and worst things in the subject's life and then handed them a pamphlet about self-regulation (p. 157). Subjects were then asked to help to improve the pamphlet by trying to apply its principles to their own lives and then reporting on the results at the next visit in two months' time. This was repeated six times.

To eliminate the possibility that the mere act of paying attention to the treated subjects made the improvement, 100 of the control group were given a placebo treatment which was identical except that it was based on dynamic psychotherapy principles. The printed statement in this case was a statement of dynamic psychotherapy principles. It had a non-significant effect of raising the survival rate from 15.8 per cent to 19 per cent. The group with the correct training had their survival rate raised to 68.4 per cent (see Eysenck 1991, p. 20).

8.   See Grossarth-Maticek 1985. These questions are now incorporated in the Self-regulation Index. They have also been adapted by Charles Spielberger into a rationality/emotional defensiveness test which was used by Rocio Fernandez-Ballesteros of University of Madrid. In this form of the test the answers are on a scale of 1–4 instead of yes/no, so a maximum score of 4 is like having all 'yes' answers on Grossarth-Maticek's test. The test was given to 210 students, 122 healthy women, 122 women with benign breast disease and 122 women with breast cancer. The percentage of each of these groups scoring above 3.1 on the test was 11.4 per cent, 12 per cent, 11.9 per cent and 88.3 per cent respectively. More than seven times as many women with breast cancer got high rationality scores than any of the other groups (see Fernandez-Ballesteros 1997).

9.   Everson 1996 tested 2,428 men for helplessness and found a three-fold increase in risk of death six years later. Grossarth-Maticek did three important prospective studies in the 1960s where he divided people into personality types. He was able to predict a high risk of cancer, high risk for cardio-vascular disease, and good health with amazing accuracy (see Grossarth-Maticek 1988).

See Grossarth-Maticek 1990 (p. 247). A similar study with boxing teams produced 55 losses in the trained group versus 128 in the controls.

10.   Write to Plan International, 5/6 Underhill Street, London NW1 for further information. Or phone them on 0171 485 6612.

CHAPTER 10   BEING CAREFUL CAN KILL YOU

1.   See Coffey 1994, p. 283.

2.   From Statistical Record of Older Americans, Darnay 1994. The rate of personal crime victimization for people over 65 is only 24.6 per 1,000, versus 174.8 for those aged 20–24. Rates for other age groups were 114 for ages 25–34, 76.6 for 35–49, and 44 for 50–64. Crimes of theft rated as follows: 91.5 for ages 12–15, 113.4 for 16–19, 111.6 for 20–24, 77.5 for 25–34, 57.5 for 35–49, 36.5 for 50–64, and only 21.2 for people over 65 years.

3.	See Eysenck 1994, p. 184. In a follow-up 15 years later, survival rates were 17 and 45 per cent respectively (Greer 1990).

4.	See Cohen 1991 for a complete catalogue of risks in the form of loss of life expectancy figures (LLE). These can be used to make rational decisions as to what the real dangers in your life are. LLE takes into consideration the number of years normally lost to the risk. For example, one game of Russian roulette has a 1-in-6 chance of killing you. If we assume that it would take 30 years off your life expectancy, then the LLE is 30/6 = 5 years. This is less than the 7.1-year risk of smoking 20 cigarettes a day.

5.	These calculations are based on the fact that an average life expectancy of 21 years at the time of the test would correspond to a 50 per cent survival rate at the end of the test. For other percentages the life expectancy is assumed to be linear, so expectancy/21 = %alive/50%. Solving for expectancy we get expectancy = $21/50 \times$ %alive = $.42 \times$ %alive. The raw %alive and calculated expectancy figures are as follows:

SCORE	<1.5	2	2.5	3	3.5	4	4.5	5	5.5	6	6.5
% ALIVE	5	14	20	27	35	56	64	70	75	74	80
EXP YRS	2.1	5.9	8.4	11	15	23	27	29	31	31	34

Note that the average age at the time of the test was 58, so the actual life expectancies are 58 plus the numbers on the chart above. Our approximation is thus most accurate if you are 58 when you take the test. The average life expectancy was taken to be 25 years, which corresponds to the mean score of 4.3.

6.	See previous note for how these are calculated.

7.	This percentage is simply calculated by dividing the two risks 69.5/3,290 = 2 per cent. We can push the example even further by also giving you, in addition, a new dangerous career. Either championship auto racing or becoming a high-wire performer would only subtract an additional 100 hours from your life expectancy – still only 169.5/3,290 = 5 per cent of your cancer and heart danger.

8.	Having a cancer-prone Type One personality (Grossarth-Maticek 1988) makes your cancer risk 4.4 times the average. These are very rough estimates based on the 2,225 subjects of two experiments relating deaths to attitudes. They were calculated by adding the data from the normal Heidelberg and the Yugoslav (Grossarth-Maticek 1988, p. 486) studies together and comparing the total Type One cancer risk per Type One person (140 + 19/109 + 303 = 38.6 per cent) with the total cancer risk for all types together (29 + 166/872 + 1,353 = 8.76 per cent). Dividing these two gives 38.6/8.76 = 4.4. The additional loss of life expectancy was thus 3.3 × the standard loss of life expectancy figure for cancer. A similar calculation tells us that having a Type Four personality reduces cancer risk to 3/482 + 391 = .34 per cent, which is .34/8.76 = 1/26th of the average risk. Coronary disease risk is 2.9 times higher if you are a Type Two personality compared to the average for all types together. The additional risk is thus 1.9 times the average coronary risk. Being Type Four reduces your cancer risk to 1/26th of the average and your coronary risk to 1/8 of the average for all personality types together. This translates into 3.4 × 1,247 = 4,240 days of additional life expectancy! A Type Two cardiac-prone personality reduces your life expectancy by 1,838 days from the average, while having a healthy Type Four personality increases your life expectancy by 2,987 days. The total change if you could change yourself from a Type One to a Type Four personality would thus be 4,250 + 2,987 = 7,237 days! The tiny risks most people worry about pale in comparison to the positive effects of a strong, confident attitude.

9.   In the 25- to 44-year age group these probabilities drop to .019 per cent and .027 per cent (data from Statistical Abstract of the United States 1991 chart number 127).

10.   'Hot reactors' have dangerously high blood pressure during stressful situations which is way above anything measured in the doctor's surgery. This can cause permanent contraction band scarring in the heart (see Elliot 1994).

11.   American coastal commuters who do a weekly return journey from coast to coast (250,000 mi/yr) lose 64 days of life expectancy (Cohen 1991, p. 327).

12.   Women diagnosed with AIDS in the US are 54% black and 20.5% Latina. These groups are 12% and 9% of the population respectively (Amaro 1995, p. 438).

13.   See Urquhart 1984, p. 69. Melanoma has doubled in the past 15 years, but is not a major killer. The delayed rise of women's lung cancer is still the most convincing indication that smoking directly causes it. Other personality factors that go along with smoking certainly cause smoking's effect to be overstated. For example, university-educated women smokers are four times as likely to be non-virgins at 19 than non-smokers (Eysenck 1991b, p. 26).

14.   Cohen 1991, p. 319.

15.   These figures are low, for example, compared to the 400-day difference in accident rate between living in New Mexico or New York, or the 207-day difference between driving large cars and small cars. Even more important, there is some evidence that a little poison may be better for you than none at all because it keeps your defences working (see Johnson 1996).

16.   See the *Washington Post* April 15, 1993 for the award-winning article on this subject.

17.   *Los Angeles Times* August 28, 1995.

18.   Here is a graph of the actual interactions of risk behaviours with self-regulation scores.

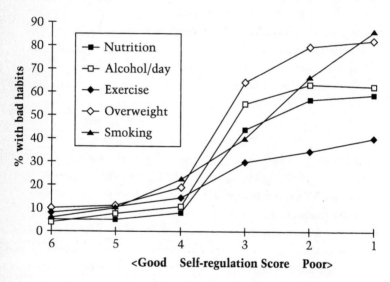

19.   Here is a tabulation of the actual results (from Grossarth-Maticek, 1995b):

	HEALTHY LIFESTYLE no smoke, drink, good diet, 1.5 hr/day exercise	**UNHEALTHY LIFESTYLE** >20 cigs, 60g. alco/day, bad diet, little exercise
Good Self-regulation	83.6 years (n=378)	71.8 years (n=287)
Bad Self-regulation	63.3 years (n=336)	56.8 years (n=216)

20.   Here is the complete test:

	SMOKERS	NON-SMOKERS
Drinking has Positive Effect	77% (n=528)	73% (n=514)
Negative Effect	3.5% (n=454)	50% (n=437)

EFFECTS OF DRINKING ON SELF-REGULATION

I. Improved self-regulation from alcohol
Drinking alcohol:

1. relaxes me
2. improves my well-being
3. stimulates me in a positive way
4. has a positive influence on my feelings
5. improves my sex life
6. helps me to converse better with other people
7. improves my mood (e.g. leads to euphoria and makes me feel good)
8. intensifies the feeling of having an emotional bond with others
9. improves my self-esteem
10. improves my relationship with other people

II. Diminished self-regulation from alcohol
Drinking alcohol:

1. makes my personal problems and difficulties worse
2. makes me feel even more unwell
3. increases anxiety, insecurity and other problems in the mind
4. increases my worries/grief and sorrow
5. isolates me from people who mean a lot to me
6. inhibits me from doing things which are important to me
7. makes me too aggressive and difficult for others to tolerate
8. intensifies negative recollections and experiences
9. disturbs my concentration and memory

10. leads to poor physical health (e.g. sleep disorders, itch, fatigue)
11. leads rapidly to drunkenness of considerable duration

(Scoring: At least one yes to the first group of questions, *no* yes answers to the second group required to be assigned to the 'alcohol improves self-regulation' group.)

21. The table below shows how these factors determined the chances of remaining alive and free of chronic disease 20 years on:

22. The table below shows how self-regulation and drinking interact with health.

	POSITIVE DRINKERS	NON-DRINKERS	NEGATIVE DRINKERS
Bad SR 1.6–2.5	53% 89g (n=95)	32% 0g (n=102)	7% 0g (n=20)
Fair SR 2.6–3.5	70% 88g (n=163)	49% 0g (n=121)	20% 40g (n=61)
Better SR 3.6–4.5	80% 71g (n=361)	71% 0g (n=351)	50% 45g (n=105)
Best SR 4.5–5.5	93% 63g (n=166)	90% 0g (n=162)	68% 45g (n=50)
Combined	75% 75g (n=785)	59% 0g (n=736)	26% 43g (n=236)

23. Cohen 1991. Also see *Newsweek* September 25, 1995 for some bad news. A recent study of 115,000 nurses in the US found that maximum longevity actually occurred at a weight that was 15 per cent *below* the current standard guidelines. A medium-boned, 5'5" woman lived longest if she weighed 8 stone 8 pounds. Weighing 9 st 9 increased death rate by 20 per cent, 12 st 2 by 60 per cent, and 13 st 13 by 100 per cent. The increased mortality came mostly from increased cardiovascular disease, but diabetes, digestive

disorders and cancer were also problems. Overweight also strains the joints, causing more arthritis, hip replacements, etc. See Manson 1995 for the original *New England Journal of Medicine* article describing the study.

24.   One experiment found that smokers' survival rate 13 years later correlated with their beliefs about the dangers of smoking. **74 per cent** of those who believed that smoking didn't injure their health survived, compared to **12 per cent** survival among 72 who thought it did injure their health only because of information from the media. 66 per cent survived among those who believed from their own experience that it did injure their health. The media reports may literally be scaring people to death (see Grossarth-Maticek 1989).

CHAPTER 11   EXPANDING YOUR BOUNDARIES

1.   Cushman 1990, p. 603.

2.   In Sweden and Germany the percentage is even higher. 30 per cent of people over 65 in the US and 39 per cent in Germany live alone.

3.   See Shaffer 1987 and also Eysenck 1994, p. 186. Scores on 14 personality tests given to 972 Johns Hopkins medical students were compared with their freedom from cancer 30 years later. The researcher used the personality test results to classify the students into five personality type clusters. Thirty years later they were amazed to find that the students classified as 'loners' by the tests were *16 times* more likely to have developed cancer than the group whose tests indicated that they gave vent to their emotions. 'Loners' were defined as people who suppressed their emotions 'beneath a bland exterior'. This study is particularly convincing because its original purpose was to study the effects of attitude on coronary heart disease – the cancer correlations were therefore not influenced by anybody's expectations.

4.   Both suicide and drug use is actually higher in rural areas than in the city. Though some have argued that other interactions cause the observed higher mortality of people living alone, see Gove 1980 for a convincing argument refuting this notion.

5.   See Berkman 1979. This massive study of the importance of close human connections was done in 1965 on a random sample of 4,725 adults in Alameda County, California. Interviews were conducted to determine the degree of social and community ties of each subject. A questionnaire asked if they were married, how many close friends and relatives they had, and how often they saw them. Church and club memberships were also considered. These factors were combined into a 'social network index'. Nine

years later names were matched up with death certificates and it was found that when the bottom quarter was compared with the top, 2.8 times as many women and 2.3 times as many men had died. Having more social connections can thus more than double your chances of survival. Certainly at least part of this effect is the fact that friends and relatives can help cushion the effects of stressful events.

Also see Elliot 1994, p. 117. Also The Harvard Grant study classified selected second-year university students as 'lonely' or 'friendly' and then interviewed them 30 years later. 46 per cent of the 'lonely' men had chronic physical illness versus 4 per cent for the 'friendly' men (Vaillant 1977, p. 306).

6.　　These figures on depression are from a 1970 US Government-sponsored study led by Gerald Klerman. They interviewed 9,500 randomly selected people (Seligman 1993, p. 106).

7.　　See Baumeister 1987, p. 169. Also for more on privacy see Taylor. 1989, p. 291.

8.　　See Schoeman 1984, p. 63.

9.　　Seligman 1993, p. 106.

10.　　The teen suicide rate has tripled in the past 30 years. Victims tend to be solitary boys over the age of 12 (see Berk 1989, box 11.1).

11.　　See Cushman 1990, p.603 for the original article on the empty self. See also chapter 12 of Blakeslee 1996.

12.　　If you don't have this problem please excuse this section. I did, but I think I'm improving.

13.　　See Guisinger 1994, p. 107.

14.　　These points are borrowed from Pennebaker 1990, p. 202.

CHAPTER 12　DEVELOPING OPTIMISM AND COMPLEXITY

1.　　See Seligman 1993, p. 114. About 35 per cent of the people taking Prozac find that it lowers their libido.

2.　　One study (Peterson 1988) tested 172 students for 'explanatory style' and found that the pessimists lost twice as many days to sickness and made four times as many visits to their doctor's surgery as the optimists. Success in business, particularly sales and politics, has also been shown to go primarily to optimists (Seligman 1994). People whose mother dies before they are 11 have been found to be at higher risk for depression. Since the mother never comes back, Permanence and Pervasiveness can become a habit (Seligman 1995, p. 109).

3.　　In 1840 it was up to 41 years (Cohen 1991, p. 317).

4.　Another cognitive error that caus8es much depression and disappointment is the idea that visualizing a goal will make it happen. If you visualize a parking space and the drivers directly in front of and behind you are doing a similar visualization, who will get the space? You can't all get it, so two of you will be disappointed. Visualization of reality only works in a world that exists only for you alone.

5.　See chapter 4 of Seligman 1995.

6.　Depression among teenagers is endemic. One researcher studied 3,000 12- to 14-year-olds in the southeastern US and found that 9 per cent of them were depressed (Seligman 1995, p. 40).

7.　For a complete development of how the mind is made up of many specialized modules, see Blakeslee 1996.

8.　Suicide among men increases linearly as they age, while the rate among women stays static. This is probably because only men put all of their eggs in one basket, which is their job. Suicide rates for men per 100,000 go from 18 at age 25–34, to 39 at 55–64, to 65 above the age of 85 (Kimmel 1974, p. 327). In California the rate above the age of 85 is 105.5 per 100,000 of the population (Friedan 1993, p. 175).

9.　Complexity can be measured by having the subject select from 33 cards, each of which bears the name of a personality trait (e.g. quiet, assertive, emotional, etc.). Applicable traits are selected for each sub-personality and then the complexity score is determined as a measure of how greatly the sub-personalities vary. One study found a correlation between complexity and depression, and also with symptoms of illness (Linville 1987).

CHAPTER 13　SEX, SENSUALITY AND FOOD

1.　Murray, *Longevity* December 1994, p. 28.

2.　Bacon, C., Remeker, R. and Ertler, M., 'A psychosomatic survey of cancer of the breast' *Psychosomatic Medicine* 14 (1952): 453–60. Also see Eysenck 1994, p. 170. Thirty of the 40 were also found to have no healthy way to discharge anger.

3.　See Money 1980, p. 147. More than half of women with spinal cord injuries can masturbate to orgasm (Sipski 1995). Male cockroaches actually continue to copulate after they are decapitated by the female (see Dretske 1988, p. 196).

4.　For a good article on habituation, see Kastenbaum 1993.

CHAPTER 14   AGEING AND CULTURE

1.   See Leaf 1975, p. 12. Also 45 per cent took long strolls daily out of their gardens, 24 per cent walked from one mountain village to another, and 24 per cent walked only in their own garden.

2.   Fischer 1977, p. 15.

3.   See Fischer 1977, p. 24.

4.   See Bortz 1991, p. 126.

5.   See *Runner's World*, August 1994, p. 51.

6.   See Bortz 1991, p. 127.

7.   See Bortz 1991, p. 125.

8.   This was originally said slightly differently in 1873 by Edward Stanley, Earl of Derby.

CHAPTER 15   PRINCIPLES OF RUT-BUSTING

1.   Try ringing 01252 344161 for some free brochures.

2.   For a free brochure ring 0990 134 227 in the UK or (800) 243-8520 in the US.

3.   For information ring 0171 494 1105.

4.   VSO's phone number is 0181 780 2266. They are located at 317 Putney Bridge Rd, London SW15 2PN.

APPENDIX I   THE PLEASURE AND WELL-BEING TEST

1.   This translation from the original German retains the original meanings but changes the format somewhat. The original format was to have each question followed by a key to the numbered responses. I have retained this format only where it adds precision, for example in question where time periods are specified. It was felt that weak, medium-weak, medium-strong, etc. only complicated the test. We have translated the German word *lust* as 'pleasure', and *wohlbefinden* as 'well-being.'

THE ATTITUDE FACTOR WEB SITE

1.   Another purpose of the site is to gather data for a massive prospective study. Questionnaire results will be archived in a safe place and health status of users over 45 will be checked in 5 and 10 years' time. Correlation of mortality to initial test scores and to scores after training will be plotted. A randomly-assigned control group of 1,000 users aged 55 or older will be given the tests but will not be offered any information or training.

Expected results are as follows:

1. Replication of Grossarth-Maticek's Self-Regulation (Eysenck 1994) and Pleasure studies (Grossarth-Maticek 1997) and Andas 1993 hopelessness study. All questions will be used unchanged, with a few questions added. Plots will be made of %alive vs initial test score.
2. Replication in principle of Grossarth-Maticek's intervention studies (Eysenck 1991). A family of survival curves will be plotted. Better survival is expected for those achieving more improvement in their training retests and/or those spending more time in training and following it for one year.
3. *The Attitude Factor* (book) can be ordered through the site. Purchasers will be asked to rate the book after reading it and a family of %alive vs self-regulation curves will be plotted. Highest book ratings are expected to be associated with better survival than predicted by self-regulation scores before purchase.
4. Data on national variations in mean scores on rationality, expression of feelings and other factors will be tabulated. National mentalities are expected to correlate with regional variations in life expectancy. Foreign-language versions will be created.